Labor Rights and Multinational Production

Labor Rights and Multinational Production investigates the relationship between workers' rights and multinational production. Layna Mosley argues that some types of multinational production, embodied in directly owned foreign investment, positively affect labor rights. However, other types of international production, particularly subcontracting, can engender competitive races to the bottom in labor rights. To test these claims, Mosley presents newly generated measures of collective labor rights, covering a wide range of low- and middle-income nations for the 1985–2002 period. *Labor Rights and Multinational Production* suggests that the consequences of economic openness for developing countries are highly dependent on foreign firms' modes of entry and, more generally, on the precise way in which each developing country engages the global economy. The book contributes to the academic literature in comparative and international political economy and to public policy debates regarding the effects of globalization.

Layna Mosley is associate professor in the Department of Political Science at the University of North Carolina at Chapel Hill. She is the author of *Global Capital and National Governments*, and her articles have appeared in *American Political Science Review*, *International Organization*, *International Studies Quarterly*, and *Comparative Political Studies*, among other publications. Her past research has been funded by the German Marshall Fund of the United States, the National Science Foundation, and the Social Science Research Council.

Cambridge Studies in Comparative Politics

Other Books in the Series

David Austen-Smith, Jeffry A. Frieden, Miriam A. Golden, Karl Ove Moene, and Adam Przeworski, eds., *Selected Works of Michael Wallerstein: The Political Economy of Inequality, Unions, and Social Democracy*

Andy Baker, *The Market and the Masses in Latin America: Policy Reform and Consumption in Liberalizing Economies*

Lisa Baldez, *Why Women Protest: Women's Movements in Chile*

Stefano Bartolini, *The Political Mobilization of the European Left, 1860–1980: The Class Cleavage*

Robert Bates, *When Things Fell Apart: State Failure in Late-Century Africa*

Mark Beissinger, *Nationalist Mobilization and the Collapse of the Soviet State*

Nancy Bermeo, ed., *Unemployment in the New Europe*

Continued after the Index

Labor Rights and Multinational Production

LAYNA MOSLEY

University of North Carolina, Chapel Hill

CAMBRIDGE
UNIVERSITY PRESS

CAMBRIDGE UNIVERSITY PRESS
Cambridge, New York, Melbourne, Madrid, Cape Town, Singapore,
São Paulo, Delhi, Dubai, Tokyo, Mexico City

Cambridge University Press
32 Avenue of the Americas, New York, NY 10013-2473, USA

www.cambridge.org
Information on this title: www.cambridge.org/9780521694414

First published 2011

Printed in the United States of America

A catalog record for this publication is available from the British Library.

Library of Congress Cataloging in Publication data
Mosley, Layna.
    Labor rights and multinational production / Layna Mosley.
        p.   cm. – (Cambridge studies in comparative politics)
    Includes bibliographical references and index.
    ISBN 978-0-521-87281-2 (hardback) – ISBN 978-0-521-69441-4 (pbk.)
    1. Employee rights – Developing countries.   2. Investments, Foreign – Developing
    countries.   3. International business enterprises – Developing countries.   I. Title.
    HD8943.M67 2010
    331.01′1–dc22   2010030878

ISBN 978-0-521-87281-2 Hardback
ISBN 978-0-521-69441-4 Paperback

for Andy

Contents

Tables and Figures

Acknowledgments

What is the impact of the global economy on workers in developing nations? Does multinational production represent an opportunity for improvements for those in low- and middle-income countries, or ought we to worry about the competitive pressures unleashed by firms' use of global supply chains? This book is motivated by a desire to understand the conditions under which economic globalization helps citizens of developing nations as well as the circumstances under which economic openness negatively affects such individuals. While my framework is a theoretical one, based on the organization of production globally, the issue is very much an empirical one, as activists and policymakers grapple with how best to reconcile the competitive pressures of the global economy with considerations of workers' rights and conditions.

This project had its genesis when I was a faculty member at the University of Notre Dame, and one of the graduate students in my International Political Economy seminar – Saika Uno – asked about the connection between labor rights and economic openness. She pointed out that, despite the importance of this issue to both policymakers and academics, there was very little cross-national time series evidence examining the potential link between the two. Our initial conversation launched a collaborative project resulting in a journal article. It also spurred my interest in tying together international political economy research on multinational corporations with comparative and international politics investigations of human rights outcomes. The result is *Labor Rights and Multinational Production*, which focuses on the role of the international economy in affecting the collective labor rights of workers in low- and middle-income nations.

Along the way, many individuals and institutions have supported this research. At the University of Notre Dame, the Institute for Scholarship in the Liberal Arts and the Kellogg Institute for International Studies funded the initial data collection and coding of the labor rights indicator. In 2002–2003, a faculty research fellowship from the German Marshall Fund facilitated a larger-scale effort to code the labor rights indicator and to frame the project in theoretical terms. The College of Arts and Sciences at the University of North Carolina at Chapel Hill (UNC) also provided pre-tenure leave in Fall 2005. A Workshop Grant from the International Studies Association, along with contributions from several units at Duke University and UNC, allowed me to organize a faculty workshop on labor rights, held at UNC in September 2006. I was fortunate to be a Faculty Fellow at UNC's Institute for the Arts and Humanities during Fall 2008, which allowed for the completion of the penultimate version of the manuscript as well as the opportunity to present my research to an interdisciplinary audience.

While funding is certainly an important part of any academic project, the opportunity to present, debate, and refine one's research is even more fundamental. I am grateful for many opportunities to gain feedback on various elements of this project. These include talks at Columbia University, the Duke University Seminar on Global Governance and Democracy, the Duke University conference on Foreign Direct Investment (April 2006), the Frontiers of Comparative Politics conference at Duke University (April 2007), the Kellogg Institute at the University of Notre Dame, UNC–Chapel Hill, the University of South Carolina, the University of Southern California, and the University of Virginia. Papers related to this project also were presented at meetings of the American Political Science Association, the International Studies Association, and the Midwest Political Science Association. Portions of Chapters 5 and 7 were first published in *Comparative Political Studies*. Participants in a seminar hosted by the Center for the Comparative Historical Analysis of Organizations and States (CHAOS) at the University of Washington carefully read and extensively commented on the penultimate version of the manuscript.

Saika Uno collaborated on the initial set of conference papers and the resulting *Comparative Political Studies* article. More recently, as my collaborators on work involving the role of trade and FDI in the diffusion of standards, Brian Greenhill and Aseem Prakash have pushed me to think more clearly about the causal mechanisms connecting labor rights with multinational firms and transnational labor rights advocates. Aahren

DiPalma, Kathryn Gelder, Robin Macklin, Sarah Moore, and Jason Warner were all excellent as research assistants, performing tasks ranging from photocopying labor rights reports to coding labor rights violations and collecting materials related to Costa Rica's labor rights situation. Gary Thompson, in the Department of Sociology at Duke University, provided advice about compiling export profile data as well as much of the actual data. Lewis Bateman of Cambridge University Press was enthusiastic about a book-length treatment of globalization and labor rights from the beginning, and I thank him for his patience as I worked to complete the manuscript. Margaret Levi has been particularly enthusiastic about this manuscript, and I deeply appreciate her support and encouragement.

Although I am certain to forget to mention some of the many individuals who offered comments and advice along the way, I would be remiss if I did not attempt to list and thank them. They include Susan Aaronson, Rodwan Abouharb, Jennifer Bair, David Brady, Sarah Brooks, Tim Büthe, David Cingranelli, Gary Gereffi, Debra Glassman, Brian Greenhill, Emilie Hafner-Burton, Nathan Jensen, Frances Hagopian, Evelyne Huber, Judith Kelley, Robert Keohane, Herbert Kitschelt, Margaret Levi, Quan Li, Mary Anne Madeira, Victoria Murillo, John Odell, Guillermo O'Donnell, Aseem Prakash, Karen Remmer, Graeme Robertson, Nita Rudra, Andrew Schrank, John Stephens, Emmanuel Teitelbaum, Michael Ward, Susan Whiting, Erik Wibbels, and several anonymous journal reviewers.

The last decade witnessed important transformations in the global economy, the implications of which we are still seeking to understand. The global economic crisis that began in 2008 may, as I discuss in Chapter 8, alter the linkages between multinational production and labor rights. The last decade also has been one of important changes for me: I arrived at UNC Chapel Hill in 2004. UNC has been a wonderful place for research and teaching. My broader circle of friends and colleagues in Carrboro, Chapel Hill, and Durham has provided me with just the right mixture of companionship, motivation, and distraction, much of it on the single-track trails of Carolina North Forest.

Most importantly, my family is an inspiration both to work harder *and* to stop working. My two stepchildren, Atticus and Madeline, make being an "evil stepmother" a real joy; they even ask about my research, a somewhat remarkable feat for two teenagers. My daughters, Cecilia Jane and Tess Caroline, arrived after I had begun to work on this project, and they always give me plenty of reasons to smile, even in the face of grim reports regarding labor rights abroad. They inspire me to work to better understand the world around us. Lastly, my partner, Andrew Reynolds, is a constant source of laughter, love, support – and competition. To thank him for these things (and not simply because it is an unwritten rule for second books), this book is dedicated to him.

Chapel Hill, NC
February 2010

Workers in the Global Economy

> Multinational companies have turned back the clock, transferring production to countries with labor conditions that resemble those in the early period of America's own industrialization.
>
> (Collinsworth et al. 1994, p. 9)

In every region of the world, workers often are treated poorly: Some are denied the rights to unionize and strike by their governments, while others are blacklisted from employment if they assert their legally mandated right to organize. Still others work very long hours with no overtime pay, with exposure to noxious chemicals or to sexual harassment by management. For instance, in its 2007 annual survey of trade union rights, the International Trade Union Confederation (ITUC) documents the deaths of 144 trade unionists; nearly 5,000 arrests for union-related activities; and over 8,000 dismissals from employment for reasons related to unionization. These violations of collective labor rights are concentrated in some countries; for instance, Colombia leads the world in trade unionist disappearances and deaths. At the same time, though, the ITUC documents denials of collective labor rights in 138 nations, including both developed and developing countries, and in sectors ranging from bananas and coffee to electronics and pharmaceuticals.[1]

Violations of individual labor rights – working hours, overtime pay, health, and safety – are similarly widespread. A decade ago, reports of abuses in many of Nike's supplier factories received widespread public

---

[1] The ITUC report is available at http://survey07.ituc-csi.org/getcontinent.php?IDContinent=0andIDLang=EN

attention; these included the underpayment of wages by subcontractors in Indonesia, the use of child labor in the production of soccer balls in Pakistan, and exposure of workers in China and Vietnam to a variety of dangerous chemicals (Locke 2001). Activists routinely document the abuse of agricultural sector workers, such as the widespread use (and abuse) of child workers in Ecuador's banana sector (Human Rights Watch 2002). Additionally, the expansion of China's exports has been accompanied by a growth in reports of abuses in Chinese factories, in sectors ranging from apparel to toys to electronics.

Despite the recent attention of transnational and local human rights activists to the plight of workers around the world, labor rights abuses are not a new phenomenon. In many nations, agricultural production often has employed child labor, and it has involved repressive relationships between land owners and agricultural workers, many of whom are (illegal) migrants with little capacity to assert their rights. Manufacturing has similarly witnessed centuries of abuses. Indeed, the International Labour Organization (ILO), which is at the forefront of efforts to promulgate international standards for the treatment of workers, has itself existed since the early 1920s.

Is economic globalization to blame for the perilous plight of many of the world's workers? Globalization's critics would suggest that this is the case, whereas its proponents would argue that the rising tide of economic integration will lift all boats, including those of workers in low- and middle-income countries. Yet neither globalization's supporters nor its detractors accurately capture the causal links between workers, on the one hand, and the global economy, on the other. The impact of multinational production on labor rights depends on the precise ways in which a country and its firms and citizens participate in the global economy. While production directly owned by multinational corporations (MNCs) should lead to improvements in labor rights, production that takes place in the context of subcontracting relationships will be associated with deteriorations in labor rights.

The central aim of this book, then, is to identify the precise way in which violations of workers' rights are related to recent increases in international economic integration. Many activist campaigns link the globalization of the production process with the mistreatment of workers, as multinational firms and their subcontractors seek to minimize labor costs, and as governments aim to attract foreign businesses via lower standards. However, while it certainly is true that the trends of increased economic integration (trade, foreign direct investment [FDI], and production) and of greater abuses – or, at least, identification and awareness of abuses – of labor rights are correlated, we should exercise caution in assuming that they are causally related. Indeed, proponents of corporate social responsibility argue that multinational firms have material incentives to promote the protection of labor rights, not only in their home countries but also in their various host locations. Given that these firms want to avoid the spotlight (Spar 1999) and the negative effects it can have on shareholder and consumer perceptions, they may be inclined to pressure their affiliates and suppliers to adhere to internationally recognized core labor rights.

Moreover, while the World Trade Organization (WTO) has long resisted addressing issues related to labor rights, governments have begun to include labor rights provisions in bilateral and regional trade agreements. Recent free trade agreements, such as the U.S.-Cambodia Trade Agreement on Textiles and Apparel (1999–2004), the U.S.-Jordan Free Trade Agreement (2000), the Central American Free Trade Agreement (CAFTA-DR, 2005), as well as the proposed U.S.-Colombia Free Trade Agreement, contain a range of explicit labor rights provisions. Certainly, this inclusion is related somewhat to pressures from developed nation labor unions, such as the American Federation of Labor – Congress of Industrial Unions (AFL-CIO) in the United States; labor rights provisions are a means of convincing these groups that free trade agreements will not be (as) harmful to labor-intensive manufacturing industries (Hafner-Burton 2009). At the same time, though, the inclusion of some labor rights provisions suggests that trade-related mechanisms may be effective at monitoring and protecting workers' rights (Greenhill et al. 2009).

There are reasons to believe, then, that economic globalization may be either good or bad for labor rights. I seek to identify the conditions under which either is the case, and I posit that the effect of multinational production on workers' rights is a mixed one: Some elements of economic openness bode well for labor rights, while others seem to generate increased violations of workers' union-related rights. Moreover, the effects of economic openness on labor are by no means constant within nations: In some industries, pressures generated by the global economy lead to downward pressure on labor rights. In other sectors, engaging the global economy has allowed workers in developing countries to experience improvements in collective rights as well as in wages and benefits. The short answer, then, is that economic globalization is *somewhat* related to labor rights, but in a much more nuanced way than many policy debates and activist campaigns suggest.

In the remainder of this chapter, I briefly situate the topic of global production and workers' rights in broader discussions of the impact of economic globalization on outcomes in developing nations. I then introduce the book's main theoretical claim: The way in which multinational firms organize their overseas production affects labor rights outcomes. Directly owned production augurs positively for labor rights, while subcontracted, arm's-length production has negative consequences for workers' rights. Given the prevalence of both modes of firm organization, multinational production has both positive and negative consequences for workers in developing nations. I summarize the factors that may mediate the influence of multinational production on workers in developing countries; these include domestic politics and institutions, as well as the economic sector and nature of production of the multinational production in which a given country is involved.

The empirical analyses presented in this book focus on the capacity of workers to act collectively – their legal right as well as their de facto ability to organize, bargain collectively, and strike. These rights are correlated with, but analytically distinct from, broader measures of human rights, which also include considerations of civil and political rights (i.e., Abouharb and Cingranelli 2008). Moreover, collective labor rights are distinct from individual working conditions, as I discuss in Chapter 4. The former (sometimes referred to as "core standards") are correlated with individual conditions (sometimes labeled "cash standards"), such as wage levels, payment of overtime wages, and occupational health and safety. Individual conditions, however, are beyond the scope of this book. I do assume, though, that there is a positive – albeit not perfect – correlation between collective labor rights and improvements in wages and working conditions (e.g., Aidt and Tzannaos 2002; Blanchflower and Bryson 2003; Flanagan 2006; Huber and Stephens 2001). Moreover, given that approximately one-quarter of the world's nonagricultural workers are members of labor unions (Visser 2003) – and that still more workers are covered by collective agreements – the potential for workers to act collectively is central to current debates regarding the impact of economic globalization on domestic outcomes.

I. THE DIVERSITY OF GLOBAL PRODUCTION

Much popular literature continues to treat globalization as a monolithic process, one that encompasses trade as well as finance, and one in which nearly all national economies are involved. Arguments describing a flat world suggest that factor-price equalization has reached, or is about to reach, its endpoint (i.e., Friedman 2005): That is, global economic markets are almost perfectly integrated, generating a very different set of competitive dynamics within the global economy.

Academic analysts repeatedly note that a homogenous view of globalization is inaccurate, along at least two dimensions. First, despite general global trends toward economic liberalization, government trade and financial policies continue to vary markedly across countries. Countries that are open to trade are not necessarily as open to finance, and vice versa (Garrett 2000). Additionally, some governments restrict flows of foreign direct investment into particular industries, whereas others welcome direct investment of all stripes. Some governments maintain high barriers to some types of imports, while allowing relatively unfettered access to others. These differences often reflect varying domestic interest groups and domestic political institutions. That is, the competitive pressures emanating from the global economy interact with country-specific factors to generate national policies regarding economic openness (i.e., Plümper et al. 2009). In sum, scholars who treat economic openness – or specific facets of economic openness – as a dependent variable suggest that there remains substantial variation to explain, and that such variation has domestic as well as international roots (Rodrik 2007; Simmons et al. 2008).

Second, in terms of the impact of international economic forces on national policy outcomes, the precise pattern of a country's involvement in the global economy – for instance, the extent to which it is open to trade *and* to finance, or the extent to which it relies on short-term versus long-term capital inflows – determines the impact of economic integration on national policy outcomes. Recent work in this area has pointed to the heterogeneity of economic integration at a relatively macro-level – that is, trade versus finance, or portfolio capital flows versus foreign direct investment versus remittances.

Indeed, a substantial body of literature in comparative political economy during the last two decades has considered the causal connections between global capital markets and national government policy choices (e.g., Mosley 2003). While early studies in this vein considered the impact of financial globalization writ large, or focused on the reactions of one type of investment to government policies, more recent scholarship has identified differences among types of investors. For instance, Mosley and Singer (2008) compare the response to various political and economic factors of equity market valuations, on one hand, and government bond interest rates, on the other. For a sample of thirty-seven developed and emerging-market economies, they find that many of the political and economic factors deemed highly salient to bond investors are not associated with stock market valuations, and vice versa. Similarly, Ahlquist (2006) compares the reaction of foreign direct investors, on the one hand, and portfolio market investors, on the other, to changes in government policy outcomes in the developing world. Again, he finds marked differences across investors. Portfolio (stock and bond) investors are sensitive to past government behavior, such as fiscal and monetary policy outcomes. Foreign direct investment flows, though, do not seem to react to macroeconomic policies; rather, they are sensitive to political institutions, with a revealed preference for more democratic governance mechanisms.[2]

While these studies advance our knowledge by theorizing about heterogeneity within international capital markets, they do not go far enough in disaggregating the concept and consequences of economic openness. This book further disentangles one element of the contemporary global economy – multinational production, in which thousands of firms operate in multiple national markets, producing goods in multiple locations; trading inputs and finished products among affiliates and subcontractors; and selling finished products to consumers in an array of national markets.

Scholars of international political economy have treated multinational production as a type of capital flow that is distinct from shorter-term portfolio investment (bank lending, corporate and government bonds, and equities). Foreign direct investment refers to longer-term cross-border investment, which provides the investor (a multinational firm) with a management interest in an enterprise (an affiliate) and direct control over its production activities. Direct investment is distinguished from portfolio investment by its longer time horizon and by its direct control of assets. Various scholars have envisioned both negative and positive consequences of direct investment for developing countries generally and for workers in developing nations specifically. The negative accounts focus on the relative power of investors vis-à-vis governments, particularly governments of capital-poor (developing) nations. Some observers maintain that multinational firms are likely to respond to greater demands from workers in developing nations (i.e., to unionization efforts, as in Silver

---

[2] Other studies that disaggregate international capital markets include Bernhard and Leblang (2006); Maxfield (1997); Santiso (2003); Shambaugh (2005).

2003) by threatening to relocate, or actually relocating, production to other developing countries. Another set of studies, however, notes the generally positive consequences of FDI for economic growth and technology transfer. These analyses suggest that direct investment's effects on workers generally will be positive (i.e., Bhagwati 2004; Brown et al. 2004; Flanagan 2006).

Yet, on each side of this divide, there exists a tendency to treat multinational corporations as an undifferentiated set of actors – to assume, for instance, that no matter how a firm or a sector organizes its global production, the implications for workers, the environment, or economic growth will be similar. However, just as various component elements of economic globalization affect social policy, tax policy, and fiscal policy differently, variation in the organization of global production has important consequences for labor rights (also see Gallagher 2005; Hafner-Burton 2005a). The main distinction I draw with respect to global production is that between directly owned production (accomplished via foreign direct investment from one country to another) and arm's length production (accomplished via subcontracting relationships and generating flows of goods across national borders, but not resulting in flows of direct investment).

This variation in firm organization and ownership structure has implications for labor rights: MNC-owned global production affects labor rights in a positive fashion, whereas subcontracted production is associated with less respect for workers' rights. In other words, the "mode of entry" employed by multinational corporations has important – and under-theorized – consequences for workers' rights and working conditions. Scholars of management and industrial organization have explored the causes of firms' modes of entry decisions (see Chapter 3), but political economists have paid scant attention to the implications of this choice for national policies. Empirically, this framework predicts that, as "racing to the top" accounts suggest, directly owned multinational production – captured empirically by cross-border flows of foreign direct investment – will have a positive effect on collective labor rights. However, at the same time, arm's-length production (offshoring or subcontracting, operationalized as trade openness) will tend to affect collective labor rights negatively. In the remainder of this chapter, I situate my approach in the broader literature that explores the effect of economic openness on national policy outcomes. I then summarize my claims in greater detail and conclude with an overview of *Labor Rights and Multinational Production*.

II. RACES TO THE BOTTOM AND CLIMBS TO THE TOP

A wide recent literature in comparative and international political economy investigates the linkages between the global economy, on the one hand, and policy outcomes in developing nations, on the other. This research generally focuses on the extent to which, and the ways in which, openness to global trade and finance influences policy choices in developing nations. The starting assumption is that developing nations are, by virtue of their relative lack of capital, their desire for economic growth, and their relative lack of voice in intergovernmental economic institutions, quite prone to the influence of global economic forces. While advanced democracies may, under some circumstances, be able to resist pressures emanating from the global economy (Scruggs and Lange 2002), low- and middle-income nations will not have this luxury (Mosley 2003; Rudra 2008; Wibbels 2006).

From this general orientation, analysts take divergent views regarding the strength and scope of globalization-induced pressures. Some, for instance, point out that the pressures from global capital markets to keep fiscal deficits small, coupled with the exposure of developing nations to exogenous shocks, renders their governments much less able to smooth consumption. Several studies find empirical support for this claim, as trade openness is linked with declines in social spending (i.e., Kaufman and Segura-Ubiero 2001). Rudra (2002) argues that, in contrast with labor in the developed world, workers in developing nations have been less able to prevent the dismantling of the welfare state in the face of economic openness. Where there is a large surplus of labor, and where the labor force is more unskilled than skilled, economic openness appears to be associated with downward pressure on social spending. Building on this work, Wibbels (2006) points out that governments of developing countries are likely to cut social spending when it is most needed – as recession occurs. His empirical analyses, focused on Latin America, support the general notion of pro-cyclical budget deficits; he also finds that public spending on human capital – rather than on social security – is most likely to be cut in a downturn.

Others maintain that, while the global economy has effects on policy outcomes in developing countries, these effects are less consequential than one might imagine. In her analysis of social policy, for instance, Rudra (2008) reports that economic integration tends to result in lower social spending. However, as she notes, social spending in developing nations tends to benefit the upper classes; as a result, the pressures on social policy that result from globalization should not be expected to render poverty or income inequality any *more* severe (also see Avelino et al. 2005).

Still others argue that, despite – or even because of – the pressures emanating from the global economy, domestic politics and institutions play a key role in determining policy outcomes in developing countries. One variant of this literature argues that because the global economy exposes individuals to greater income volatility, and because individuals demand protection from such volatility, more open economies tend to have larger public sectors. Rodrik (1998), for instance, reports a positive and significant correlation between an economy's exposure to international trade and the size of its government. Adserà and Boix (2002) add a layer of nuance to this argument, positing that regime type influences the response of governments to externally induced volatility. Democratic regimes in the developing world are likely to increase public spending as trade openness grows, while authoritarian governments have no domestic political need to do so.[3] If developing democracies maintain competitive export sectors, then they can use the proceeds from international trade to fund greater social protection. Turning specifically to education and social security policy, Avelino et al. (2005) report that financial openness does not appear to limit social spending in Latin America; that democracy is associated with greater levels of social spending; and that increasing trade openness tends to bring about increased spending on education and social security. In short, the pressures emanating from the global economy either are insignificant or they push in an upward direction. Moreover, even at similar levels of exposure to trade and financial openness, countries vary in their public policy outcomes. Brooks (2005), for instance, finds that the occurrence and extent of social security privatization in developing and transition countries is due not only to international pressures, but also to existing social security commitments and to political competition domestically.

Many conceive of this broader literature as a test of the "race to the bottom" claim, grounded in the imperatives of cross-national competition and economic efficiency. Extant research in political science finds little strong support for such a claim (i.e., Spar and Yoffie 1999); indeed, it has taken on the role as a favorite straw man of empirically based work on globalization and national policies. One possible lesson

---

[3] On the validity of the link between externally induced volatility and trade openness, see Kim (2007).

to draw from such studies is that the international economy simply plays little role, positive or negative, in the determination of policy outcomes. Indeed, this study (Chapters 5 and 7, in particular) suggests that domestic politics and institutions continue to play an important role, so that outcomes in developing countries reflect a mix of internal and external factors. Some of the variation in the extent to which workers are able to form unions certainly is explained by the type of political regime in office, by the nature of production (agricultural versus manufacturing versus services), and by the country's relative level of economic development. Indeed, domestic variables are particularly important in the area of labor rights practices – that is, in determining whether or not governments successfully implement and firms routinely comply with various labor laws. I discuss this argument in more detail in Chapter 3.

At the same time, however, another possible – and a more plausible – lesson from the extant literature is that the terms of the debate have been too stark: It is not a question of whether economic globalization has negative or positive consequences for workers in developing nations. Rather, it is an issue of "under what conditions." Therefore, I take the view that international factors *are* important influences on labor rights in developing nations,[4] but that their impact is varied and contingent. In addition to the nature and extent of multinational production, other important international influences on labor rights include demands from transnational advocacy groups and competitive pressures from other nations in a country's (geographic or income) peer groups.

In considering these external influences on labor rights, an important starting point is to disaggregate economic globalization. Too often, in both the popular press and in academic analyses, "globalization" is used as an all-encompassing term, referring to trade, short-term capital, and long-term direct investment. Yet there are many reasons to believe that each of these factors could have different effects on country-level outcomes. If some elements of globalization have positive effects, while others have negative effects, studies that use overall measures of economic openness may well report "no effects," when this is not the case. Given that countries are integrated differently into the global economy, it is important to consider each type of integration as distinct.

---

[4] Similarly, Abouharb and Cingranelli 2007 argue that more attention to the international dimensions of human (and labor) rights outcomes is necessary.

III. LABOR RIGHTS AND MULTINATIONAL PRODUCTION

Returning to the specific issue of labor rights in the developing world, academic literature on the impact of multinational corporations on labor-related outcomes offers reasons for both optimism and pessimism. In part, this reflects the fact that much of this literature is based on detailed country or industry case studies, rather than broader cross-national (and time series) analyses. While such studies are an excellent means of tracing the causal mechanisms that underlie labor-related outcomes, they are less useful when it comes to generalizing across countries. A major contribution of this book, then, is to provide systematic large-N analyses of the link between workers' rights and the global economy, with specific attention to low- and middle-income nations.

Additionally, many studies have – for reasons of data availability as well as longer democratic and labor market traditions – tended to focus on advanced industrial democracies. While the linkages between economic globalization and labor-related outcomes in countries like Germany, Sweden, and the United States may hold some relevance to contemporary low- and middle-income countries, there are many reasons to expect a different causal process at play in developing countries, which face distinct competitive pressures (and domestic political constellations). Advanced democracies also differ in how they engage the global economy: They tend to have large amounts of trade and direct investment activity (OECD nations continue to attract the lion's share of global direct investment). This, coupled with these countries' generally low levels of labor rights violations, might bias our conclusions toward a finding that economic openness is associated positively with labor rights.

The empirical focus of *Labor Rights and Multinational Production*, then, is developing nations from Africa, Latin America, Asia, and the Middle East; our data cover the 1986–2002 period. The late 1980s and 1990s are periods of growing – and often high – economic openness and, therefore, the years for which the impact of globalization on labor rights should be most pronounced; these years also provide the broadest data coverage on key variables.[5] At the same time, we exclude developed

---

[5] Also, Nunnenkamp and Spatz's (2002) study, based on twenty-eight developing nations, suggests that the determinants of FDI do not change much between the late 1980s and the early 2000s.

and transition countries[6] from our analyses. We expect that many of the independent variables of interest will have different effects in developing nations than they will in wealthy, historically democratic countries (Blonigen and Wang 2005). With respect to transition nations, during the first part of our sample period, these nations were under Communist rule; reliable data on economic indicators are not available. In the latter part of the sample period, data availability improves, but these countries remain very different from the others in our sample (Bunce 1995). While they are not necessarily exceptional in their simultaneous economic and political transitions, they are quite unique in their Communist legacy (and the attendant treatment of workers) as well as in their degree of economic restructuring (mass privatizations and the movement away from a closed, command economy) and in the efforts of many former Communist countries to join the European Union.[7]

My main theoretical argument is that firm decisions regarding how to organize overseas production will affect labor-related outcomes. I expect that directly owned multinational production will generate pressures for the protection of collective labor rights. MNCs have material incentives to standardize practices across their operation; to bring "best practices" to their foreign affiliates; and to invest resources in monitoring and promoting the provision of internationally recognized core labor rights. Empirically, then, the overall impact of direct investment on workers' rights is likely to be a positive one, promoting a "climb to the top" among developing nations.[8]

At the same time, arm's-length production relationships, in which MNCs place transactions in the market rather than within the firm and in which they rely on subcontractor firms to assemble and produce goods, will have negative consequences for workers' rights. Subcontracting relationships often are driven by cost considerations, and they are more prevalent in labor-intensive industries. As such, subcontracting brings

---

[6] Developed nations include Western European countries, Australia, Canada, Japan, New Zealand, and the United States. Transition nations are those in Eastern Europe and the former Soviet Union.

[7] On membership conditionality related to European Union accession, see Kelley (2004); Vachudova (2005). The importance of Communist legacies to labor rights outcomes in post-Communist states should diminish over time, so that the exclusion of post-Communist nations will be less necessary for future studies that employ more recent (i.e., 2000s and after) data.

[8] This book's theoretical framework does not consider short-term financial flows, as these are less likely to be causally related to labor rights. See Mosley and Uno (2007) for an empirical test of this expectation.

to the fore a desire to lower production costs. Collective labor rights play an important role in production costs, given the empirical linkages between unions and collective bargaining, on the one hand, and wage levels and non-wage benefits, on the other (Aidt and Tzannaos 2002; Gallagher 2005; Graham 2000; Murillo and Schrank 2005). Firms can reduce demands for wages and non-wage benefits by restricting collective labor rights; governments can further serve investors' interests (O'Donnell 1988) by not providing, or not enforcing, these rights. For instance, many developing nations have attempted to meet the demands of firms for lower-cost production locations by establishing export processing zones (EPZs). These zones specialize in the manufacture of goods for export, often via subcontracting; jobs in these areas are low-skilled and labor-intensive, and labor rights often are restricted (Madami 1999; Mandle 2003; Moran 2002). While it is nearly impossible to measure subcontracting flows at the national level, we can use trade to proxy for its occurrence. Given this, I expect that trade and collective labor rights may well be negatively related: Once we account for the positive effects of direct investment on labor rights, the "residual" effect of trade (which captures the movement of imports and exports, often via subcontracting) will be a negative one.

Ultimately, workers in developing nations may experience a range of effects related to multinational production. Trade openness presents governments and firms with one set of pressures, wheras capital market openness exposes them to a different – and often contradictory – set of demands. As a result, a country that is very integrated into the global economy in terms of production for export, but whose production facilities are mostly operated by local firms that subcontract for foreign multinationals, is likely to experience worse labor outcomes than a nation with high levels of foreign direct investment. Additionally, within countries, changes over time in the balance between directly owned and arm's-length (or subcontracted) production will lead to changes in the treatment of workers. Ownership structures and sectoral production patterns, then, are a key part of the globalization-workers' rights nexus.

In the mid-1990s, for instance, Mauritius was very involved in global trade, with its exports (and imports) twice as large, relative to its economy, as the average low- and middle-income nation. At the same time, though, Mauritius received very little direct investment relative to its peers; most production for export took place in the context of locally owned firms that subcontracted for foreign multinationals or sold directly to export markets. By 2002, Mauritius remained similarly integrated into global product markets, but the extent of direct investment in its economy had more than doubled. In the mid-1990s, then, Mauritius was more likely (relative to other developing nations) to experience the negative consequences for workers of economic openness. By the early 2000s, however, some of these tendencies were offset by the increased presence of multinational firms.

IV. THE PLAN OF THE BOOK

In the next chapter, I discuss the main independent variables in *Labor Rights and Multinational Production* – international trade, subcontracting, and foreign direct investment. I describe trends in each of these, and I discuss the way in which firms' investment and location decisions interact with national political institutions and practices. As such, Chapter 2 begins to consider the causal connections between labor rights and multinational production, and it refines the notion that economic globalization may have varying effects on developing nations, depending on the precise ways in which they participate in the global economy.

Chapter 3 addresses the determinants of labor rights outcomes, with a focus on multinational firms' mode of entry into foreign markets and their resulting ownership patterns. It develops and presents the book's central hypotheses. I also discuss other potential external influences on labor rights outcomes, including transnational advocacy networks, consumer pressures, and the recent interest in (at least the appearance of) "corporate social responsibility." In the second half of the chapter, I turn to domestic politics: While the main focus of *Labor Rights and Multinational Production* is on the linkages between the global economy and labor rights outcomes, domestic political institutions often play a central role in mediating the pressures emanating from the global economy. Indeed, domestic institutions and politics have contributed markedly to many countries' moves toward economic openness; these same institutions and interests can refract – or reinforce – the pressures generated by global production networks.

In Chapter 4, I describe the book's main dependent variable: the protection and provision of collective labor rights. I discuss the broad concept of collective labor rights, which focuses on the ability of workers to organize, bargain collectively, and strike. This chapter also describes the measure of collective labor rights employed in the book's empirical analyses. In doing so, it highlights an important empirical contribution, which is the creation of a cross-national, time series dataset measuring violations of workers' collective rights. This measure, which is based upon coding of documents from various sources for each country-year, provides a measure of collective labor rights that improves substantially upon previous quantitative measures. As such, it facilitates a shift from considering labor rights anecdotally to considering them systematically.[9]

The remaining chapters of the book provide empirical assessments of the theoretical claims advanced in Chapters 2 and 3. Chapter 5 contains the central cross-national empirical tests of the book's claim that foreign direct investment is positively associated with labor rights outcomes, wheras trade openness often is negatively linked with collective labor rights. The focus of Chapter 5 is the national level of analysis. This chapter confirms the claim that different facets of economic openness have different implications for workers' rights outcomes. In Chapters 6 and 7, I shift from explaining cross-national variation to considering variation within countries. Specifically, I consider how different types of global production and direct investment may have varying implications for collective labor rights, and how these factors interact with domestic political institutions and histories to produce labor rights outcomes.

These chapters represent a second cut in the effort to disaggregate economic globalization: I note that, wheras differentiating between direct investment and subcontracting (operationalized as trade openness) is a worthwhile initial step, another level of distinctions is necessary. I develop the notion that investors' preferences vary across industry and sector, so that different types of FDI (and different export profiles) have different implications for collective labor rights. After developing this theoretical argument in Chapter 6, I present various empirical illustrations of the argument, based on survey as well as case study evidence. In Chapter 7, I consider the case of Costa Rica, which has seen dramatic shifts in its export and foreign direct investment profiles during the last decade. In many ways, Costa Rica is a "most likely" case for the industrial (and labor rights) upgrading that can accompany multinational production. The case study also illustrates the important role that domestic political institutions and histories play in mediating the effects of the global economy. The country's experiences serve as a useful illustration of how the sectoral nature of global production – and not simply its overall

---

[9] Along these lines, Flanagan points out that there "is an extraordinary difference between the conclusions of the research community and the views of globalization skeptics about working conditions in multinationals. To some extent the difference in views reflects a tension between anecdotes and evidence." (Flanagan 2006, p. 124). Construction of the labor rights measure represents an attempt to resolve this tension.

extent – plays an important role in determining its implications for labor rights.

Chapter 8 offers concluding observations on the linkages between collective labor rights and the global economy. I consider how the empirical and theoretical arguments advanced in *Labor Rights and Multinational Production* might change as we move further into the twenty-first century. What, for instance, are the implications of the shift of much foreign direct investment from manufacturing to services? How does the continued economic growth – and competitive prowess – of China and India affect labor rights outcomes (and market pressures) elsewhere in the developing world? And perhaps the most important question: What do this book's findings imply for those who want to work to improve the status of workers in developing countries?

2

Producing Globally

A hallmark of the contemporary international system is the multinational nature of production: Goods and services are produced in a variety of locations, as different nations – and different regions within nations – specialize in varying types of production. As a result of both technological and policy changes, developing nations increasingly participate in global production networks, receiving substantial amounts of foreign direct investment (FDI), participating as subcontracting partners, and importing and exporting a variety of commodities.

It is this expansion of global production, both in terms of its scale and its geographic scope, that has generated interest in the causal linkage between multinational corporations (MNCs), on the one hand, and labor and human rights outcomes, on the other. A long literature has explored the bargaining relationship between multinational firms and national governments (potential or actual host countries). Much of this literature takes as its starting point a concern with the asymmetry in bargaining power: Firms are able to choose from a variety of production locations, and their technologies tend to be cutting-edge; developing country governments are anxious to attract capital as well as to promote employment growth and the transfer of new technologies.

In the 1970s, for instance, many scholars investigated the impact of MNCs on developing host nations. Analysts – both those sympathetic to dependency theory as well as adherents to liberal or mercantilist schools of thought – often were concerned with imbalances in bargaining power between foreign firms and host governments (i.e., Cardoso and Faletto

1971; Evans 1971; Moran 1974). Such imbalances suggested, among other things, that MNCs would form alliances with local elites, sharing their profits with this narrow group in a way that did not benefit society more broadly (Evans 1979), and that local elites would be inclined to change government policies in ways that benefited MNCs but that did not necessarily benefit workers.

More recent analyses echo some of these concerns: Whereas foreign direct investment may bring a range of benefits to host economies, there also can be imbalances in bargaining power between host country governments and MNCs. This is particularly true when MNCs are able to choose among a variety of potential investment locations ("footloose" foreign capital) and when a given country is – perhaps by virtue of its relative level of economic development, its current account position, or its need to increase employment and boost tax revenue – particularly in need of foreign capital.[1] At the same time, though, participation in the global economy – as a host of foreign investment, an exporter of finished and intermediate products, or as a recipient of subcontracting activity – offers a range of benefits to developing nations. At issue for those interested in social policies in developing countries, then, is the ultimate balance between these potential costs and benefits.

In this chapter, I summarize the broad trends in global production that have characterized the last two decades. I consider three main elements of these trends – foreign direct investment, trade, and subcontracting. These are the main independent variables for this book's analysis: The main question is whether, and to what extent, these trends are associated with collective labor rights outcomes. After describing these trends, I briefly review the theoretical literature regarding the determinants of multinational production: Why do firms elect to go abroad, and what do the factors that motivate them suggest about their impact on labor rights outcomes?

---

[1] A related literature examines the existence, and political impact of, a natural resource curse in developing nations. The "curse" refers to the fact that countries that are heavily dependent on resource-related exports tend to exhibit lower rates of economic growth. The economic rationale for the curse centers on positive wealth shocks in the resource sector, which limit competitiveness of the rest of the economy. The political explanations note that resource wealth provides the government with a non-tax revenue source, while also creating incentives for predation and corruption. See Ross (2001, 2008) and Sachs and Warner (2001).

I. TRENDS IN GLOBAL PRODUCTION

Taken broadly, the central independent variable of this book is multinational production, in which goods are produced in one (or more) jurisdiction and sold in other countries. This production could occur through directly owned affiliates of MNCs, through local firms with contractual relationships with multinational firms, or simply through domestically owned firms that export their products. Global production networks are facilitated by several factors, including the standardization of many manufactured goods, the liberalization of trade, improvements in technology, and the decline in long-distance transportation costs (Gereffi et al. 2005; Gereffi and Korzeniewicz 1994; Henderson et al. 2002). In these networks, the value chain of production is spread across multiple locations, often distant from one another. An MNC may purchase inputs for production in one country, process these inputs into component parts in another country, assemble components into final products in yet another country, and sell these finished products to consumers in multiple markets. Multinational production, then, concerns three important and interrelated facets of global production: trade, foreign direct investment, and subcontracting.

Each of these activities has intensified during the last two decades. Most developing nations have liberalized their rules regarding longer-term investment flows (foreign direct investment), and many offer generous investment incentives to multinational corporations (i.e., Li 2006). Particularly during the last decade, governments have increasingly signaled their interest in attracting foreign firms, not only by offering various incentives to these firms, but also by concluding a range of bilateral investment agreements often intended to signal credibility (and to offer compensation in the event of nationalization or expropriation) to foreign investors (Elkins, Simmons, and Guzman 2006). Similarly, trade openness in developing nations has increased dramatically since the late 1980s; these changes are due to external pressures for economic reform, increased international cooperation on trade, and domestic willingness to embrace openness as a means to economic growth. At the aggregate national level, higher levels of openness to trade often are associated with higher rates of economic growth. Despite recent critiques of this finding (see Garrett 2000; Rodrik and Rodriguez 2001; Rodrik 2007), governments generally have embraced outward-oriented trade policies during the last two decades. The third element of global production is perhaps most recent – subcontracting with (or outsourcing to) local suppliers. Many manufacturing firms now rely more heavily on locally owned subcontractors than on their own affiliates for overseas production.

A. Foreign Direct Investment

Foreign direct investment encompasses longer-term cross-border investment. This investment is traditionally taken to reflect a lasting interest by the parent company, which is headquartered in one country, in an enterprise that is located in a different country. FDI is the mechanism through which MNCs establish affiliates abroad ("greenfield" FDI) and by which MNCs acquire or merge with existing firms located abroad (mergers and acquisitions or "brownfield" FDI). In both cases, direct investment is distinguished from shorter-term portfolio investment by its longer time horizon as well as by its direct control of assets.[2]

The last decade was characterized by record global FDI inflows: In 2000, global inflows amounted to a then-record $1.4 trillion. Following a global economic slowdown, flows recovered during the middle of the decade. By 2006, FDI inflows worldwide had reached a new global high, roughly equivalent to 12.7 percent of global gross domestic product (GDP). FDI continued to increase, reaching nearly $2 trillion in 2007. With the "Great Recession" of 2008–2009, FDI declined, largely as a result of a drop in merger and acquisitions activity. Even with this decline, however, global FDI inflows were greater in 2008 than in 2000, and another recovery of flows was expected. As a result of the growth in FDI inflows, global FDI stocks have expanded steadily, with inward stocks accounting for 8.1 percent of world GDP in 1990, 18.1 percent in 2000, and 24.5 percent in 2008.

The expansion in FDI flows and stocks occurred in developed, developing, and transition economies. Table 2.1 documents the current importance of direct investment as well as the growth in the role of direct investment over time. Not only has FDI grown in absolute terms, its importance relative to the size of economies (GDP) and relative to overall investment (gross fixed capital formation) also has increased. The

---

[2] Foreign direct investment statistics usually include the initial transaction between a parent firm and a foreign affiliate, as well as all subsequent cross-border flows of funds, such as expansion of operations abroad. Given that FDI is conceptualized as a controlling interest in a foreign enterprise, the usual criterion applied is 10% or more of the ordinary shares of voting power, or its equivalent. Not all countries, however, use this criterion in generating FDI statistics (UNCTAD 2007).

TABLE 2.1. *Global Trends in FDI, 1982–2008*

	1982	1990	2005	2006	2008
FDI inflows (billions of current $)	59	202	946	1306	1697
FDI inflows (percentage of gross fixed capital formation)	2.4%	4.3%	9.9%	13.4%	12.3%
FDI stock (inward, billions of current $)	790	1942	10051	12404	14909
FDI stock (inward, percentage of GDP)	5.31%	8.10%	22.59%	25.3%	24.5%
Assets of foreign affiliates (billions of current $)	2206	6036	42637	51187	69771
Exports of foreign affiliates (billions of current $)	688	1523	4197	4707	6664
Exports of foreign affiliates/total exports of goods and services (percent)	32.39%	35.18%	33.34%	33.34%	33.33%
Employment of foreign affiliates (in thousands)	21524	25103	63770	72627	77386

Source(s): Data taken from, or calculated based upon, UNCTAD World Investment Report 2007, Table I.4, p. 9; UNCTAD World Investment Report 2009, Table I.6, p. 18; and WIR Annex Tables database (www.unctad.org).

growth rate of accumulated direct investment averaged 16.9 percent in the late 1980s, 9.4 percent in the early 1990s, and 17.4 percent in the late 1990s.

In concert with the growth in FDI, recent years also have witnessed an increase in the importance of MNCs to sales, production, and exports. In 2008, the estimated 82,000 MNCs and their 810,000 foreign affiliates worldwide accounted for approximately one-third of global exports of goods and services; generated sales equivalent to about 10 percent of world GDP; and employed 77 million people directly. Approximately 425,000 of these affiliates are located in developing nations, with China playing host to 286,000 of them. While the percentage of global exports accounted for by MNC affiliates has remained fairly constant since the early 1980s, this has occurred in the face of marked increases in total exports. The growth in global trade and the activities of foreign affiliates, then, are inextricably linked. Moreover, foreign affiliates' employment is now three times greater than it was in 1990; these firms employed approximately 77 million workers in 2008, a number that equated to about three percent of the total global workforce. In some countries (including Ireland and Singapore), foreign affiliates account for almost half of total employment (UNCTAD 2007). The significance of directly owned production to workers is particularly pronounced in developing and transition nations, where the employment impact of a given amount of FDI tends to be greater than that in the developed world (FDI tends to be more labor-intensive in such regions).

Developed nations continue to account for the bulk of global direct investment inflows and outflows. While developing nations – particularly large, middle-income nations such as Brazil and China and relatively wealthy countries such as Hong Kong and Singapore – increasingly generate outward direct investment (also see Gibbon et al. 2008), their share of global FDI outflows remains small. In 2006, for instance, MNCs based in developed countries accounted for 84% of total FDI; the largest source economies were the United States, France, Spain, Switzerland, the United Kingdom, and Germany (UNCTAD 2007). Although the role of developed nations as sources and destinations of FDI declined in relative terms in 2008 and 2009, this decline was not expected to persist (UNCTAD 2009).

Developed nations also represent the major destination for direct investment. In most years, the United States is the leading recipient of FDI; the majority of FDI flows continue to move from one developed country to another (North-North investment). At the same time, however, direct investment is particularly important to the economies and labor forces of developing nations. Since 1990, net capital flows to developing nations have expanded dramatically, reflecting both the liberalization of capital accounts and technological changes. During this time, direct investment flows have accounted for the largest proportion of these flows, outpacing commercial bank loans, portfolio investment (equity and bond) flows, and official development assistance (foreign aid). In many years, FDI has accounted for more than half of total capital flows to developing economies. While a small group of emerging economies – including China, Brazil, and Mexico – attracts the majority of direct investment dollars destined for developing countries, direct investment also is important (especially relative to the size of national economies) to a broad range of low- and middle-income nations. Of the nearly 12,000 greenfield FDI projects undertaken globally in 2006, for instance, over 5,000 of these were located in the developing world, especially in Latin America and Asia.[3] In the face of financial crises (1997–1998 as well as 2008–2009), direct investment flows to developing nations remained stable or increased, while shorter-term flows declined markedly.

The global expansion of FDI flows has been mirrored and facilitated by an expansion of the governance of direct investment: While there remains no global agreement that governs host country and MNC behavior (as envisioned in the late 1990s by the framers of the Multilateral Agreement on Investment), there exists a growing network of bilateral and multilateral arrangements. At the end of 2008, UNCTAD (2009) identified over 5,700 international investment agreements, including 2,676 bilateral investment treaties; 2,805 double taxation treaties; and 273 free trade agreements and economic cooperation agreements with provisions related to direct investment (also see Büthe and Milner 2008; Elkins et al. 2004; Henisz 2000). Bilateral investment treaties, which generally cover principles for the admission of FDI, the treatment of MNCs by host governments, expropriation, and dispute settlement, increased fourfold from the early 1990s. UNCTAD's longer-term survey of FDI-related policies (such as sectoral restrictions on foreign ownership, corporate taxation, and investment incentives) finds that the majority of regulatory changes related to FDI have liberalized, rather than restricted, inward investment. From 1992 to 2008, an average of sixty-nine countries per year made changes to national FDI regulations. Of these regulatory revisions (numbering 2,659 in total), 90 percent were in a direction more favorable to direct investors.[4]

In addition to reforming the overall regulatory climate for foreign direct investment, many developing nations have expanded their use of export processing zones (EPZs). These zones, which also are known as free trade zones or *maquiladoras*, are defined by the International Labour Organization (ILO) as "industrial zones set up to attract foreign investors, in which imported materials undergo some degree of processing before being (re)-exported ..." (International Labour Office Governing Body 2003, p. 1). In 1975, 25 countries used EPZs, with a total of 79 zones worldwide. By 2002, the number had grown to 116 nations, with approximately 3,000 EPZs, employing 43 million workers. By 2006, the

---

[3] The number of greenfield projects continued to rise through 2008, with a total of 15,551 projects; in that year, however, only 2,534 of these projects occurred in developing nations. See UNCTAD 2009, Annex Table A.I.1.

[4] Based on data in UNCTAD (2009), Table I.14, p. 31.

governments of 130 nations had established a total of 3,500 EPZs or similar types of zones, accounting for 66 million employees worldwide. Many of these zones are located in China, where approximately 40 million workers are employed in such areas. However, the zones also are common across the developing world; in Central America and Mexico, for instance, EPZ firms employ 5.3 million individuals (Boyenge 2007).

In terms of the effects of FDI on developing countries, some observers argue that, because the majority of FDI continues to flow among developed nations, MNCs are unlikely to have pronounced effects on social policies and institutions in developing nations (i.e., Flanagan 2006). While it is true that global FDI flows are biased toward wealthy economies, FDI remains important to many developing nations. If we think about developing-nation FDI as a percentage of *all* direct investment, it indeed is relatively small. However, if we consider FDI as a percentage of host country GDP, or as a fraction of total host country gross fixed capital formation, a different picture emerges. For low-income, capital-poor nations, amounts of FDI that are globally small can be locally very significant. This generates great interest in attracting direct investment, and it may endow MNCs with significant bargaining power vis-à-vis developing country workers and governments, especially in institutional climates in which left-labor power is far less entrenched than in developed democracies (see Garrett 1998; Huber and Stephens 2001). This is a point we return to in Chapter 3.

B. Trade

The second element of global production is international trade: When firms undertake foreign operations, they often do so with an eye to selling their products in home- or third-country markets. Additionally, MNCs with complex production chains may extract and process raw materials in one location, produce intermediate goods in another location, and create final consumer products in still other locations. MNCs often subcontract with numerous firms in diverse locations, agreeing to purchase a specific type and quantity of product at a predetermined price. Each of these activities generates trade flows, as subcontractors and affiliates export their intermediate and finished products to MNCs and to consumer markets.

Like foreign direct investment (Lipson 1985), international trade has long played an important role in the global economy. The last two centuries have witnessed a steady growth in world trade, averaging 3.5 percent

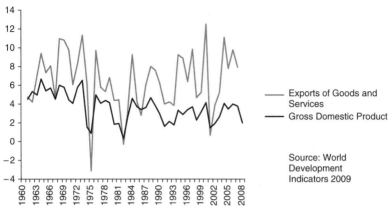

FIGURE 2.1. Growth rates of global exports and output, 1960–2008.

per year, and were marked by extensive (albeit incomplete) convergence in the prices of like goods (Findlay and O'Rourke 2003). Particularly prior to the World War II, much of the expansion in trade was driven by technology as decreases in transportation costs (and improvements in refrigeration, for instance) rendered long-distance shipping more affordable. The growth of trade also was facilitated by domestic political changes in various countries, as groups that would benefit from trade (i.e., in the nineteenth century, urban consumers of agricultural products) gained greater influence over government policies.

In the post–World War II era, the growth of trade also reflects the growing institutionalization of trade relationships at both the global and the regional or bilateral level. The World Trade Organization (WTO) and its predecessor, the General Agreement on Tariffs and Trade (GATT), have played an important role in this growth,[5] as have various regional trade arrangements. More recently, trade openness in developing nations, like FDI activity, has increased dramatically since the 1980s, sometimes as a component of structural adjustment programs and other times in an effort at export-led development.

Figure 2.1 charts the growth of global exports from the early 1960s. In nearly every year, global exports have expanded more rapidly than global output (measured in terms of growth in gross domestic product). During the 1950–2005 period, global exports grew at an average rate of 6.2 percent per annum, compared with an annual GDP growth rate of 3.8 percent. Export growth was even more pronounced in manufactured goods,

[5] See Rose 2004 for a dissenting view.

where annual growth averaged 7.5 percent during the same period (WTO 2007). In many years, exports have far outpaced the rate of GDP growth, suggesting that national economies have become increasingly dependent on global trade. This trend has continued in more recent years, with merchandise trade expanding by an average of 5.7 percent per annum during 1998–2008, compared with a 3 percent annual expansion in global output.[6] Trade growth did slow in 2008 in the wake of a global recession (2 percent, in real terms, compared with 6 percent in 2007), but trade still expanded faster than did global output (1.7 percent, compared with 3.5 percent in 2007).

As part of this trend, the last decade brought increases in merchandise exports across regions. The annual rate of growth of global merchandise exports averaged 11 percent during 2000–2006, before slowing later in the decade. Rates of export growth were even higher in South and Central America (14 percent during 2000–2006), Africa (16 percent), and Asia (12 percent, including a 25 percent annual rate of growth in China and a 19 percent average growth rate in India). While these rates of growth declined in 2008, they remained positive; and export growth was notably higher in developing – versus developed – nations. Additionally, developing countries' share of world merchandise exports climbed to 38 percent in 2008, an all-time high. On the import side, developing nations accounted for 34 percent of global merchandise imports in 2008, the highest level in nearly 30 years (WTO 2009).

The expansion of exports from developing nations also relates to the growth of export processing zones. For many countries, goods produced in EPZs – of which garments and electronics are presently the most common – account for a sizeable percentage of export earnings (International Labour Office Governing Body 2003). The ILO's recent report on EPZs notes that exports from these zones account for 38 percent of export value in Sri Lanka, 41 percent in Mexico, 42 percent in Mauritius, 52 percent in Tunisia, and 87 percent in Kenya (Boyenge 2007).[7]

Contemporary trade openness often goes hand in hand with direct investment. In the 1970s and 1980s, FDI often substituted for trade:

---

[6] These averages are for merchandise trade in volume terms, which exclude price and exchange rate fluctuations. See WTO 2009.

[7] Of course, not all of the value of the exports is added in the EPZ country, as the zones are intended to add value to imported products and then to re-export finished (or intermediate) goods. The ILO's database (Boyenge 2007) summarizes information on EPZs, including the number of zones, total employment, proportion of female employees, major investors and industries, and key exports.

A multinational that wanted to sell its products in a foreign country could manufacture at home and export to its foreign markets; or it could make a direct investment in foreign countries and produce for those domestic markets.[8] Where tariffs or transportation costs were high, firms often chose the latter strategy, so that investment flows substituted for trade flows. While this tariff-jumping, horizontal FDI still occurs, the last two decades have witnessed the growth of another sort of direct investment. Global production networks are facilitated by the standardization of many manufactured commodities, the liberalization of trade in manufactures, improvements in technology, and the decline in long-distance transportation costs (Gereffi and Korzeniewicz 1994). In these networks, the value chain of production is spread across multiple locations, often distant from one another (Gibbon et al. 2008). Multinational firms rely on their subsidiaries, or on local subcontractors and partners, to handle different stages of the production process. Each element in the production chain results in imports and exports so that direct investment and trade are positively correlated (Aizenman and Noy 2005). While many observers have noted the growth in services trade during the last decade, that period also has witnessed a growth in trade in intermediate inputs (as opposed to finish products; Helpman 2006; Hummels et al. 2001). This input trade has occurred both as part of arm's-length subcontracting relationships (see Section IC) and within the boundaries of multinational corporations.[9] Indeed, various studies estimate that approximately one-third of all global trade now occurs *within* firms.

C. Subcontracting

The final element of contemporary global production is subcontracting, which involves an arm's-length relationship between a lead firm and one or more supplier firms.[10] This practice is sometimes known as outsourcing (which can refer to a market-based relationship with a domestic *or*

---

[8] For a discussion of why firms choose a strategy of foreign direct investment versus exporting, see Melitz (2003), Helpman et al. (2004), Helpman (2006), and Tybout (2000). These models imply that the most productive firms serve foreign markets via FDI, while firms with intermediate productivity serve foreign markets via exports; the lowest productivity firms serve only domestic markets. Also see Chapter 3.

[9] Literature in economics refers to the practice of sourcing inputs from affiliates in foreign locations as "offshoring."

[10] I use the term "subcontracting" to refer to arm's-length relationships between lead firms in one country and supplier firms in a second country. In the economics literature, this practice – "the acquisition of an input or service from an unaffiliated company" – often is

a foreign firm). This is part of a more general phenomenon, in which firms decide to conduct some of their operations in the market (outsourcing) rather than within a firm (integration). Subcontracting may be entirely domestic: In the early post–World War II period, for instance, Japanese automakers developed a multi-level system of subcontracting. Automobile firms retained some core functions and employees, while relying on an arm's-length supply network for many key inputs. This shift allowed for the "lean production" that characterized Japanese automakers in the 1970s, and it was, at least in some ways, emulated by European and American firms beginning in the 1980s (Silver 2003).

In the contemporary period, many manufacturing firms produce a large proportion of their goods overseas but rely more heavily on locally owned subcontractors than on their own affiliates (Navaretti and Venables 2004; UNCTAD 1999, 2004). In such situations, no direct investment flows across national borders; rather, subcontractor sales and purchases generate imports and exports (Aizenman and Noy 2005). During the last two decades, some MNCs from developed nations have expanded the scope of their outsourcing activities to include not only the manufacture of components, but also the assembly of subsystems and even finished products. This shift in the nature of global production means that industrial capacity in developing nations often is owned by a country's nationals rather than by foreign firms (Gibbon et al. 2008).

The growth in outsourcing abroad has been facilitated by technological changes, such as computer-aided design and computer-assisted manufacturing, which render it easier for supplier firms to manufacture products that fit the specifications of lead firms. Outsourcing – a "post-Fordist transformation in the organization of production" (Silver 2003, 15) – also allows firms to take advantage of lower marginal labor costs in foreign locations. Furthermore, trade liberalization plays a role: It offers lead firms access to a broader set of suppliers; all else equal, when more potential suppliers are available, firms are more likely to choose outsourcing rather than integration (Helpman 2006). Through an arm's-length mode of entry, then, firms often are able to realize many of the benefits of producing abroad (such as lower unit costs) without the risks associated with direct ownership of facilities (Markusen 1995; Meyer 2001).

---

referred to as "outsourcing," with a distinction drawn between outsourcing at home and outsourcing abroad (Helpman 2006, fn. 55). In the popular press, "outsourcing" often refers specifically to subcontracting in the services sector.

This decision to outsource, whether at home or abroad, often is driven by firm-level considerations, many of which vary by industry. In components-intensive industries (such as electronics), firms benefit more from outsourcing than from integration. Firms have incentives to subcontract in labor-intensive sectors, but to keep production in-house (generating intra-firm trade) in capital-intensive sectors. Indeed, among U.S. manufacturing industries, the level of intra-firm trade is positively correlated with capital intensity; in cross-national analyses, more capital-abundant countries display higher levels of intra-firm trade (Helpman 2006). For firms and countries that tend toward the outsourcing model (generating extra-firm trade), corporations may hire dozens of subcontractors at each stage of the production process.[11] The internationalization of production through market-based mechanisms is perhaps most advanced in labor-intensive sectors (Gibbon et al. 2008; also see Silver 2003).

Yet, in empirical terms, very little systematic information about subcontracting relationships exists. Governments do not collect these data, and firms are – for proprietary and other reasons – hesitant to report it (WTO 2005). One reasonable proxy for this activity, then, is trade. A nation that is very involved in textile production for the world market may receive little foreign direct investment, but it will generate substantial imports of raw materials and exports of finished products. Consistent with this phenomenon, during the first half of the 2000s, global inflows of direct investment declined, but global exports and employment by firms' foreign partners continued to rise (UNCTAD 2004a). I discuss the operationalization of subcontracting (using trade openness as a proxy) in greater detail in Chapter 3.

II. MULTINATIONAL PRODUCTION AND FIRM DECISION-MAKING

Global production is a process that should be understood in terms of both longer-term finance and trade. Multinational corporations are at the center of global production networks; multinational firms, their domestic affiliates, and their local subcontractors generate significant movements of long-term capital, as well as large quantities of imports and exports. While not all global trade and finance involves MNCs, a substantial portion of it does. As a result, the motivations of multinational firms – both

---

[11] Firms appear more likely, all else equal, to outsource to countries with higher concentrations of suppliers. See Helpman 2006.

in terms of what drives the decision to become multinational in the first place, as well as in terms of *how* and *where* to invest internationally – are central to considering the impact of the global economy on workers' rights.

We can begin by considering why firms opt to become involved internationally at all – either through arm's-length relationships or through direct ownership of production. These initial decisions generally are driven by some characteristic(s) of overseas markets that renders them attractive from the firm's point of view. These fall under the general category of locational advantages (Dunning 1992). They include a desire to access natural resources (central in the extractive sector); an interest in accessing particular consumer markets (important especially where such markets are large and/or expanding, as in Brazil, China, and India; or where trade barriers and transportation costs render export from the home market prohibitively expensive); and a desire to improve the efficiency of production. Efforts to increase efficiency often involve a range of country and sector characteristics, including unit labor costs, economies of scale, tax policy, and the availability of skilled workers.

A. Control: Choosing a Mode of Entry

The second stage of firm decision-making involves a choice between involvement in foreign markets through subcontracting relationships (essentially, keeping transactions in the market) and direct investment (making transactions internal to the firm) – the "make versus buy" or "mode of entry" decision.[12] Whereas extant literature treats the decision regarding control of a firm's operation as separate from its locational choices (i.e., Helpman et al. 2004), the two certainly are related: Weak intellectual property protections or political instability, for instance, may increase the perceived costs of direct ownership and, therefore, increase the appeal of an arm's-length production model (also see Agarwal and Ramaswami 1992; Meyer 2001). The general argument of the mode of entry literature is that firm- and sector-level characteristics are key determinants of the means by which internationally active firms engage foreign

---

[12] A large literature explores why multinationals choose wholly owned (directly invested) or arm's-length (trade, licensing, subcontracting) production strategies. See, among others, Antràs (2005), Buckley and Ghauri (2004), and Henisz and Williamson (1999);. Gibbon et al. (2008) point out, though, that there also are several "hybrid" possibilities involving longer-term relationships between lead firms and particular suppliers (also see Agarwal and Ramaswami 1992; Locke et al. 2007; Meyer 2001).

markets. If we take John Dunning's (1992) classic "eclectic" framework for FDI (also known as the OLI approach) as a starting point, we would assume that firms consider organizational factors, location-specific characteristics, and internalization-related advantages when structuring their overseas operations.[13] Organizational factors relate to the control of firm-specific, often intangible assets (Williamson 1985). Internalization refers to the potential benefits of placing transactions within the firm rather than in the broader market. This literature suggests that it is microeconomic concerns that influence firms' decisions about *how* to operate abroad.[14] When firms face concerns about control of intangible assets or access to specific factors of production, their operations abroad are more likely to follow the foreign direct investment, rather than the subcontracting and exporting, model.

Empirical observation bears out many of these predictions. Direct ownership is more prevalent in knowledge-intensive industries, particularly when operating in locations with limited protection of intellectual property. At the firm level, direct ownership (FDI) tends to be employed by firms that are larger, more productive, and more experienced internationally. Subcontracting, on the other hand, is widely used in sectors such as apparel and textiles (note that Nike owns none of the approximately 900 overseas facilities that produce its goods). Arm's-length production also is relatively common in electronics (where some firms, like Dell, subcontract for nearly all of their computer components, maintaining ownership of only the final assembly process; see Berger 2005). It is also sometimes observed in the automobile sector, where firms like General Motors work closely with components suppliers (such as Delphi), sometimes going as far as to share factory floor space (but not ownership) with them. Subcontracting arrangements appear strongly influenced by

---

[13] Agarwal and Ramaswami (1992) explore how these three sets of factors interact to influence firms' mode of entry decisions. For a summary of Dunning's original OLI theory, as well as a discussion of how inter-firm alliances might affect that framework, see Dunning (1995). A Marxist-inspired view of the mode of entry decision might suggest that firms facing labor resistance will opt for subcontracting rather than direct ownership, so as to minimize the level of threats to their production. Silver (2003) refers to such a change in the nature of production as a "technological fix;" changes in firms' production locations can be considered "spatial fixes."

[14] In the contemporary era, of course, firms may simultaneously pursue – and have firm-level incentives to pursue – horizontal *and* vertical integration. One recent study, for instance, finds that 69 percent of U.S. multinationals with affiliates in Canada pursue "complex integration strategies," rather than purely vertical or purely horizontal integration (see Helpman 2006).

efficiency considerations: Surveys of MNCs suggest that, across industries, concerns about costs are the major influence on subcontracting and outsourcing decisions (UNCTAD 2004a). In this context, a nation's ability to produce a good at the lowest possible cost is central to increasing export share and winning business for local subcontracting firms.

Firms that elect to retain ownership, then, tend to be concerned about various market imperfections (also see Henisz 2000; Jensen 2006). These concerns increase the utility of a directly owned production chain that is integrated horizontally, vertically, or along both dimensions. Horizontal integration involves replicating each stage of the production process in each production location, with affiliates under the central control of the MNC. An automobile manufacturer might produce cars in South Carolina for sale to the United States (or North American) market, while producing cars in Germany for sale to the European Union market. This type of integration is attractive to MNCs that want to expand abroad (and, specifically, want to produce for various markets abroad), but that also want to retain control of intangible assets (Markusen 1995). These assets usually involve knowledge of the production process (the technical specifications for a pharmaceutical product or an electronics device, for instance); such assets can be difficult to value and price (information about their underlying value is, almost by definition, asymmetric). Retaining firm control of those intangible assets, then, allows the firm to capture their true value via the production process.

Vertical integration, on the other hand, refers to separating a single production chain (for the global supply of a given product) into distinct stages of production; locating each stage in the location (or locations) where productive efficiency is greatest; and retaining direct firm ownership over the various stages.[15] This last feature is essential, as it represents an internalization of transactions: Rather than purchasing inputs from a firm under different ownership, inputs are purchased from an affiliate or subsidiary firm. Firm decisions to vertically integrate are driven not only by efficiency considerations (in which comparative advantages might motivate a decision to produce microprocessors in

---

[15] Another means of differentiating (by product or sector, rather than by firm) relies on the distinction between producer-driven and buyer-driven commodity chains, with the latter more common in labor-intensive sectors (Gibbon et al. 2008). For a recent typology of the governance of value chains, see Gereffi et al. (2005). They identify five means of governing global production networks: market-based, modular, relational, captive, and hierarchy. Market-based models imply high levels of subcontracting, while hierarchical models entail a focus on directly owned production.

South Korea and flat panel display screens in China, but conduct marketing and customer service in the United States), but also by the desire to retain control over assets that are specific to the production process. The main idea is that firms may want to guarantee their access to a specific input or service (e.g., microprocessors or railroad shipping); they may worry that dependence on suppliers – especially on a small set of suppliers – may leave them in a vulnerable bargaining position vis-à-vis owners of key inputs. Internalizing transactions removes this bargaining issue: Firms do not have to worry that a supplier with a monopoly on producing a specific asset will be able to exploit their need for that asset.

The mode of entry literature has thus far received little attention within political science. Whereas some scholars have noted the connections between political institutions and firms' desire for control of the production process – such as Meyer's (2001) analysis of firm operations in post-Communist countries – little attention has been paid to the political and social implications of the mode of entry. One innovation of this study is to link the mode of entry – specifically, direct investment versus subcontracting – with labor rights outcomes.[16] In developing expectations regarding these links, it is useful to consider another related body of scholarship focused on firms' location decisions.

B. Location: Choosing Where to Invest

If we turn to the issue of *where* abroad to operate (rather than *whether* and *how* to operate abroad), the role of political and social institutions and the reciprocal causal relationship between MNC activities and institutional structures, quickly become evident. Indeed, Dunning's third factor – location – highlights the fact that firms seek not only to go abroad generally, but also to go abroad to specific countries and regions because these confer particular advantages. These potential advantages are diverse, ranging from the availability of specific natural resources or workers with a certain skill set, to investor-friendly legal and regulatory systems, to large and growing consumer markets. Again, most research in this area has focused on direct investment and

---

[16] Firms may use multiple modes of entry: That is, they may engage in both subcontracting and direct ownership, depending on the locations in which they operate as well as the stage of the production process. I focus on the distinction between subcontracting and direct ownership, leaving "mixed" modes of entry as a subject for future research.

wholly owned subsidiaries, rather than on subcontracting and export operations; this is due, at least in part, to the difficulties associated with measuring the latter.

The literature on firms' location decisions provides insights regarding the potential importance of labor rights to global production decisions (both in terms of direct investment and of subcontracting). If multinationals do consider collective labor laws and practices as part of their location calculus, and if developing country governments are interested in attracting multinational investment and trade, then there exists a clear causal pathway for a relationship between global production and workers' rights. If, on the other hand, factors other than labor rights are those that are most important to multinationals' location decisions, or if multinationals have varying views regarding the importance of (and direction of importance of) labor rights institutions, then the causal pathway is much murkier. What, then, does extant literature suggest about the relative importance of political and social institutions, generally, and labor rights, specifically, to firms?

A large literature in economics suggests that economic considerations are paramount determinants of firms' location decisions (e.g., Feng 2001; Kobrin 1987; Leahy and Montagna 2000), and that firms pursue foreign direct investment for a variety of reasons (Hanson et al. 2002). MNCs expand their operations abroad as a way of accessing natural resources, as a means of gaining access to new consumer markets, or as a means of improving their productive efficiency. Firms that seek access to natural resources are, of course, most concerned about the presence of raw materials as well as about infrastructure and property rights (see Chapter 6). Firms concerned with accessing markets (the horizontal model) tend to make direct investments in locations with large national (or regional) markets, where expectations of future economic performance are high. Recent surveys of MNCs confirm that market access remains an important determinant of FDI flows for many firms (Hatem 1998; MIGA 2002), so we might expect an association between market size, economic growth, and income per capita, on the one hand, and direct investment, on the other. For instance, various multinational automobile companies made significant investments in India during the second half of this decade. Their main motivation was to access India's growing (and, eventually, large) domestic car market (UNCTAD 2007). Similarly, in a recent study of U.S. multinationals' direct investments in seven economic sectors and twenty-two countries, Bognanno and colleagues' (2005) find that host country market size is the most important determinant of multinationals' location decisions.

Firms with efficiency motivations, operating under a vertical model of FDI, will consider the comparative productive advantages of various locales. For these direct investors, multinational production is a means of lowering costs (e.g., Feng 2001; Leahy and Montagna 2000; Markusen 1995; Mutti 2003; Navaretti and Venables 2004). FDI allows them to take advantage of cross-national differences in productivity, agglomeration, and the costs of various inputs. The latter could include labor as well as taxation and environmental regulation. Of course, "cost" often is a broad category, encompassing not only labor and infrastructure costs, but also the availability, productivity, and skill of labor; the structure of corporate taxation; and the availability of suppliers in complementary sectors. There is little evidence that one single cost-related consideration drives investment decisions; for instance, most studies report that tax avoidance alone does not motivate direct investment flows (i.e., Markusen 1995).

Some efficiency-seeking direct investors, then, will be drawn to locations with better-developed infrastructure and better-educated labor forces, which tend to characterize nations at higher levels of socioeconomic development. To take an example, Cooke and Noble (1998) analyze FDI outflows from U.S. parent firms, at the industry level, for the early 1990s. They focus on flows to thirty-three industrialized and developing nations; their aim is to assess the impact of various labor-related factors on MNC investment decisions, all else equal. They find that high-skill, high-wage countries are most effective at attracting FDI, even in the presence of restrictions on employee layoffs and the centralization of collective bargaining. Whereas firms might prefer, all else equal, systems with more flexible labor regulations, they are willing to accept regulations in the presence of other attractive factors – political stability and highly skilled and educated workers, for instance. Likewise, another recent study of U.S.-based MNCs finds that wages and the industrial relations system[17] of host nations have a significant influence on firm locations (more flexible systems are positively related to FDI), but that the magnitude of this influence is much smaller than that of host country market size (Bognanno et al. 2005).

---

[17] Bognanno et al.'s (2005) measure of industrial relations is a composite that includes information on union density, strike intensity, collective bargaining structure, works councils, and layoff restrictions. The study covers twenty-two countries, almost all of which fall into the high-income category.

Political institutions also can play an important role in firms' cost calculations and in investment risk assessments more generally. An earlier generation of literature suggests that authoritarian governments, by virtue of their ability to repress labor and control access to resources, attract more direct investment (e.g., Evans 1979). Whereas multinationals worry less about direct expropriation than they did a generation ago, they remain concerned with property rights, the rule of law, and the stability of national policies (such as taxation and market access). More recent studies find that better-developed legal and regulatory frameworks render countries more attractive to MNCs and better able to achieve economic growth (e.g., Keefer and Knack 1997; de Soysa and Oneal 1999). Li and Resnick (2003), for instance, demonstrate a positive association between the "rule of law" aspects of democracy and inflows of direct investment (also see Richards et al. 2001).[18] Additionally, in their study of direct investment flows to Latin America, Biglaiser and deRouen (2006) find that property rights enforcement (as well as financial sector reform) is significantly and positively associated with investment flows.[19]

Along similar lines, Jensen (2003, 2006) posits that, all else equal, more democratic nations attract more foreign direct investment. For a large sample of developed and developing nations, in the 1990s, Jensen (2003) finds that democratic governments attract as much as 70 percent more direct investment than their authoritarian counterparts, after controlling for cross-national differences in economic characteristics. This result hinges on democracy as a commitment device: Popularly elected governments can more credibly commit to future market-friendly policies.[20] Additionally, if democratic governments pursue policies contrary to multinationals' interests, firms can threaten not to renew their investment. Voters will react negatively to such threats, pressuring their governments to maintain policies that please MNCs and, therefore, offer higher

---

[18] Li (2009) finds that, in the midst of a general decline in the prevalence of expropriation in recent decades, there remains a difference across political systems in the risk of expropriation. Less democratic governments and governments with shorter time horizons are, all else equal, more likely to engage in expropriation.

[19] Biglaiser and deRouen (2006) report that, once property rights protections are taken into account, there is no statistically significant impact of other types of economic reforms (taxation, privatization, capital account liberalization) on FDI flows. On the links in post-Communist countries between FDI and government policies, see Bandelj (2008).

[20] Büthe and Milner (2008) argue that the positive impact of international institutions (i.e., preferential trade agreements) on foreign direct investment inflows is conditioned by regime type. When signed by democratic governments, bilateral or multilateral trade agreements encourage greater direct investment inflows, all else equal.

economic growth. Jensen maintains that this positive effect of democracy outweighs any potential negative effects of democracy on investment.[21]

Jensen also argues that political federalism serves to encourage foreign direct investors (also see Jensen and McGillivray 2005; Weingast 1995). Again, this effect stems from the link between direct investment and economic growth: Sub-national governments are likely to enjoy geographically specific benefits from direct investment. Whereas national governments might be tempted to renege on their commitments to MNCs *ex post*, subnational political units are more likely to continue MNC-friendly treatment, as they want to continue to reap the benefits of increased local employment and investment (Jensen 2006).[22]

Although the link between democratic political regimes and FDI flows remains a subject of some debate, the more general claim that MNCs prefer institutional environments that facilitate credible commitments by host governments receives consistent support. Büthe and Milner (2008, 2009) report that once a measure of political constraints on the national executive is included as a regressor, the impact of democracy on FDI flows is no longer statistically significant. The political constraints measure may be a more accurate measure of the political institutions that matter to investors – those that help prevent unanticipated changes in national government policies.[23]

Similarly, Li's (2006) study of tax incentives in developing nations suggests that these instruments often are used to compensate investors for a lack of democratic governance. His analyses, based on cross-sectional data for fifty-two developing countries, suggest that authoritarian governments are more likely to offer tax incentives, perhaps as a means of counteracting the credibility or property rights problems associated with such regimes. Where firms encounter weaker rule of law, tax incentives tend to be greater (also see Henisz and Macher 2004).

---

[21] Resnick (2001) argues that democratic transitions generate uncertainty regarding the rule of law, reducing FDI flows. Li and Resnick (2003) suggest that democracy has contending effects on direct investment: There is a positive "property rights" effect and a negative "reduced scope for rents" dimension.

[22] Malesky's (2008) study of provincial-level policymaking offers an interesting twist: He finds that provinces with a greater stock of existing direct investment were, all else equal, more likely to ignore the dictates of national investment rules, and instead act in ways that were more favorable to foreign firms – essentially, direct investment facilitated "fence-breaking" by sub-national authorities.

[23] Büthe and Milner (2008, 2009) also point out that the link between democracy and FDI flows in past analyses may be an artifact of the trend – upward, in both instances – in each series, rather than of a causal relationship.

Domestic political and social institutions also can have a more direct influence on investors' calculations via their immediate impact on production costs. For instance, countries with better developed domestic financial sectors can offer MNCs easier access to local credit, thereby reducing one type of operating costs. Additionally, nations characterized by better developed vocational training systems can offer a more skilled (and, perhaps, more specifically skilled) pool of workers, thereby improving firms' productivity (Hall and Soskice 2001; Mares 2003). It is in this way – as a direct influence on production outcomes and, therefore, on the efficiency of direct investment – that we might best think of domestic labor laws and practices. Labor laws and practices encompass a wide range of factors, from the status of labor unions and the rights to bargain collectively (the focus of this book), to working conditions and minimum wages, to prohibitions on forced, dangerous, or child labor.

Given the varying motivations of MNCs, we could envision differences in firms' responses to – and resulting pressures on – collective labor laws and practices. On the one hand, labor institutions may serve to increase wage and non-wage costs, thereby reducing the savings that could accrue from multinational production. Because there is an empirical linkage between collective labor institutions and wages, as well as to non-wage benefits (see Aidt and Tzannaos 2002; Gallagher 2005; Graham 2000; Murillo and Schrank 2005), foreign investors might prefer locations with fewer collective labor rights (either in terms of laws on the books or in terms of enforcement of those laws). Indeed, Silver's (2003) exploration of the connections between levels of labor protest and the movement of capital internationally, which spans the late nineteenth and entire twentieth centuries, suggests one way in which firm location decisions may relate directly to labor issues. The general pattern, illustrated by Silver's analyses of the automobile and textile industries, is that pronounced increases in strike activity motivate firms to relocate production abroad. Other reports suggest that U.S. firms have responded to unionization campaigns by threatening to relocate – or actually relocating – their operations abroad (Bronfenbrenner 2000).

The possibility that firms will avoid countries with better developed collective labor rights, and that governments will be tempted to reduce the provision or enforcement of such rights in order to make themselves more attractive to investors, underlies "race to the bottom" concerns of many anti-globalization activists (Drezner 2001; Elliott and Freeman 2003; Spar and Yoffie 1999). This perspective is reminiscent of dependency theory in its view of the exploitative tendencies of MNCs (e.g., Cardoso and Faletto 1971; Evans 1979; Maskus 1997; Smith et al. 1999). As evidence of this dynamic, observers point to the fact that governments often limit collective labor rights in export processing zones, presumably as an added incentive for direct investors (Madami 1999; Mandle 2003). For example, in her study of foreign-owned Chinese firms, Gallagher (2005) reports increasing labor rights violations in the early 1990s, particularly in labor-intensive industries in coastal regions. Furthermore, a few cross-national studies suggest that competition to attract foreign capital results in the reduction of social welfare and respect for human and labor rights (e.g., Rodrik 1997).

Accounts that predict a negative relationship between collective labor organization and direct investment tend to focus on the competition among nations to attract and retain MNCs. Developing nation governments, which tend to be capital-poor, have a variety of reasons for wanting to convince firms to locate in their jurisdictions.[24] Firms, which seek to maximize profit, are inclined to choose the investment destinations that provide the best (and cheapest) combination of the factors that matter to them. Multinationals will bargain with potential host country governments in order to receive the best possible bundle of these items; in doing so, they are likely to play national (and sometimes sub-national) governments off against one another, using race to the bottom dynamics to improve the bargaining outcome. While foreign direct investment is more stable than portfolio investment, it is not entirely "sunk:" Particularly in response to negative changes in government policies or economic outcomes, MNCs may move from one production location to another (of course, the capacity to do so will vary across firms and sectors) or, more modestly, reduce the level of follow-on investments in a given nation.[25]

According to this view of labor institutions and FDI, repression of workers' rights is likely to persist after foreign firms have invested in a particular nation. Given the growing ease of moving operations, particularly labor-intensive ones, MNCs are increasingly able to threaten exit *ex post*. In response, workers who want to preserve their employment might disavow union organization, collective bargaining, or efforts at better working conditions. If this account holds, where labor rights are

---

[24] There is a broad literature on the positive economic consequences of FDI for host countries, some of which I review in Chapter 3.

[25] This logic contrasts with the obsolescing bargain model of direct investment, in which MNCs originally have power vis-à-vis national governments (as MNCs compare across potential investment locations) but lose power over time as their fixed assets in a given location increase. See Vernon (1971) and Kobrin (1987).

better protected, foreign direct investment flows will be lower, all else equal. In the longer run, nations that are more involved in global production also will exhibit more limited labor rights.

It also is possible, however, that the opposite relationship between direct investment and labor rights obtains. Collective labor institutions may serve as a mechanism by which governments persuade workers to invest in sector-specific skills, by which firms encourage their employees to acquire firm-specific skills, and by which employers retain their most productive workers, particularly when labor markets are tight. In this logic, it ultimately is the quality of labor, rather than its cost, that matters (see Chapter 3). To the extent that labor market regulations create a more appealing environment for workers, MNCs will either be neutral or favorably disposed toward them (Cooke and Noble 1998). To return to Silver's (2003) claim that MNCs sometimes choose to relocate in response to labor activism, these relocations have mixed effects for workers. While they harm workers in the original host country locations, they simultaneously advantage workers in new host countries, as the latter experience improved employment prospects and increased wages.

If these optimistic "climb to the top"[26] accounts are accurate, we should find that greater protections of labor rights are associated with higher inflows of FDI, controlling for other economic and institutional factors. Relatedly, while wages in export processing zones located in developing nations generally are low by the standards of developed democracies, they tend to be higher than wages elsewhere in the country (ILO 1998; Moran 2002; U.S. Department of Labor 2000). Even in textiles and footwear, foreign firms may aim to hire and retain reasonably well-educated workers: Their focus is near the top, rather than the bottom, of the local labor market. Locke et al. (2007) find that, among Nike supplier factories, those producing more complex products have higher levels of compliance with labor-related codes of conduct – so that, even within a relatively low-skilled area of production, skill intensity of production can provide incentives for firms to protect workers' rights.

Additionally, wages in foreign-owned facilitates often are higher than wages in otherwise similar domestically owned plants (Graham 1996; Lipsey 2002). Along these lines, Feenstra and Hanson's (1997) analysis of wages in Mexican affiliates of U.S. firms concludes that the growth in foreign direct investment in the 1980s accounts for as much as half of the

---

[26] Spar and Yoffie (1999) label such a view "governance from the top," as national governments, firms, and nongovernmental organizations (NGOs) improve labor standards.

increase in the skilled labor wage during that period. More recently, studies of wages in China indicate that the average wage per worker in MNC-owned facilities is one and one-half times that in state-owned firms, and more than double that paid in collectively owned enterprises. American and European firms were found to pay the highest wages, and these differences existed *within* particular economic sectors (Flanagan 2006). These studies, then, underlie Flanagan's recent conclusion that the empirical evidence is "remarkably clear: on average, multinationals improve labor conditions in host countries" (2006, 124).[27] If MNCs generally pay higher wages, and if they hire from the more skilled segment of the labor force, we can expect FDI to be associated with rising income inequality (Jensen and Rosas 2007). Whereas this may have negative social implications, it is consistent with workers *benefiting* from the arrival of MNCs (also see Chapter 3).

Another alternative – to the predictions that MNCs will avoid countries with better labor rights, or that MNCs will be attracted to such locations – is that, while some firms are attentive to labor costs (perhaps particularly in labor-intensive sectors, in which subcontracting is very prevalent), labor issues generally are less important determinants of firm location decisions than other factors. For instance, a Multilateral Investment Guarantee Agency (MIGA 2002) survey asked firms to rank the most important factors in their selection of investment sites. Seventy-seven percent of firms ranked market access among the top five factors. Other factors cited were a stable social and political environment (ranked among the top five factors by 64% of firms, and consistent with the broad institutional accounts above); reliability of infrastructure (50%); the ability to hire technical professionals (39%); the cost of labor (33%); the ability to hire skilled workers (32%); labor relations and unionization (23%); and taxation (32%).

Whereas a few studies (e.g., Bognanno et al. 2005; Javorcik and Spatareanu 2005) suggest that firm location decisions are influenced positively by labor market flexibility,[28] the balance of evidence supports the assertion that domestic labor institutions and practices often have

---

[27] Some of these differences likely stem from the fact that MNCs have a different profile than domestically owned firms. They are concentrated in sectors such as manufacturing and mining (which often pay higher wages relative to other industries), and they tend to be larger firms (see Helpman 2006). Studies that control for such selection effects, however, still tend to report an MNC wage premium.

[28] Javorcik and Spatareanu (2005) examine firm location decisions in nineteen Western and Eastern European nations.

little effect – and, if anything, a positive effect – on FDI.[29] For instance, a Trade Union Advisory Council (TUAC 1996) study suggests that multinationals from developed nations do not consider core labor standards when assessing investment opportunities.[30] In their study of FDI outflows from U.S. parent firms, Cooke and Noble (1998) report mixed effects of national labor practices: Countries that ratify more ILO conventions, and industries that require works councils, receive *more* direct investment, all else equal. At the same time, restrictions on employee layoffs and levels of unionization are negatively related to FDI flows. However, the negative effect of the latter is outweighed, in substantive terms, by the positive effects of both the former and of workers' skill levels.

More recently, Elliott and Freeman (2003) point out that none of the studies that uses the OECD's four-point labor rights index (see Chapter 4) as an explanatory variable supports the claim that MNCs seek out nations with low labor standards (Oman 2000; Rodrik 1996). Morici and Schulz (2001) do report a correlation between labor standards and labor costs (standards raise costs), but not between labor standards and direct investment. Flanagan (2006) considers variation in countries' share of global FDI flows during the 1991–1996 period. He concludes that "there is no evidence consistent with the view that countries with less skilled labor attract more FDI" (p. 135). Similarly, Kucera's (2002) and Neumayer and de Soysa's (2006) analyses imply that there is no significant relationship between labor rights and direct investment. If anything, these studies suggest that labor rights institutions and practices are related positively to foreign direct investment, supporting the assertion that MNCs often are interested more in retaining skilled workers than in paying the lowest possible wages.[31]

The bulk of evidence regarding what motivates FDI, then, suggests little systematic cause for pessimism regarding the impact of MNC-owned production on labor rights. Three caveats apply, however. First, most studies to date rely on very limited measures of labor rights institutions

[29] Also see Cooke and Noble (1998) and Flanagan (2006) for a review of some of these studies.
[30] The report also points out, though, that governments in some developing nations *believe* that restricting labor rights makes them more attractive to foreign firms.
[31] Kucera (2002) reports that, in some specifications of his model, there is a statistically significant and positive relationship between labor rights and foreign direct investment. This relationship, however, is not robust and does not occur consistently across models. Neumayer and de Soysa (2006) ultimately are interested in the reverse causal relationship, testing whether higher levels of economic globalization generate better (or worse) labor rights.

and practices. As I suggest in Chapter 4, measures based on ratifications of ILO conventions, or on a three-point scale,[32] are likely to obscure much of the cross-national variation in labor rights. While a few studies employ more comprehensive data (Kucera 2002; Neumayer and de Soysa 2006), even these are somewhat limited, in that their measure covers only a single point in time rather than a time series. Empirically, then, the hypothesis that labor rights play little role in determining direct investment requires further assessment using better data.

Second, there are many reasons to expect that the views of firms regarding labor institutions vary among MNCs. We might expect, for instance, that efficiency-seeking firms worry more about production costs (narrowly or broadly conceived) than market-seeking firms.[33] Also, multinationals involved in labor-intensive production (e.g., apparel) may well be more concerned with labor costs than multinationals involved in capital- or technology-intensive sectors (Hatem 1998; Nunnenkamp and Spatz 2002). In such industries, wage costs are a large portion of firms' overall budgets, creating greater incentives for repression, or for avoiding those locations with stronger labor rights protections (Elliot and Freeman 2001; Herzenberg 1996). Firms in such sectors may move repeatedly, seeking out those locations with lower labor costs and less stringent regulations (Mandle 2003; Mutti 2003). In capital-intensive sectors, however, labor costs are a relatively small portion of firms' overall costs, and it is important for employers to attract and retain skilled labor (Gallagher 2005; Hall and Soskice 2001; Moran 2002; Spar 1999). As capital-intensive industries entail larger sunk costs, it is more difficult for firms to threaten exit *ex post*. I explore these within-country, cross-sectoral variations in Chapter 6.

Third, and related to the issue of cross-sectoral distinctions, almost all extant literature considers the link between directly owned affiliates (FDI) and labor institutions, rather than between subcontracting and labor outcomes. In terms of political institutions broadly, it is reasonable to expect that firms engaging in cross-border outsourcing will be

---

[32] Given the paucity of data on labor rights, most analyses focus on human rights (e.g., Apodaca 2001; de Soysa and Oneal 1999; Hafner-Burton 2005; Meyer 1998; Poe and Tate 1994; Poe et al. 1999; Richards et al. 2001; Spar 1998a). In these studies, FDI often is linked with human rights via economic growth or via rule of law and investment risk (Jensen 2003; Li and Resnick 2003).

[33] Santoro (2000) and Gallagher (2005) make such an argument about China: Some foreign MNCs are interested in lowering overall costs, using a "sweatshop" model; others are interested in accessing the domestic Chinese market and in retaining skilled workers.

concerned about the quality of the legal system in countries where their suppliers are located. Countries with better rule of law have been found to export relatively more in "contract intensive" sectors (those characterized by high degrees of subcontracting activity) than countries with weaker legal protections (Helpman 2006; Meyer 2001). We also might imagine that outsourcing could be a reaction to political risk: Where the risk of expropriation, nationalization, or civil conflict is high, firms might be more inclined to engage suppliers via outsourcing rather than direct ownership, as this puts their capital and technology less at risk.

While international outsourcing has increased dramatically in recent decades, there have been few empirical efforts to assess its effects. There are few analyses, for instance, that compare wages in subcontractor factories with those in MNC-owned or purely domestically oriented facilities.[34] If cost considerations are more important to subcontracting location decisions (as compared with FDI location decisions; see Anner 2001), we might expect that contemporary outsourcing has less benign consequences for workers and for their collective rights. In this vein, Anner's (2001) case studies of Hungary and Mexico point to a decline over time in unionization rates, coinciding with the growth of the export-oriented and *maquila* sectors; he notes that unionization rates in subcontractor facilities are substantially lower than those in similarly sized factories in the traditional (directly owned, or for domestic production) manufacturing sector. Furthermore, research on buyer-driven commodity chains (particularly prevalent in labor-intensive sectors) highlights the dominant position of lead firms (see Gibbon et al. 2008), which can pressure their suppliers regarding production standards, timetables for delivery, and costs – all of which may well relate to collective labor rights. This implies that focusing solely on direct investment does not capture the entire picture: If subcontracting decisions are made in response to (a lack of) labor rights protections, the impact of labor-related institutions and practices may be in trade flows or in business alliances, rather than in investment flows.

---

[34] Flanagan (2006) takes a more optimistic view of the linkage between subcontracted production and labor-related outcomes. He notes that most studies of EPZs – where some facilities are foreign-owned, while others are subcontractor-owned – find that workers producing for export earn more than workers elsewhere in the domestic economy. Lim (2001) finds that workers in Nike subcontractor factories in Indonesia are paid significantly higher wages – by a factor of three to five – than workers elsewhere in the economy.

To address this issue empirically, we can use trade as a proxy for subcontracting. Once we control for a country's foreign direct investment activity, we can assume that much of its remaining trade activity reflects participation in global production chains. Because such production networks rely on the movement of goods between nations, they generate large import and export flows. This expectation – that subcontracting and directly owned production may have different implications for labor rights in developing nations – is at the center of the hypotheses developed in the next chapter.

III. CONCLUSION

This chapter summarizes the main independent variables that comprise multinational production and are analyzed in *Labor Rights and Multinational Production* – trade, foreign direct investment, and subcontracting activities. I note how each of these activities has, as a result of both political and technological changes, intensified in recent decades. This chapter also suggests potential pathways through which labor rights could be affected by these trends in global production, in terms of the impact of labor rights on firms' production costs and location decisions. In the next chapter, I describe the hypothesized causal relationships between global production and labor rights. In Chapter 4, I turn to describing the book's main dependent variable – collective labor rights.

3

Inside and Out

The Determinants of Labor Rights

The previous chapter sets the stage for considering the impact of multinational production on workers' collective rights. In this chapter, I develop a set of hypotheses linking the two. My main hypotheses focus on the implications of different modes of production – directly owned versus subcontracted – for labor rights outcomes in developing nations. In addition to theorizing about the effects of international economic participation on labor-related outcomes, I also consider the impact global learning and advocacy, as well as domestic political institutions, have on labor rights. Whereas the main focus of this book is on the impact of the global economy on labor rights, I discuss the potential direct and mediating effects of the latter two factors.

The main theoretical argument I advance is that participation in the global economy has varying effects in developing countries. Some elements of global production, such as directly owned investments, are likely to promote better respect for labor rights. However, other elements of global production, particularly arm's-length subcontracting relationships, may have negative consequences for workers as a result of the cost competition they engender. Ultimately, then, the impact of economic openness on workers' rights will depend on how each country is integrated into the global economy, and this varies across countries and over time.[1] Variation in multinational firms' modes of entry will be associated with differences in firms' attitudes toward, and practices regarding, collective labor rights. Empirically, subcontracting

---

[1] For a similar empirical finding related to forced labor and economic globalization, see Busse and Braun 2003.

and high trade openness may present governments with one set of pressures, while foreign direct investment and capital market openness could expose them to a different – and perhaps contradictory – set of demands.

In the first section, I develop hypotheses regarding the linkages between global production and labor rights. In doing so, I draw upon two bodies of academic research – the first focuses on the implications of economic openness for national policy outcomes, and the second focuses on variation in the ways in which firms organize their global production activities. The first refers to debates centered on the possibility of a cross-national race to the bottom. Although scholarship increasingly has called into question this possibility, it remains prevalent in broader discussions of globalization. I suggest that, despite mixed empirical evidence on the general claims of such arguments, there are some conditions under which global production will be associated with a competitive lowering of standards. The key causal connection, highlighted in the second body of literature, is subcontracting relationships. This mode of organization generates pronounced cost concerns for governments and firms in developing countries, thereby placing downward pressure on collective labor rights. I also discuss the extent to which other types of trade-related factors, such as regional trade agreements, could come to be associated with improvements in labor rights and working conditions.

Next, I turn to the impact of directly owned production on labor rights outcomes. Here, I offer the "climb to the top" logic as an alternative to a trade-related race to the bottom. I assert that, given the way in which directly owned foreign investments are organized and managed, we are likely to observe a positive relationship between FDI and labor rights. Through a variety of mechanisms, direct investors have incentives to encourage the observance of core labor standards in their overseas production facilities. In the remainder of the first section, I discuss other mechanisms that may influence labor rights at the international level; I focus on the role of international human and labor rights advocacy groups, as well as the more general phenomenon of the cross-national diffusion of norms and practices.

In the final section of this chapter, I focus on internal influences on collective labor rights. Specifically, I discuss the mediating and direct influence of domestic economic conditions, as well as political institutions and ideology, on labor rights outcomes. I suggest that domestic factors, including the structure of the economy, the degree of political representation, and the ideology of the governing party or parties, can serve to filter the influences of the global economy. Political interests and institutions may be particularly important for the implementation of collective labor rights: In situations in which economic resources are limited, political will is essential to the domestic monitoring and enforcement of core labor rights.

I. THE GLOBAL ECONOMY AND LABOR RIGHTS

Is economic globalization to blame for the perilous plight of many of the world's workers? Much of this debate is captured in the more general concerns regarding a race to the bottom, a concept frequently invoked, both in academic literature and the popular press, during the 1990s and 2000s. The phrase reflects a concern that economic globalization has, in concert with technological changes, produced a competition among governments, firms, and workers. Its underlying assumption is that competitive pressures trump all sorts of other considerations, including the ideology of governments and political parties and the varying preferences of citizens and firms. Also, its prediction for a "flat" world (Friedman 2005) suggested a narrowing, or even a disappearance, of cross-national differences in areas ranging from social security systems to welfare provision to labor rights.

Many proponents of the race to the bottom view have worried about its implications for citizens of developing (as well as developed) nations in terms of wages, job quality, and economic inequality. Some note that citizens, as they experience the negative consequences of economic openness, are likely to demand increased trade protectionism, putting at risk the global trend toward integration (i.e., Rodrik 1997). For instance, Stephen Roach, the long-time managing director and chief economist at Morgan Stanley, has commented repeatedly on the process of "global labor arbitrage," in which competitive pressures, coupled with innovations in information technology, drive firms to continually search for lower labor costs, both for unskilled and highly skilled workers. In his analysis, the result has been "increasingly brutal wage compression," producing "mounting disparities in the income distribution – for developed and developing countries alike" (Roach 2006). In his analysis, the tide of globalization has failed to lift all, or even most, boats; in the political realm, this is likely to imperil the decades-long movement toward openness. Many critics of economic globalization, of course, cite race to the bottom pressures as the key problem, undermining the policymaking autonomy of national governments and giving too much control over domestic policies to mobile firms and investors.

Among scholars of international and comparative political economy, however, the race to the bottom hypothesis has received only limited empirical support. Indeed, at its most extreme – external factors dominate domestic ones under nearly all circumstances – the thesis is more a foil for empirical researchers than a scholarly claim about the causal linkages between economic openness and domestic policy choices.[2] Empirical researchers have reported a variety of findings with respect to the race to the bottom in developing nations. These include the claims that developing nation governments are less able to act autonomously than their developed-nation counterparts (Mosley 2003; Wibbels 2006); that economic globalization is associated with lower social spending in developing nations, but that such spending has never been pro-poor in its effects (Avelino et al. 2005; Rudra 2008); that economic globalization increases pressures for compensation, so therefore is associated with *more* public spending (Rodrik 1998); and that the pressures from economic openness often are outweighed by domestic political institutions and ideology (Brooks 2009; Huber and Stephens 2001).

To what extent is the race to the bottom a valid claim in the area of labor rights? A more general concern with cross-national competitive pressures and the welfare of workers has a long history. The founders of the ILO, for instance, worried about the effect of one country's labor rights practices on peer countries. The Preamble to the Constitution of the ILO, adopted at the April 1919 Paris Peace Conference, justifies the creation of a global labor organization on the grounds that "the failure of any nation to adopt humane conditions of labor is an obstacle in the way of other nations which desire to improve conditions in their own countries."[3] At the same time, a race to the bottom effect runs counter to the predictions of neoclassical economics: As trade openness generates factor-price equalization, wages (and, more generally, the conditions) of workers in the developing world should increase.[4] The globalization of production, then, could harm some workers (those who lose their jobs

---

[2] For more detailed discussions of the race to the bottom claim in the political economy literature, see Drezner 2001, Mosley 2003, and Rudra 2008.

[3] Quoted in Elliott and Freeman 2003, p. 4.

[4] Indeed, there is some evidence of an "export wage premium" in both developed and developing country studies: Workers in export industries tend to earn higher wages than those in non-export industries. There is likely an important process of selection at work, however: Firms that become exporters are different from those that do not, and these

as multinational firms relocate some production) but advantage others (those who gain employment opportunities as new direct investors arrive; see Silver 2003). Yet theories based in neoclassical economics tend to assume competitive labor markets, without government intervention and without large reserves of surplus labor. Such conditions often do not obtain in developing nations, generating the potential for a negative impact of subcontracting (the role of which usually is neglected in such theories; see Flanagan 2006) and trade-based competition.

I discuss the link between subcontracting and labor rights in Section B below. More generally, though, neither globalization's supporters nor its detractors accurately capture the causal links between workers, on the one hand, and the global economy, on the other. The impact of multinational production on labor rights depends on the precise ways in which a country, and its firms and citizens, participate in the global economy. As a result, economic globalization is *somewhat* related to labor rights but in a much more nuanced way than many scholars (and activist campaigns) have suggested. Specifically, the effect of multinational production on workers' rights depends on the ways in which multinational production is organized – whether it is characterized by direct ownership of production facilities abroad, or by subcontracted arm's-length relationships between lead firms and supplier firms. While scholars of economics and industrial organization have sought to explain the *causes* of firms' mode of entry decisions, they have paid scant attention to the *consequences* of these decisions for labor rights outcomes. Moreover, while comparative and international political economists have considered the relationship between economic globalization and policy outcomes in developing nations, they have done so at a very aggregate level, examining the impact of overall economic openness on domestic policy outcomes. By considering variation in how firms organize production, and in how developing nations are integrated into the global economy, I offer a more nuanced theoretical view of the causal connections between global production and labor rights.

A. Multinational Corporations and the Climb to the Top?

As Chapter 2 describes, foreign direct investment has become an increasingly important feature of the global economy during the last two

---

differences likely include worker productivity and technological intensity, both of which also will affect wages. Also see Flanagan 2006, chapter 4.

decades. Given existing empirical literature regarding the links between MNCs and policy outcomes in host countries, as well as a variety of theoretical propositions regarding MNCs' operating behavior, I expect that multinational corporations' directly owned activities will generate positive pressures for the adoption and observation of collective labor rights. As such, developing nations with high levels of direct investment (relative to the size of their economies) can be expected to exhibit fewer violations of collective labor rights, all else equal – a positive, climb to the top effect on labor rights.

Certainly, some observers take the opposite view, maintaining that FDI has negative consequences for workers' rights. Such claims are based on the race to the bottom logic, as well as on an older literature that worries about the exploitative tendencies of MNCs, especially in collusion with local elites (i.e., Evans 1979; O'Donnell 1988). As part of such collusion, local governments and capital owners may attempt to repress organized labor and limit the legal rights of workers. This view overlaps with dependency theory, which worries more generally about the inequality between core states (and their companies) and peripheral nations (Cardoso and Faletto 1971; Hymer 1979; Smith et al. 1999). The negative view of MNCs' impact also relates to concerns about the relative voices of investors, home governments, and local labor forces. If the capacity to threaten exit provides voice to political actors (see Mosley 2003 for a summary of this argument), then foreign investors are likely to have more voice than governments or workers. Whereas direct investment is less liquid than shorter-term portfolio investment, and therefore less able to make credible threats of exit, technological change has rendered at least some FDI more footloose. MNCs may threaten to relocate developing country facilities or not to reinvest in existing facilities (allowing them to eventually become outdated). Moreover, even if FDI is relatively illiquid *ex post*, the *ex ante* (pre-investment) competition among governments to attract direct investment provides bargaining leverage for such firms. In terms of labor rights, this line of reasoning implies that workers who want to preserve their employment might disavow union organization, collective bargaining, or efforts for better working conditions. According to this view, then, FDI will be associated with increases in labor rights violations, particularly in labor-intensive sectors where unskilled workers have little bargaining power.

Negative accounts of FDI and workers' collective rights cite numerous anecdotal accounts in which developing country governments ignore, or actively flout, core labor standards as a means of attracting and retaining foreign multinationals. Mexican *maquiladoras* and Southeast Asian sweat-shops are perhaps the most visible examples (e.g., Iglesias Prieto 1997). More recently, studies of the natural resource curse sometimes point to collusion between corrupt host country governments and multinational corporations (Stiglitz 2007). Additionally, a few cross-national studies suggest that competition to attract foreign capital results in the reduction of social welfare and respect for human and labor rights (Rodrik 1997) as well as in the reduction of corporate tax rates (Mutti 2003).[5] Yet systematic support for this view is limited.

Furthermore, such a view runs counter to the large literature – found mostly in economics and political science – that establishes a variety of positive effects (particularly at the aggregate national level) of direct investment in developing nations (Bhagwati 2004; Brown et al. 2004; Frankel 2003; Graham 2000; Leahy and Montagna 2000; Moran 2002; Mutti 2003; OECD 2002; Santoro 2000). These include technology transfer, job creation, and economic growth. While low- and middle-income nations may indeed be characterized by a dearth of labor rights – and the more general occurrence of repression – this likely has less to do with the presence of MNCs than with trade openness and with internal political and economic factors (see Part II, this chapter). We expect that, *ceteris paribus*, FDI is related positively to workers' rights.

There are three specific causal pathways through which directly owned production (FDI) could enhance the capacity of workers to demand – and to achieve – improvements in their collective rights. Each predicts that directly owned production is a mechanism for a climb to the top rather than a race to the bottom. First, MNCs may urge governments explicitly to improve the rule of law, protect the vulnerable, and invest in social services and infrastructure (Ahlquist and Prakash 2008; Biersteker 1978; Richards et al. 2001). Foreign corporations are likely to encourage improved rule of law, not out of altruism, but out of concern for corporate profitability: Stronger rule of law lowers investment risk for MNCs as they become more confident in the stability of their rights of ownership and in the local legal system (on FDI and democracy, see Jensen 2006; Li and Resnick 2003; Li 2009). In this pathway, improved labor rights are a perhaps unintended product of national governments' efforts to improve governance and, therefore, to lower MNCs' investment risk.

---

[5] Likewise, Javorcik and Wei (2004) report that there is some, albeit weak, evidence that MNCs engaged in high-pollution activities locate in areas with low environmental standards.

Second, whereas unit labor costs – that is, labor costs controlling for differences in productivity – often play a role in MNC's location decisions, the bulk of MNCs are concerned with the hiring and retention of skilled workers. As Brown et al. (2004) point out, the Heckscher-Ohlin model suggests that multinationals will leave the "low" (less skilled) end of production in developed countries; as they move to the developing world, these same industries will be at the "high" (more skilled) end. As a result, multinationals find themselves wanting to attract the best workers in developing nations. Given that MNCs are competing with local firms to hire skilled workers, they may want to avoid the competitive disadvantage that would result from a reputation for repressing labor rights (Flanagan 2006). A recent report on the global electronics industry, for instance, noted that some firms that moved to China from various Southeast Asian nations are now reversing course. Their moves (back) to Malaysia, Singapore, and Vietnam were motivated by the difficulty of attracting and retaining *skilled* workers in China's booming coastal provinces (*New York Times*, February 27, 2006).[6] More broadly, as the available supply of Chinese workers in many industries has declined (due to a variety of factors, including government efforts at rural development in the inland provinces), wages are rising, and firms are providing new benefits to workers (*New York Times*, April 3, 2006).

In this logic, firms *do* care about overall productive efficiency in their directly owned facilities; but efficiency includes not only wage costs but also the productivity of labor, as well as the sunk costs associated with training workers, particularly when production involves firm- and sector-specific skills. It is ultimately the quality of labor, rather than its cost, that matters (Moran 2002; Santoro 2000; Spar 1999; Spar and Yoffie 1999; World Bank 1996).[7] In such cases, corporations are likely to invest in countries with higher education levels, to expend resources on training and benefits for employees, and to pay higher wages to reduce turnover (Gallagher 2005; Garrett 1998; Hall and Soskice 2001; Moran 2002; Santoro 2000). This is likely true particularly when FDI is motivated

---

[6] For a similar example from India, see James Surowiecki, "India's Skills Famine," *The New Yorker*, April 14, 2007.

[7] Along these lines, Blanton and Blanton (2007, 2009) argue that human capital formation is the mechanism that generates a statistically significant relationship between human rights and direct investment. Where human rights are better protected, human capital development is greater, and the majority of MNCs are attracted to locations with higher levels of human capital.

by access to specific consumer markets rather than by efforts to lower production costs.

Even in sectors with mostly unskilled workers, many firms may believe that workers whose core rights are protected (and whose working conditions meet minimum standards) are more likely to remain on the job and more likely to work efficiently. For example, in the Dominican Republic, foreign direct investors that were involved in producing more high-technology products located their operations near Santo Domingo (the capital) so that they would have access to more skilled labor (Moran 2002). More recently, consulting firm Grant Thornton surveyed multinationals regarding the issue of attracting and retaining workers. Firms were most concerned about hiring and keeping skilled workers in Vietnam (with China second; Bradsher 2008); even in destinations perceived as "cheap labor," concerns about retention may push firms to improve working conditions.

In the post-MFA period, for instance, Better Factories Cambodia (the new name for the ILO-backed monitoring initiative; see Section IC below) has tried to draw a connection between corporate responsibility to workers and productive efficiency (Chiu 2007). More generally, collective labor institutions – labor unions – serve as a mechanism by which governments can persuade workers to invest in sector-specific skills, by which firms encourage their employees to acquire firm-specific skills, and with which firms retain their most productive workers, particularly where labor markets are very competitive. In this vein, empirical evidence suggests that wages in foreign-owned facilities often are higher than wages in equivalent domestically owned plants (Brown et al. 2004; Graham 1996; Lipsey 2002; Moran 2002; also see Helpman et al. 2004).[8] Some qualitative analyses of EPZs suggest that, even in textiles and footwear, foreign firms seek out reasonably well-educated workers who live close to industrial hubs and commercial centers – again, reflecting a desire to hire and retain the most skilled employees (Moran 2002). We often observe, then, that multinational firms aim at the high end of local labor markets in developing nations, something that is very much at odds with a race to the bottom view.

The third causal mechanism linking direct investment with higher levels of collective labor rights draws on the fact that foreign multinationals

---

[8] Similarly, Locke et al.'s (2007) study of labor conditions in Nike supplier factories finds a significant relationship between the ownership (foreign versus domestic) of the facility and compliance with Nike's labor code. Foreign-owned suppliers have higher rates of compliance, all else equal.

often transfer new technologies to host economies. In many cases, these technologies help to improve the capital and skill intensity of production and, therefore, lead to higher wages for workers. These new technologies are initially used in directly owned production facilities but then often diffuse to a broader set of firms within the economy. In her analysis of the affiliates of U.S.-owned chemical firms in Brazil and Mexico, for instance, Garcia-Johnson (2000) finds that MNCs tend to bring higher-end technology to their developing world operations. Rather than using developing-nation facilities as a means to avoid home country regulations, MNCs standardize technologies across their facilities. Firms engage in this practice because it makes productive sense: They tend to find that it is more efficient to standardize across facilities. Standardization of management practices across facilities allows firms to limit the fixed costs associated with operating subsidiaries abroad (see Helpman et al. 2004). One result of this efficiency-minded strategy is a sort of "California effect," in which the more stringent regulations of some production location become the de facto practice throughout a firm's operations (Levy and Prakash 2003; Vogel 1995).[9]

The extent to which developing-country firms adopt more advanced environmental management practices depends, of course, on the use of such practices in the countries from which they receive direct investment. Prakash and Potoski (2007)'s quantitative analyses reveal that, when developing nations receive a greater proportion of direct investment from nations with high rates of ISO 14001 adoption, those countries are themselves more likely to adopt ISO 14001 at a higher rate.[10] Here, the practices are environmental rather than labor-related, but the mechanism is similar: MNCs' desire for standardization – and for being

---

[9] Locke et al.'s (2009a) study of labor conditions in global supply chains reveals a similar pattern, although their focus is on explaining differences among supplier firms (all of which have subcontracting relationships with a lead firm). In case studies of firms in the Dominican Republic, Honduras, and India, the authors find that the local firms that are best able to effect improvements in labor conditions are those that have a long-term relationship with a particular lead firm. Given this relationship, the lead firm appears more concerned with transferring best practices and with helping suppliers find cost-effective means of complying with individual labor rights provisions. Also see Locke et al.'s (2007) analysis of Nike supplier factories for a similar finding.

[10] Prakash and Potoski (2007) report that only the bilateral FDI context – that is, the level of standards adoption in home countries, weighted by their share in a given host country's total direct investment flows – is significantly related to ISO adoption. A host country's total stock of direct investment is not significantly associated with levels of ISO 14001 adoption.

able to describe their affiliates' practices as "advanced" – generates an "investing up" in standards. If this mechanism holds more generally, affiliates in low- and middle-income countries will be provided with more up-to-date technologies than they would have otherwise. Given the variety of firms' operating locations, such a desire for harmonization may well create a race to the top rather than to the bottom, particularly for firms from wealthy, democratic nations with strong labor rights protections.

In terms of labor-related issues, we can expect MNCs to bring "best practices" for workers' rights to host countries (Finnemore 1996; OECD 2002). Given that the vast majority of MNCs continue to be headquartered in developed nations, where core labor standards are well observed both in law and in practice, the labor rights technologies brought to developing nations are likely to include participatory labor-management relations as well as corporate codes of conduct with labor-oriented provisions. Again, such practices stem not from MNCs' altruism toward their labor forces in host countries, but from their desire to achieve a high level of productive efficiency. As Moran argues, "the [subsidiary] plants are designed to capture all potential economies of scale, and to sustain a position at the cutting edge of industry best practices" (2002, 117). Similarly, the literature on global value chains points to the role played by particularly powerful companies ("lead firms") in global economic governance. Such firms often are able to set standards, not only for products and components (Gibbon et al. 2008), but also for the behavior of affiliates and subsidiaries. In this vein, Prakash and Potoski (2006) describe how multinational firms pressure subsidiary firms in developing countries to adopt voluntary environmental standards (ISO 14001). As such, we can expect a fair amount of "parental supervision" within directly owned production networks. Moreover, we can expect most MNC parent firms to be concerned – for reasons related both to productive efficiency and to the "spotlight" from shareholders and consumers – with labor practices in their facilities.

Consistent with the "best practices" argument is empirical evidence regarding compensation in MNC-owned facilities. While wages in foreign-owned developing country firms may not be as high as those in developed nations,[11] they often are higher than in locally owned

---

[11] What is less clear, however, is the extent to which wages and productivity spill over from MNC-owned affiliates to locally owned firms in the host economy. See Flanagan 2006 for a review.

developing country firms.[12] Multinationals also may have material incentives to standardize their operations across their affiliates and subsidiaries so that the highest standards are taken abroad. Indeed, a variety of studies suggests that affiliates of foreign firms have higher levels of labor productivity than do their domestically owned counterparts and that this holds in developing as well as developed nations (Flanagan 2006).[13]

Furthermore, MNCs' tendency to bring best practices for workers' rights to developing countries is enhanced by attention from shareholders, human and labor rights activists, and consumers. Indeed, the last decade has witnessed a marked increase in attention to corporate social responsibility (CSR), in which firms make commitments to a certain set of environmental, labor, and social practices throughout their supply chains. The rise of corporate codes of conduct, as well as the creation of various industry-wide standards, can be seen as part of the broader rise of private-sector-based governance arrangements, which either supplement or substitute for governmental regulation (Bartley 2003 2007; Mosley 2009; Vogel 2009). Particularly where host-country governments lack the technical resources or the political will to implement collective labor rights, such private-sector-based systems may be an effective alternative (see Rodríguez-Garavito 2005).[14]

This trend has occurred alongside a heightened attention to labor rights on the part of national governments. Bartley (2003) argues that, as developed nation governments found themselves unable to pursue labor rights issues in intergovernmental organizations (given the conflict

---

[12] In their comparative study of two Nike plants in Mexico, however, Locke and Romis (2009b) find that labor conditions are worse at the foreign-owned than at the domestically owned facility. There are, however, other differences between the facilities (such as the level of development of the surrounding area, the proximity to corporate headquarters, and the size of the work force) that might explain this pattern.

[13] On the relative productivity of MNCs versus exporters, see Helpman et al. 2004. On the productivity of domestically owned versus foreign-owned firms, see Un and Cuervo-Cazurra (2008).

[14] Croucher and Cotton (2009) posit that international framework agreements, which are agreements between labor unions (or union federations) and multinationals' management, may be an alternative to codes of conduct, particularly when a given MNC is active in multiple jurisdictions. While only sixty-four such agreements were concluded in 2008, this represents a marked increase from 2000 (nine international framework agreements) and 2004 (thirty-two such agreements). Union activists sometimes prefer such agreements, as organized labor tends to have more input regarding their content. These agreements also offer the opportunity to match the level (supranational) of labor politics to the level of production (Silver 2003). However, like corporate codes of conduct, the impact in practice of international framework agreements is thus far unclear.

between developed and developing countries over whether "labor rights" issues were little more than veiled protectionism), they instead dedicated resources to private-sector-based efforts.[15] Private-sector-based regulations have the advantage of falling outside the WTO's realm: Multinational firms can make demands of suppliers (in terms, for instance, of labor conditions) that importing jurisdictions cannot, given global trade rules, make of their trade partners. Along these lines, in 1996, the Clinton administration backed – politically as well as fiscally – the formation of the Fair Labor Association (FLA), via the Apparel Industry Partnership; and in 1997, the United Nations launched the Global Compact program. Both sought participation from firms that were willing to commit to certain practices throughout their operations and supply chains (also see Bartley 2007).

The mid-1990s also witnessed the development of other umbrella organizations that developed codes of conduct and created third-party monitoring systems, including the Ethical Trading Initiative (ETI), Workers' Rights Consortium (WRC), Social Accountability International (SAI; the SA8000 standard), and the Worldwide Responsible Apparel Production Certification Program (WRAP). These initiatives, which also include the FLA, were intended to provide some uniformity in codes of conduct (at least, at the industry level) and to address the credibility problems associated with self-monitoring of codes by MNCs. The variation across these third-party monitoring systems, however, may diminish their overall impact. For instance, while the FLA, WRC, and SAI all include the freedom of association and collective bargaining as part of their standard, WRAP does not. Only the WRC and the FLA have the capacity to sanction members (Rodríguez-Garavito 2005; also see Bartley 2003, 2007; Brown et al. 2004).

While the CSR movement may reflect a change in firms' underlying perceptions regarding the most appropriate labor rights practices (Keck and Sikkink 1998; Brown et al. 2004), or an effort based more in image and marketing than in substantive commitment to workers' rights, it also may reflect a straightforward response to material incentives (Barrientos and Smith 2007; Bhagwati 2004; Frankel 2003; Gereffi et al. 2005; Haufler 2000). Multinational corporations can come under pressure

---

[15] Bartley also notes that the Clinton administration proposed to the ILO, in mid-1996, a "global social label" for apparel. The ILO considered a similar proposal the following year, but it was criticized by developing-nation representatives as a disguised form of protectionism.

from a variety of directions to ensure ethical conduct and practices within their supply chains (Baron 2003; Becker and Sklar 1999; Blanton and Blanton 2007; Brown et al. 2004; Spar and La Mure 2003; Vogel 2009). For many firms, the threat of political action by human rights groups in home countries concerned about buying goods from countries with exploitative labor practices, the ensuing media scrutiny, and the possibility of consumer backlash create strong incentives to pay attention to labor issues abroad.[16] Additionally, shareholder activism by ethically focused investment funds, as well as large institutional investors such as Calpers, encourages firms to adopt codes of corporate social responsibility whose obligations extend to their overseas subsidiaries (Bartley 2005; O'Rourke 2003).

Another source of pressures may be competitor firms in the same industry: If firms engage in mutual monitoring of one another's behavior, firm-level codes of conduct may diffuse, even absent consumer pressure (Sabel 2007).[17] And, of course, providing better conditions for workers can head off protests, not only from transnational activists, but also from local workers. In the Mactan EPZ in the Philippines, for example, firms undertook self-policing in the 1990s, carried out via a human resource association comprised of various firms' personnel department staff. The intent was to use compliance with national labor regulations as a means of avoiding the labor unrest that had characterized other parts of the country (Moran 2002).

Therefore, even without a change in underlying beliefs, pressure from shareholders, consumers, or the media may result in a new level of attentiveness to labor rights and working conditions (Anner 2001). For instance, Colonomos and Santiso's (2005) analysis of French firms' attention to the notion of corporate social responsibility finds that shareholder pressures play an important role. French companies with significant share ownership by U.S. investors appear more attentive to general CSR principles than do other listed French companies.[18] More generally,

---

[16] Bartley (2007), however, argues that market pressures alone are an insufficient explanation for the specific *type* of regulatory response (based in the private sector but with some third-party enforcement) that emerged in the late 1990s.

[17] This process relates to the "rolling rule" regime. It also is consistent with the fact that Social Accountability International's use by firms as a certification organization has increased markedly during the last decade despite the fact that it does not offer a label for consumer products. I thank Tim Bartley for pointing this out.

[18] Also see Margolis and Walsh (2001), who report a link between MNC share prices and reports of labor abuses.

when firms perceive a "market for labor standards" (Elliott and Freeman 2003), they will be more likely to consider the extent to which their affiliates are located in countries with legal protections for labor rights, as well as the degree to which such legal protections are effective in practice. Such attentiveness can serve to further underscore the climb to the top influences of firms' interest in retaining workers and in favoring developing nations with strong rule of law. We might expect, of course, that the extent to which MNCs fall under the spotlight of attention regarding their practices varies. This attention will be strongest in cases of branded and luxury products, where firms are concerned with maintaining a positive brand image and where (given costs of marketing and design) wages represent a relatively small proportion – perhaps even less than one percent – of a product's final cost (Moran 2002).

The general pattern, then, has been one in which a variety of firms have adopted corporate codes of conduct, with an increasing focus over time on third-party monitoring. Vogel (2009) notes that there now exist over 300 industry or product codes, nearly all of which address labor or environmental practices; more than 3,000 global firms now issue reports on their social and environmental standards.[19] In 2003, a World Bank study estimated that 1,000 labor-related codes existed (Smith and Feldman 2003).[20] Labor-related codes of conduct vary in scope, stringency, and emphasis; some focus on health and safety issues; others focus on environmental issues; and still others emphasize payment of minimum

---

[19] The general effectiveness of voluntary codes is open to debate. Potoski and Prakash 2009 examine ISO 9000, a set of standards for quality management systems and practices. They find that developing countries with higher levels of ISO 9000 adoption export more products, all else equal, than countries with lower rates of adoption. Firms in developing countries, then, may benefit from this voluntary standard because it provides foreign buyers with information regarding the ways in which their products are manufactured. Barrientos and Smith 2007 find, in their study of twenty-nine companies with operations in a range of industries and countries, a mixed track record for labor-related corporate codes.

[20] A 2001 OECD study of codes of conduct reported that 246 major firms had corporate codes. The OECD study also reported variation by nationality: U.S. firms accounted for 68 percent of the total, while British and German multinationals each accounted for 5 percent. A 2005 study by KPMG notes the marked growth in firms' reporting on CSR-related issues. In 2002, 45 percent of global Fortune 250 firms issued corporate responsibility reports. By 2005, this share had increased to 63 percent. Over 80 percent of the 100 largest Japanese firms, and over 70 percent of the 100 largest British firms, issued such reports. While "sustainability" was the most popular type of corporate responsibility report in 2005, the study also documented a near-doubling (between 2002 and 2005) in the share of firms that released "environmental and social" (including labor issues) reports.

or living wages. Many of them, however, take the core labor standards promulgated by the ILO in 1998 as a key starting point (ILO 2005). As such, the freedom of association and right to bargain collectively, as well as the elimination of child and forced labor, are central elements.[21]

The codes also vary in their provisions for monitoring and enforcement. In recent years, though, the general trend has been toward monitoring via third-party auditors (which could be private firms such as Ernst and Young, or NGOs that work on labor rights issues); increasingly, these auditors are certified or trained by multi-stakeholder initiatives (representing industry as well as activists). For instance, companies affiliated with the Fair Labor Association (FLA) agree to implement the FLA Code of Conduct, which draws on the ILO's core labor standards. FLA members also are required to establish an internal monitoring and compliance program; this program is supplemented with unannounced external monitoring visits to a randomly selected sample of firms, concentrated in footwear, apparel, and equipment (FLA 2005; also see Locke 2007; Rodríguez-Garavito 2005).[22]

Such codes of conduct and monitoring programs could be viewed either as a supplement to, or a substitute for, public-sector-based regulation of workers' rights. Indeed, we might expect that private-sector-based regulatory efforts are undertaken when firms believe that public sector regulatory efforts are imminent (Spar and Yoffie 1999). Alternatively, these codes of conduct may provide a means of implementing collective and individual labor rights in situations in which local governments lack either the political will or the technical capacity to do so effectively. Or, in some cases, codes of conduct allow firms to make more specific their commitments to protect workers' rights. Of course, codes are fraught with their own compliance issues, so that simply signing onto or announcing a code may be no guarantee of greater respect for workers' rights. In some cases, firms respond to this concern by hiring independent auditors, but some observers question whether accounting

---

[21] Barrientos and Smith (2007) note, however, that many corporate codes are focused on outcome-based standards rather than on process-oriented rules. More specifically, CSR programs tend to emphasize worker health and safety or working hours rather than collective bargaining and freedom of association.

[22] FLA members fall into two categories, those that commit to implementing the code of conduct throughout their supply chains (fifteen "Participating Companies" as of 2005); and university and college licensees, who agree to implement the code in the factors that produce collegiate-licensed products (thirteen "Category B Licensees" in 2005). In 2004, the FLA's external monitors visited ninety-four facilities worldwide, a figure that amounts to 3.3 percent of total FLA-affiliated facilities.

firms that are paid by MNCs would be likely to report violations (e.g., Moran 2002).

In the environmental issue area, Potoski and Prakash (2005) report that U.S. firms that participate in ISO 14001 experience greater declines in pollution emissions than non-participating firms. To receive or retain ISO 14001 certification, firms must submit to annual audits by accredited third parties. The audits focus on the extent to which a firm establishes and follows an effective environmental management system. The results of these audits are shared with the firm, but they are not made public. Hence, the capacity of various stakeholders (e.g., corporate stockholders, consumers) to sanction firms for non-compliance is limited, and the ISO itself has not tended to punish shirkers. Despite the relatively weak monitoring and sanctioning characteristics of the ISO 14001 program, though, there remains a significant statistical association between participation in the program and emissions reductions. Such reductions persist after accounting for firms' emission and compliance histories, as well as addressing selection dynamics. They suggest that, at least in some circumstances, voluntary programs can affect firm behavior. These effects may stem from firms' incentives to standardize practices across their production facilities, or from the internal firm performance pressures generated by external audits.

How well such a finding travels to the labor rights area remains, of course, an open question (also see Bartley 2005; O'Rourke 2003). The incentives to standardize practices, though, should exist in labor-related issues as well: A similar set of human resource practices across facilities, whether or not they are legally required, increases efficiency across the corporate structure. Moreover, in a recent cross-national, cross-industry analysis of code enforcement under the umbrella of the U.K.'s Ethical Trading Initiative, Barrientos and Smith (2007) report that lead firms have a greater influence on labor conditions when they have more direct and longer-term control of affiliates and subcontractors in developing countries (also see Frenkel 2001; Locke et al. 2007). Again, then, the mode of multinational production should affect the extent to which private-sector codes are successful. In the labor area, then, we would expect that these codes of conduct, if they have any general impact, would serve to strengthen the link between direct investment and labor rights. More broadly, multinational firms' incentives to undertake policies that are consistent with a climb to the top should lead to a positive and significant causal link between directly owned production facilities and labor rights:

Hypothesis 3.1: All else equal, foreign direct investment in developing nations will be associated with improvements in, or fewer violations of, collective labor rights, both in law and in practice.

This account also is consistent with factor-based theories of the effects of economic openness on incomes. The Stolper-Samuelson theorem treats societies as divided among land, labor, and capital; freer trade will lead societies to specialize in the production of goods that use the abundant factor intensively (Heckscher-Ohlin). This means that in countries with relatively large endowments of labor, but scarce endowments of capital – generally, in low- and middle-income nations – economic openness should increase the returns to labor (wages) and decrease the returns to capital (profits).

B. Trade, Subcontracting, and the Race to the Bottom?

Directly owned production is only one mode, of course, through which multinational firms enter foreign markets. While FDI is expected to be related positively with collective labor rights, the other main mode of entry – subcontracting – is expected to have negative implications for workers in the developing world. What explains this difference? In summary, a negative, race to the bottom effect of multinational production on labor rights is most likely to occur when firms' production decisions – and, therefore, governments' efforts to attract international firms – are motivated primarily by labor costs rather than by a range of other considerations (such as the size of consumer markets, the retention of skilled workers, or the political stability of a given production location). When participation in global commodity chains forces developing nations (and their workers) into competition with one another (also see Cao and Prakash 2010), a race to the bottom can occur.

Recall that, all else equal, the presence of unions and the use of collective bargaining appear to increase production costs via their effects on both wage levels and non-wage costs (benefits to workers or employer contributions to social security protections; see Aidt and Tzannaos 2002; Blanchflower and Bryson 2003; Flanagan 2006; Gallagher 2005; Graham 2000; Murillo and Schrank 2005). These effects could reduce the cost savings to firms – at least in terms of labor costs – that accrue from multinational production and sourcing. This suggests that, where labor costs are the key concern of firms, such firms will prefer to transact with locations with lower levels of collective labor rights (either in terms of laws on the books or in terms of enforcement of those laws). In their efforts to attract business from such cost-motivated firms, governments will be tempted to reduce the provision or enforcement of such rights.

What sorts of multinational firms are motivated most by labor costs? Extant literature suggests that these firms will be located in labor-intensive sectors, such as footwear and apparel, where subcontracting (rather than directly owned production) is the prevalent form of multinational production. The microeconomic motivations for subcontracting (see Helpman 2006) often involve taking advantages of small differences in marginal costs, and of moving in response to changes in such costs. Moreover, in labor-intensive sectors, wage and non-wage costs (as opposed to capital equipment or research and development costs) often account for a large portion of firms' total production costs, rendering such firms more sensitive to labor-related issues. For instance, Moran's (2002) examples include an Indonesian footwear producer for which labor costs are 20 percent of pre-tax profit, a Nicaraguan blue-jeans maker for which the figure is 46 percent, and a Nike footwear subcontractor where the ratio is 250 percent. Each of these subcontractors can be expected to be under substantial cost pressures on the labor side (also see Brown et al. 2004). In the context of such subcontracting, then, a nation's ability to produce a good at the lowest possible cost is central to increasing export share as well as to winning business for local producers (also see Bartley 2007).

Given these sensitivities, we might expect local subcontractor firms to restrict collective labor rights, or we might predict that governments would serve such firms' (and the lead firms in their supply chains) interests by not providing, or not enforcing, these same collective labor rights (e.g., O'Donnell 1988). Indeed, we sometimes observe such a dynamic in the context of export processing zones, which include a mix of directly owned production facilities and export-oriented, locally owned subcontractor firms. In some EPZs, jobs are low-skilled and labor intensive; and, either by government decree or by practical occurrence, labor rights are restricted (Madami 1999; Mandle 2003; Moran 2002). In her study of foreign-owned firms in China, Gallagher (2005) reports increasing labor rights violations in the early 1990s, particularly in labor-intensive industries located in the coastal regions. Foreign investors sought to lower costs by employing a less contentious labor force. Moreover, if we consider the numerous anecdotal accounts of poor working conditions or violations of core labor rights in low- and middle-income countries, we find that many of these occur within the subcontractor-owned facilities of multinational firms *rather than* in directly owned production facilities. Public attention to problems in Nike or Gap factories, for instance, reflects violations associated with outsourced, rather than directly owned, production.

In April 2008, for instance, a *New York Times* reporter visited several factories in China. The clothing factory he visited, in the Kun Shan industrial zone (northwest of Shanghai), fit the stereotype for such factories with run-down facilities and equipment. The owner, who manufactures inexpensive clothing for various European suppliers, complained about the impact of China's recently reformed labor laws on his costs. He noted that, in response, many orders were going to factories in Vietnam and Mexico, rather than coming to Chinese factories like his. This was the classic low-cost producer concerned with attracting foreign orders and perceiving himself as ever squeezed by cost pressures (Nocera 2008). Similarly, Ngai (2005) studied two foreign-owned (one Taiwanese, one Hong Kong) factories in China, both of which subcontracted for European and U.S. multinationals. Managers at both factories reported that, while codes of conduct existed, their perception was that, "when production and codes clash, we should emphasize production." One factory supervisor interviewed reported that, "once I phoned the TNC and asked, 'Do you still want your products in time?' The [code of conduct] monitor then left our company alone" (p. 107). The more general conclusion of Ngai's study is that, while suppliers are willing to implement the formal provisions of MNCs' codes of conduct (including better record keeping as well as a formalized complaints procedure for employees), they do so in order to win subcontracts, and not because of any intention to comply in practice. Ultimately, most of the substantive provisions of codes of conduct (such as the investigation of and response to workers' complaints) are not implemented because they would raise production costs in what is a very cutthroat competitive market.

Of course, it may be that multinational firms are aware of, but elect to ignore, the occurrence of labor-related problems in supplier factories. Or it may be that the contemporary segmentation of production – the movement away from the Fordist-era model of placing the entire value chain of production in a single location – makes the monitoring of core labor rights by lead firms (and activists) much more difficult. Subcontractor firms often are small (and a single lead firm may deal with hundreds or even thousands of such firms) and spread across numerous political jurisdictions. This segmentation can render union organization more difficult, as it implies that workers are no longer able to threaten large-scale industrial action as a means of disrupting a horizontally integrated production process (Anner 2001; Silver 2003). The extensive use of subcontractors also creates problems for oversight by lead firms, as those firms that have attempted to implement corporate social responsibility programs (see Section IA above) often have discovered.

All else equal, then, developing nations characterized by a greater presence of subcontracted production activity should have lower levels of protection for workers' collective rights. Empirically, however, this presents a challenge: Whereas national governments and intergovernmental organizations regularly collect data on inflows and outflows of foreign direct investment (reported as part of balance of payments accounting, among other things), no similar efforts exist for subcontracting activities. Despite a general sense that subcontracting has become more prevalent during the last decade (WTO 2005), data collection has not kept pace with this reality. In addition, given that firms' tend to view their subcontracting decisions as proprietary information (having worked to locate a given set of subcontractors, firms can be loathe to disclose the details), obtaining such information is difficult, if not impossible.

To test the claim that subcontracting negatively affects collective labor rights, then, we need an empirical proxy for subcontracting. A reasonable and widely available proxy is a developing country's flow of trade (imports and exports). Because global production networks rely on the movement of goods between nations, they generate large trade flows, as evidenced by increasing legal and actual levels of trade openness in the developing world since the mid-1980s. I predict, then, that because participation in global commodity chains, via imports and exports, often forces developing nations (and their labor forces) into competition with one another, we will observe a negative association between a country's level of trade openness and its observance of collective labor rights. This is likely to occur at the level of overall rights, as well as in terms of labor rights laws (where governments respond to subcontracting-based pressures by reducing or avoiding legal protections) and labor rights practices (where local firms have incentives to violate, or not to enforce, existing legal protections of collective rights). This effect will be particularly evident once we control for the (hypothesized positive, as in Hypothesis 3.1) effect of direct investment on workers' rights.

> *Hypothesis 3.2: All else equal, developing nations with higher levels of trade openness will exhibit greater violations of workers' collective rights, in both law and practice.*

It is on the side of trade openness, then, that I expect some empirical support for the race to the bottom assertion. Yet might trade also be a mechanism for the improvement of collective labor rights? Could the threat of trade sanctions – or the denial of trade-related benefits – motivate governments to protect the rights of workers? Or might attention from consumers in developed countries create incentives for producer firms in developing nations to guarantee a certain level of protection to their labor forces? Might the economic growth that often results from trade lead to the improvement of civil rights more generally and labor rights more specifically?

The latter mechanism is a much longer-term process, which is likely to work through domestic political institutions (i.e., democracy) and to manifest itself only under certain conditions. The former mechanisms have been touted by activists and developed-nation labor unions as offering the potential for improvements in working conditions in low-income countries. Scholars of human rights note that, in thinking about governments' calculations of whether to comply with international treaties and norms, human rights are fundamentally different from other types of commitments. Beyond the fact that few conventions provide for direct enforcement, states' human rights behaviors toward their own citizens generate few externalities for other states in the system, and there are few "competitive market pressures" for compliance (see Hathaway 2002; Simmons 2009). The linkage of trade access with labor rights conditions has the potential to introduce market pressures and material incentives for compliance into governments' calculations.

With respect to consumer pressure, the underlying argument is that consumers in wealthy nations will be willing to pay a higher price for goods that are labeled or certified as being produced under appropriate working conditions.[23] In response to perceived consumer demand for labor standards, firms will supply goods produced accordingly (Elliott and Freeman 2003), and activists in developed nations will undertake campaigns that raise public awareness of standards (O'Rourke 2005). The process, then, is one that works through international trade, assuming

---

[23] This argument sometimes is referred to as the "ratcheting labor standards," or RLS, framework. See Rodríguez-Garavito 2005.

that most consumer goods are produced in foreign locations. However, the process relies on non-governmental organizations (NGOs) as promoters and monitors of standards ("vigilantes and verifiers," in Elliott and Freeman's description), on firms as adopters or developers of standards, and on consumers as motivated not only by product and price but also by process.

For instance, during the last decade, firms in the apparel and footwear industries have faced increasing pressure to disclose their factory locations and to oversee workers' rights in such locations (Bartley 2005, 2007). This relates to the trend toward corporate social responsibility, discussed in the preceding section. One example of consumer and media attention to the production process, and of a firm's (eventual) response to such attention, is the case of Nike (Frenkel 2001; Locke 2007; also see Rodríguez-Garavito 2005). In the early to mid-1990s, the company came under scrutiny following various allegations of worker abuses at its supplier factories. The company first denied responsibility for these problems (noting that they occurred in suppliers, not in directly owned factors), but then moved toward engaging its critics. Nike sought to position itself as an industry leader in its attention to labor rights issues (and in corporate social responsibility more generally); its first corporate code of conduct was issued in 1992. All suppliers were required to sign this code and to post it in their factories. This code evolved over time, becoming more specific and creating greater obligations for suppliers. Beginning in 1997, suppliers were subject to various Nike-administered auditing programs to assess compliance with the code of conduct. The firm also was the first in its industry to disclose its list of supplier factories (Locke 2003). Nike also now requires that factories supplying inputs (i.e., blank T-shirts) to Nike subcontractors be located in countries on the company's list of approved production locations – approximately fifty nations. As such, Nike has attempted to apply its standards of conduct, not only to its own subsidiaries, but to its subcontractors, and even to its subcontractors' suppliers.

This is an especially interesting feature of Nike's code, particularly from the point of view of concerns about subcontractors and competitive pressures on labor rights. In footwear and apparel, of course, nearly all production is done via independently owned subcontractors. For instance, Nike's list of supplier factories presently includes over 700 locations, in 47 nations, and employing approximately 700,000 workers.[24] By contrast, Nike has less than 25,000 direct employees. In recent years, other

---

[24] See http://nikeresponsibility.com/#workers-factories/main; accessed August 12, 2008.

firms in the industry have followed Nike's example. In 1997, for instance, Adidas announced its supplier code of conduct; a few years later, it also began to disclose a list of its supplier factories. Not surprisingly, there has been a long-running debate about the effectiveness of Nike's monitoring programs. There also is evidence that, while many problems in supplier factories and exporting nations remain (Sabel 2007), Nike's efforts have sometimes produced increased respect for various individual and collective labor rights, particularly in countries where government respect for rule of law also exists (Locke et al. 2007).

In the area of environmental policies, recent studies also suggest the possibility of a trade-related spread of higher standards. For instance, Prakash and Potoski's (2006) study of the ISO 14001 environmental management standard[25] finds that levels of ISO 14001 adoption among exporting countries are strongly associated with the levels of adoption found among their export destination countries, even when controlling for a number of domestic and international variables (also see Frankel 2003).

While we have observed an increase over time in the use of labor-related codes of conduct and social labeling,[26] its broader impact remains to be seen. While many private-sector-based regulatory instruments have been developed during the last decade, affecting and monitoring compliance with these instruments remains a challenge (Locke et al. 2009a; Ngai 2005; Vogel 2009). Recent social labeling efforts include Fair Trade, which is employed in a range of countries and administered by a variety of nationally based NGOs; Rugmark, which certifies carpets produced in India and Pakistan as being made without the use of child labor; and "No Sweat," a certification used for collegiate-licensed apparel. Thus far, however, consumer labeling seems to be somewhat of a luxury item, at least among U.S. buyers. Whereas survey respondents report that they would be willing to pay slightly higher prices for certified goods (especially for luxury or branded products; see Flanagan 2006; Gereffi 1999; Moran 2002), or whereas higher-income individuals may be willing to actually pay more at the cash register, the majority of consumers are

---

[25] ISO 14001 prescribes broad guidelines for firms' environmental management practices. It does not impose specific requirements in terms of product standards, production technologies, or environmental outcomes. The program requires an initial external audit as well as annual certification audits. Often, compliance with ISO 14001 entails exceeding prevailing domestic laws. See Prakash and Potoski 2007 for further description.

[26] For a summary of NGO-led campaigns related to Staples, Dell, and Nike, see Bartley 2007 and O'Rourke 2005.

likely to remain motivated by price considerations.[27] The Rugmark certification, for instance, is used on only about one percent of the carpets imported from India and Pakistan to the United States (Vogel 2005).[28]

Additionally, when U.S. consumers *are* attentive to labor-related issues, they are more sensitive to working conditions and child labor than to union rights (Elliott and Freeman 2003). Again, this may be particularly true of U.S. consumers, given the weakness of American organized labor, but it diminishes the potential impact of labeling on collective labor rights outcomes abroad. Moreover, even if the median consumer were willing to take collective labor rights issues into account as part of her consumption decisions, she would require a far greater amount of information regarding the origins of products on store shelves (O'Rourke 2005). Given these issues, I do not expect positive pressures on collective labor rights resulting from consumer labeling to outweigh the negative pressures that stem from subcontracting and labor cost competition.

The final trade-related possibility for the improvement of collective labor rights concerns the inclusion of labor rights provisions in bilateral or multilateral free trade agreements. If governments decide to link access to markets with labor conditions, we might observe a change in governments' protections of collective labor rights as their material incentives change (Hafner-Burton 2005b). This might be particularly true of agreements between countries with large disparities in economic power (i.e., the U.S. and a small, low-income nation), where the more powerful country can credibly threaten to withdraw market access in instances of non-compliance.

While the WTO has long resisted involvement in labor rights issues, pointing out that trade is a second-best mechanism for regulating them (Croucher and Cotton 2009) – and likely concerned that calls for labor rights protections from developed-nation governments and labor unions may be little more than veiled protectionism (Bartley 2007; Brown et al. 2004) – the inclusion of labor and human rights-related conditions in

---

[27] Hiscox and Smyth (2005) report results from an experiment at a higher-end household goods retailer in New York City. They identified comparable products (two brands of towels and two brands of candles) and labeled one of each as produced according to good labor standards. They found that consumers were more likely to purchase the labeled product, even as the price of the product was increased (by up to 20 percent). They note, however, that their experiment was done in a retail store with a reputation for offering socially responsible products and with a well-heeled clientele.

[28] On the effort to eliminate child labor in the soccer ball industry in Pakistan, see Spar and Yoffie 1999.

trade agreements has increased markedly during the last two decades. In 1995, the European Commission began to require the inclusion of human rights standards of conduct in all trade agreements. The European Union's focus has been on the rights of voters and citizens rather than on the rights of workers; the 2003 Cotonou Convention, for instance, which governs trade between the European Union and approximately eighty African, Caribbean, and Pacific nations, identifies civil rights and democratic principles as a key element of the trading relationship (Hafner-Burton 2009).

The U.S. government also has increasingly drawn linkages between trade agreements and human rights. In the U.S. case, the focus has been on workers' rights and child labor rather than on civil and political rights.[29] To a large extent, this difference in focus is driven by domestic politics: In the United States, organized labor unions shifted in the 1990s from a strategy of opposing trade agreements outright to one of insisting on the protection of certain workers' rights in partner nations as a precondition for concluding agreements. U.S. policymakers have been willing to include labor-related provisions in trade agreements in return for congressional support of such pacts. Hafner-Burton's (2005b) data on human rights conditions in trade agreements reveals the general trend toward linking trade with rights. Following a dramatic increase that gathered steam in the mid-1990s, by 2002 approximately forty preferential trade agreements (PTAs) contained "hard" human rights conditions, while an additional thirty included "soft" human rights conditions.[30]

The formalization of such linkages builds on a longer-standing concern with production processes in exporting nations. In the United States, the linkage between market access and labor rights dates to the 1984 Generalized System of Preferences (GSP) Renewal Act. This Act, amending the Trade Act of 1974, included a labor rights clause. Developing nations' eligibility for GSP status (a nonreciprocal set of trade concessions offered by individual developed nations to developing countries)

---

[29] Since 1995, the European Union also has operated a special incentive program for its trade agreements, in which countries are rewarded for complying with ILO Conventions 87 (freedom of association), 98 (collective bargaining), and 138 (child labor). See Hafner-Burton 2009.

[30] PTAs with soft human rights conditions are those that affirm, declare, or recognize human rights principles but that do not make trade benefits conditional on the observation of such principles. Hard PTAs draw a direct material link between the observation of specific human rights principles and the granting of trade-related benefits. The former may be thought of as persuasion, while the latter represent coercion. See Hafner-Burton 2005b.

was to be based on, among other criteria, "whether a country was taking steps to afford internationally recognized workers' rights." These were specified to include the freedom of association and the right to organize, as well as individual working conditions (Compa and Vogt 2001). From 1984 to 2000, the U.S. International Trade Commission conducted approximately 100 labor-related reviews of GSP status involving forty-two nations. During this time, thirteen countries had their GSP preferences suspended, while an additional seventeen were placed on a "temporary extension with continuing review" list. Whereas GSP-linked trade comprises only a small percentage of U.S. trade, some maintain that such reviews and suspensions have ripple effects: They signal to other importing-nation governments, as well as to MNCs and activists, that a given country has difficulty with labor rights (Compa and Vogt 2001; also see Caraway 2006b).

In the early 1990s, U.S. government attention to – and domestic interest groups' focus on – labor rights issues manifested itself via the inclusion of a labor side agreement, the North American Agreement on Labor Cooperation (NAALC), in the North American Free Trade Agreement (NAFTA). NAFTA's labor and environmental side agreements, however, generally are viewed as weak (Moran 2002). The labor agreement mandates improved enforcement of existing labor and employment standards (as well as participation in a dispute settlement process), but it does not require new labor rights commitments. The agreement prevents complaints about freedom of association, collective bargaining, the right to organize, and the right to strike from being submitted to review by outside experts or arbitrators. Such labor-related issues are classified as "third tier," while issues such as child labor and occupational health and safety are first tier, and items including forced labor and employment discrimination are second tier – allowing for evaluation by outside experts and, for first tier issues, the imposition of fines.

More recent U.S. trade agreements expand the attention given to labor rights issues. Indeed, American organized labor's backlash against the weakness of NAFTA's labor-related provisions motivated President Clinton to press for stronger protections in the later years of his presidency. The U.S.-Jordan Free Trade Agreement (2000) was the first U.S. trade agreement to mention labor standards in its main text (rather than in a side agreement). The agreement does not require either party to adopt new laws, but it does obligate them to enforce each country's existing labor laws. The parties may file complaints about any alleged enforcement problems; in such instances, a dispute settlement panel issues a nonbinding ruling (see Hafner-Burton 2009; Moran 2002).

Perhaps most explicitly, the U.S.-Cambodia Trade Agreement on Textiles and Apparel (1999–2004) offered Cambodia additional textile export access to the U.S. market, in return for a guarantee that Cambodia's national labor laws would be enforced in all Cambodian factories.[31] The agreement included participation from the Cambodian ministries, the Garment Manufacturers' Association of Cambodia, and Cambodian union federations. Oversight was conducted by ILO monitors, in conjunction with the Garment Manufacturers Association of Cambodia (GMAC), various NGOs, and U.S. buyers of Cambodian apparel (most notably, the Gap). Cambodia, which depended on textiles and apparel for 80 percent of its export earnings, used this agreement to attempt to create a niche as a "sweatshop-free" location (Chiu 2007).[32] While compliance with Cambodia's relatively stringent labor code was not absolute, studies suggest a high level of respect for collective rights as well as individual working conditions (Abrami 2003; Chiu 2007). The program enticed several U.S.-based buyers to increase their imports from Cambodia (FLA 2005). Cambodian firms that wanted to sell to U.S. buyers (via increased MFA quota allocations) realized that they had to respect workers' rights; and Cambodian workers were aware that their employers would be monitored by various external agencies (also see Vogel 2009). The U.S.-Cambodia agreement, while now defunct, suggests that demands from importing nations (and, by implication, consumers and interest groups in those nations) can lead to tangible improvements in labor rights in an exporting nation (Greenhill, Mosley, and Prakash 2009). The question, of course, is under what conditions such improvements obtain.

Even more recently, labor-related provisions became a required component of U.S. bilateral and multilateral trade agreements, such as the Central American Free Trade Agreement (CAFTA-DR 2005), as well as the proposed U.S.-Colombia Free Trade Agreement. This reflects a political compromise between the U.S. Congress and the Bush Administration: The 2002 Trade Act granted trade promotion ("fast track") authority to the executive. In return, the Act required that parties to any future trade agreement with the U.S. commit, in the text of

---

[31] The agreement remained in place until January 2005, when Multi Fibre Arrangement (also known as the Agreement on Textiles and Clothing) quotas were phased out.

[32] In the wake of the MFA phaseout, Bangladesh also established a forum designed to bring together trade unions, NGOs, apparel buyers, and manufacturers; again, its aim was to retain market share by upgrading labor standards (Ethical Trading Initiative 2005).

the agreement, to enforcing their own domestic labor laws. The Act also requires that the U.S. impose some sort of sanctions in response to violations of these commitments.

The rise of trade agreements as a means of protecting human rights necessarily raises questions regarding their effectiveness: Many countries have resisted U.S. and European agreement conditionality. Economically stronger nations, with more outside options, can more easily resist such pressures. Even when agreements with conditions exist, problems of compliance and monitoring persist. The sanctions contained in many agreements are fairly weak, so that non-compliance (that is, from continuing to suppress rights domestically) is relatively cheap for signatory governments. To an extent, this reflects the fact that labor and human rights conditions are included in trade agreements, not because policymakers are directly interested in affecting human rights outcomes, but because such inclusions render trade agreements viable, given domestic political interests and institutions (see Hafner-Burton 2009). Moreover, the impact of international agreements on national practices may be greatest when such agreements reinforce pressures on governments from domestic advocates (Simmons 2009); in the most repressive societies, though, such pressures are unlikely to exist.

These issues notwithstanding, some larger-N evidence offers cause for limited optimism. In her study of PTAs with human rights-related conditions, Hafner-Burton (2005b) argues that state commitments to agreements with hard human rights standards often are effective in producing changes in a state's human rights practices. Whereas commitments to human rights agreements and to PTAs with soft human rights practices appear to have little effect on state behavior – rather, they are more "cheap talk" – membership in PTAs with hard human rights conditions is associated significantly with a decrease in the overall level of repression. Hafner-Burton reaches these conclusions on the basis of a statistical analysis of the link between repression (of physical integrity rights; see Chapter 4) and PTAs for a sample covering nearly all countries for the 1972 to 2002 period. Similarly, in a statistical analysis of the correlates of rates of child labor, Simmons (2009) reports a robust and negative association between a country's involvement in PTAs and the rate of children's labor force participation. Her analysis also is global in scope, and it covers the time period from 1985 to 2001. While Simmons does not identify the precise mechanism linking PTA participation with child labor, her findings suggest that trade agreements may provide one means of addressing labor-related issues.[33] Furthermore, changes in domestic labor laws may occur as part of the negotiation process: in trade agreement talks with Oman, as well as with Chile, U.S. officials insisted on changes to those countries' domestic labor laws. The idea was that, if the trade agreement would obligate governments to uphold their own domestic laws, their domestic laws first needed to offer greater protections to workers.

Overall, then, there are reasons to expect that trade could generate positive influences on labor rights. For the 1985–2002 period, these are unlikely to outweigh the negative pressures generated by cost-oriented competition and subcontracting. Today, the proportion of global trade governed by agreements with "hard" labor rights conditions remains relatively low. If this trend continues, however, it could alter the broader relationship between labor rights and trade. Similarly, the capacity of consumer pressure to positively affect production conditions is currently limited, but also could change in the future. To the extent that developing countries engage in trade with countries whose governments demand labor rights protections, or whose consumers pay attention to the conditions under which their purchases are produced, such pressures may generate a positive relationship between trade and labor rights. The identity of a country's trading partners (Cao and Prakash 2010; Greenhill et al. 2009), as well as the production profile of its exports, may counteract the broader downward competitive pressures that result from trade openness and subcontracting (also see Chapter 6). In the aggregate, however, and for the period under study, I expect the relationship between trade openness (empirically) and subcontracting (theoretically), on the one hand, and collective labor rights, on the other, to be negative.

C. Other International Influences: Global Learning and Advocacy

The trend toward corporate social responsibility highlights the potential importance of other international-level mechanisms in affecting the legal provision as well as the practical implementation of collective labor rights. While CSR programs are developed and implemented at the firm

---

[33] Simmons' PTA variable is the number of PTAs in which a country participates. She does not distinguish between the levels of conditionality in the PTAs, as Hafner-Burton (2009) does. Simmons also finds no significant association between the overall level of trade openness and child labor outcomes.

level, they also reflect pressures from transnational advocacy networks (human and labor rights NGOs). Some of these advocacy groups serve as monitors and enforcers, via the provision of information to shareholders, consumers, and the media, about labor rights (Barrientos and Smith 2007; Ron et al. 2005). These advocacy networks also can play an important causal role in the cross-national diffusion of labor rights practices.

Indeed, political scientists recently have paid considerable attention to the role of international economic and sociological networks in the transnational spread of a range of policies, including social security privatization (Brooks 2009; Weyland 2007); financial liberalization (Chweiroth 2007; Elkins et al. 2006; Simmons and Elkins 2004); privatization of state-owned enterprises (Brune et al. 2004; Meseguer 2004); and democratic governance (Simmons et al. 2008). Cross-national diffusion is hypothesized to result from a variety of causal mechanisms, including international economic competition, direct pressure from intergovernmental organizations, and learning among policymakers. The above discussions of trade and direct investment overlap with some of these mechanisms: Competition can put downward pressure on labor rights, whereas directly owned production can transmit labor rights practices from home to host country governments and firms.

Two additional mechanisms may be important to labor rights outcomes – governments' attention to peers' practices and direct pressure from human and labor rights NGOs.[34] The former relates to policy diffusion: If governments view themselves in competition (for investment, export markets, or both) with other countries, then those countries' labor rights practices may be an important influence. Where peer nations display greater respect for collective labor rights, we would expect upward pressures on a country's rights. At the same time, the prevalence of labor rights violations in peer nations would put downward pressure on a country's collective labor rights.

In terms of the empirical analyses in Chapter 5, I consider two types of peers – those that are close geographically and those that are similar economically. The regional variable (as in Brooks 2005; Simmons and Elkins 2004) captures the extent to which competition for FDI takes place among neighboring countries. If MNCs undertake investment because they want

---

[34] One could identify other important international factors, of course. For instance, Abouharb and Cingranelli (2006, 2008) investigate the linkages between IMF- and World Bank-sponsored structural adjustment programs and workers' rights. They argue that, largely by reducing the role of the government in the economy, such programs lead to fewer protections of workers' rights.

access to certain consumer markets, easy use of a particular set of natural resources, or low transportation costs, competition should occur within geographic regions. Moreover, if emulation and social learning play a role as diffusion mechanisms (see Simmons et al. 2008), we would expect regional networks of policymakers to have important influences.

The economic peer measurement, by contrast, considers competition among nations at similar levels of economic development and with similar factor endowments. The rationale for this measure is that, in terms of export competition, as well as some types of FDI investment location decisions, geographic similarity is less important than economic similarity. If MNCs undertake foreign investment as part of a strategy of vertical integration – that is, to locate different parts of the production process in their most efficient locations – then nations with similar resource endowments, skill levels, and infrastructure will find themselves in competition with one another. For instance, in the apparel sector, where firms are motivated primarily by lower labor costs, patterns of firm location and relocation often are cross-regional (Mandle 2003). Additionally, when Intel Corporation was deciding in the mid-1990s where to build a microprocessor plant, it considered a range of countries with similar levels of human capital formation, political stability, and transportation infrastructure. This set of countries covered a wide geographic range, including Malaysia and Costa Rica (Moran 2002).

The second global-level mechanism, the presence of human rights NGOs, highlights the potential importance of transnational advocacy networks in effecting changes in labor rights outcomes. These networks could act as independent influences on labor rights, directly pressuring national governments to improve the legal environment for workers' rights or to enforce laws on the books. Such groups might be particularly effective at highlighting situations in which governments profess adherence to a given core labor standard (i.e., they have ratified ILO Convention 98) but fail to respect the standard in practice (i.e., they allow employers to interfere in the collective bargaining process, or they require prior authorization of collective bargaining agreements; also see Hafner-Burton and Tsutsui 2005). Indeed, given that the ILO has little in the way of direct enforcement mechanisms or material resources, its main impact may be in promulgating global principles and conventions, and in providing information about compliance with its conventions, which transnational activists can then take as a basis for pointing out gaps between governments' formal acceptance of rules and their actual behavior (Brown et al. 2004; Keck and Sikkink 1998; Rodríguez-Garavito 2005).

Human and labor rights NGOs also could act in tandem with, or in response to, multinational corporations. For example, U.S.-based labor unions (especially the AFL-CIO) and human rights groups have been particularly active on labor rights issues throughout Latin America (Murillo 2005). In El Salvador in the mid- and late 1990s, firms that subcontracted with MNCs (the Gap, Liz Claiborne) faced accusations of poor working conditions and the firing of union organizers. In 1995, the Gap came under pressure regarding conditions in the Mandarin factory; this pressure came from domestic labor groups as well as from U.S.-based NGOs and activists. The latter actors not only pressured the Gap to improve conditions in its subcontractors; they also pressured the government of El Salvador to improve conditions in the *maquila* sector more generally. Ultimately, Gap forced its subcontractor to rehire those workers who had been fired and to allow independent monitors to inspect conditions at the factory. Similarly, in early 2000, thirty dismissed workers (all union leaders) were rehired at the Do All factory, a Salvadoran subcontractor that produced Liz Claiborne clothing. Again, this rehiring – the largest to that date in the El Salvador Free Trade Zone – came in the wake of foreign and domestic NGO pressures (Anner 2001; also see Abouharb and Cingranelli 2008; Rodríguez-Garavito 2005).

In order to assess empirically the impact of human rights NGOs on collective labor rights, the analyses in Chapter 5 include a measurement of the number of human rights groups active in a country in a given year. The effects of such NGOs could be direct (where more NGOs are active, governments are more inclined to respect labor rights) or interactive (where more MNCs are present, NGOs' presence could be particularly effective).[35] We account for both possibilities in our analyses. We also note that the measured effects of human and labor rights activists (see Brown et al. 2004; Keck and Sikkink 1998; Murillo and Schrank 2005) could pick up one of two contending trends. NGO activity could lead to increased reporting of labor rights violations in developing nations, even if the latent level of violations does not change (Ron et al. 2005). Or, NGO activity could produce real improvements in rights, generating a positive effect.[36]

---

[35] Another possibility, as Simmons (2009) discusses, is that international human rights agreements can serve to reinforce pressures on governments from domestic NGOs and human rights activists.

[36] Note, however, that not all studies of activists reveal a positive effect on human rights. For example, Hafner-Burton (2008) evaluates whether "naming and shaming" promotes changes in domestic human rights practices. She does so via a statistical analysis of

D. The Empirical Record: The Global Economy and Labor-Related Outcomes

To what extent are our main theoretical expectations regarding the global economy and labor rights – the overall negative effect of trade on labor rights and the offsetting positive effect of direct investment on labor rights – consistent with previous empirical analyses? In terms of foreign direct investment, the bulk of extant analyses support the climb to the top expectation. A few cross-national studies find that competition to attract foreign capital results in the reduction of social welfare and respect for human and labor rights (e.g., Rodrik 1997). At the same time, however, other empirical assessments of the impact of FDI on labor rights provide modest support for our expectations. Several studies report a positive, albeit small, relationship between FDI and labor rights (Aggarwal 1995; Busse 2003; OECD 2000; Rodrik 1996); others find no significant relationship (Kucera 2002; Neumayer and de Soysa 2006; Oman 2000; Smith et al. 1999).

Additionally, as discussed in Chapter 2, there appears to be little systematic evidence that low labor standards – either in terms of legal provisions or enforcement in practice – are a significant determinant of FDI flows to developing countries. Aggarwal (1995), for example, reports no association between lax enforcement of labor standards and the level of U.S. FDI into a given developing nation. In fact, for the ten developing nations he surveys, U.S. investments tended to flow to nations with higher labor standards and toward sectors of local economies with higher (relative to the rest of the country) labor standards. Similarly, Rodrik's (1996) study reports no correlation between labor standards and flows of FDI from the United States. In addition, a Trade Union Advisory Committee (1996) study suggests that multinationals from developed nations do not consider core labor standards a factor when assessing investment opportunities. Whereas a few scholars (e.g., Bognanno et al. 2005; Javorcik and Spatareanu 2005) report that firm location decisions are influenced positively by labor market flexibility, the balance of evidence supports the assertion that domestic labor institutions and practices have little effect – and, if anything, a positive effect – on FDI inflows.

Studies that consider the impact of direct investment on a broader set of labor-related indicators tend to reach a similar conclusion. For instance,

governments' human rights practices for 145 countries for 1972 to 2000. She reports a statistically significant and positive association between global naming and shaming campaigns, on the one hand, and levels of political terror, on the other.

Busse and Braun's (2003) cross-national analyses of forced labor and FDI flows reveals a significant and negative relationship: Nations with lower rates of forced labor receive *less* FDI, all else equal. Interestingly, this result contrasts with their findings on trade, in which there exists a significant linkage between comparative advantage in unskilled labor-intensive industries and rates of forced labor. In the area of child labor, Braun (2006) explores several potential causal pathways through which child labor might affect FDI. He finds that, if anything, nations with higher levels of child labor attract *less* direct investment. Child labor leads to a decline in human capital formation, which is likely to deter direct investment.[37] In an analysis that considers a range of labor issues, including wages, work hours, safety, and gender discrimination, Flanagan (2006) finds that labor conditions generally are unrelated to FDI flows. The one exception is rates of job fatalities.[38] In that case, nations with higher levels of fatalities (less safe working conditions) tend to attract less FDI, rather than the reverse. Anecdotal evidence involving *maquiladoras* and sweatshops notwithstanding, then, existing empirical studies highlight the potential positive effect of directly owned production on workers' rights.

On the trade side, extant studies provide some support for Hypothesis 3.2. Morici and Schulz (2001) report a positive correlation between labor standards and labor costs, indicating that greater respect for labor standards can increase firms' wage bills. In terms of workers' rights, Cingranelli and Tsai (2003) report a negative association between trade and the Cingranelli-Richards (CIRI) labor rights measure (also see Murillo and Schrank 2005; Neumayer and de Soysa 2006). In a slightly different realm, Busse and Braun's (2003) cross-national quantitative analysis finds that economies with higher rates of forced labor appear to have a comparative trade advantage in the export of goods that intensely use unskilled labor, such as clothing, toys, and footwear.[39] They conclude

---

[37] Also see Neumayer and de Soysa 2005 for a similar argument and a complimentary empirical finding. Additionally, Rodrik 1996 reports a negative relationship between the presence of child labor and manufacturing FDI from the United States; his study uses data for 1982 to 1989 and includes thirty-nine countries. Morici and Schulz's update (2001) of this analysis, based on forty-four countries for the 1982–1994 time frame, also reports no significant association between direct investment flows from the United States and child labor protections (or freedom of association rights).

[38] Note, however, that Flanagan's measures of collective labor rights are limited to Kucera's cross-sectional Freedom of Association and Collective Bargaining (FACB) measure as well as to the broad Freedom House index of civil liberties.

[39] Their causal argument is that higher rates of forced labor generate an increase in the supply of unskilled workers that, all else equal, shifts countries' comparative advantage profiles.

that a lack of compliance with global labor standards can create a type of competitive advantage in global product markets.

An older generation of analyses, however, provide less support for the negative effect of trade openness (Moran 2002). The OECD (1996) reports that the level of labor standards (high versus low) does not correlate with the price of textile exports. Instead, textile export prices are relatively similar across developing nations, despite variation in national respect for freedom of association. One possibility, though, is that prices are determined by world market conditions, whereas success in global markets – export penetration or the quantity of textiles sold rather than the price at which they are sold – could be driven by local comparative advantages. However, in his analysis of labor standards and export penetration, Aggarwal (1995) finds that variation in labor standards of developing nations (including China, India, and Mexico) is not significantly associated with those nations' success in exporting to the U.S. Indeed, this finding is consistent with Flanagan's broader claim that "countries with poor labor conditions do not obtain superior export performance" (Flanagan 2006, 132).[40] Again turning to a related area, Neumayer and de Soysa (2005) present cross-national statistical evidence suggesting that countries with higher levels of trade openness have lower rates of child labor, all else equal.

A final set of related studies are those that examine the linkage between union membership and global economic factors. These studies also engage the race to the bottom claim, as they address the extent to which cross-national as well as individual-level variation in union membership is driven by global economic factors. Put differently, these studies seek to determine the extent to which the union retrenchment that occurred in many countries in the 1990s (Visser 2003) was due to global, rather than to domestic, factors. Scruggs and Lange (2002) consider this issue in the context of sixteen developed nations during the 1960–1994 time frame. Two of their conclusions are particularly relevant to this analysis: First, the effect of "globalization" on union density varies according to the measure of the global economy used. Trade openness tends to be associated with increases in union membership, whereas direct investment and capital market openness are negatively related to changes in

---

[40] Using a dichotomous indicator of trade policy openness, Flanagan (2006) also finds that open economies tend to have superior working conditions, in terms of weekly work hours, annual pay, accident rates, child labor, and forced labor. Flanagan also reports that there is not a significant correlation between labor conditions and a country's share of exports to GDP.

union density. The effects of these variables, though, often are conditional. For instance, the negative result of FDI is most pronounced when labor unions are more institutionalized, and the positive impact of trade on union density is largest when existing labor institutions are stronger. The lesson, then, is that disaggregating economic globalization, and considering that its effects may well be contingent rather than constant, is an important empirical step. Second, Scruggs and Lange find that the effects of the global economy on union density are substantively small, especially relative to domestic politics and economic conditions. This pattern is consistent with a broader literature that argues that, rather than leading to a narrowing of cross-national differences in economic and social policies, economic globalization generates – or at least sustains – divergence among societies.

Martin and Brady (2007) address a similar issue for a set of thirty-nine developing and transition nations, using data for the late 1990s. Given the difficulty of measuring union density accurately outside the developed world (Flanagan 2006; Visser 2003), they elect to model whether (based on response to the World Values Survey) a given individual belongs to a union. They include both individual- and country-level factors (including economic globalization) in their statistical models. They report that Communist legacies are very influential: Even with a variety of controls present, citizens of post-Communist nations are significantly more likely to belong to labor unions (Bunce 1995; Robertson 2007). In terms of international factors, though, Martin and Brady find little evidence that economic globalization reduces (or increases) the incentives for union membership. Indeed, neither trade openness nor foreign direct investment is associated significantly with union membership. Rather, the most important country-level factors are the presence of an International Monetary Fund (IMF) stand-by arrangement and the level of debt service, both of which dramatically reduce the probability of union membership.

These studies suggest that the importance of domestic conditions and institutions should not be ignored, even in a study that focuses on the global economy. Indeed, this is a key lesson from the last two decades of research in comparative political economy: While global economic forces may affect domestic outcomes, especially in developing countries, domestic political and economic factors remain central to understanding cross-national variation. Therefore, it is essential to recognize the role of such factors as both direct and mediating influences on labor rights outcomes. In the next section, I examine some of the internal influences on collective labor rights outcomes. These include economic factors, such as a country's level of development and labor market conditions, as well as political factors, including the degree of democracy as well as government ideology.

II. LOOKING INSIDE STATES: DOMESTIC POLITICS AND ECONOMIC CONDITIONS

The main purpose of this book is to explore the impact of global economic conditions on labor rights – and to establish whether such an impact is present systematically. Even in economically open developing nations, many of the key influences on domestic policy outcomes remain internal. As Elliott and Freeman (2003) maintain, "Globalization does not trump local factors and the institutional and policy environment in which globalization takes place" (p. 16). For instance, where the level of democracy is higher, labor rights should be better protected throughout the economy. Anecdotally, many instances of the repression of workers' rights, especially violent repression entailing arrests, detentions, and deaths, occur in nations that are undergoing political repression generally or that are in the midst of civil war. Indeed, in its 2005 report, the International Confederation of Free Trade Unions (ICFTU) noted that the most serious violations of trade union rights in 2004 occurred in Colombia, where 99 (of a global total of 145) trade unionists were murdered. Similarly, the report singled out Zimbabwe as one of the worst violators of labor rights, with numerous arrests of leaders and members of the Zimbabwe Congress of Trade unions, which is aligned with Zimbabwe's opposition movement (ICFTU 2005; Visser 2003).

More broadly, many recent studies of globalization and national policies find that, even in economically open developing nations, the key influences on domestic policy outcomes remain internal rather than external (e.g., Brooks 2002; Huber and Stephens 2001; Mosley 2003; Wibbels and Arce 2003). According to this "domestic factors" view, it is not so much differences in economic internationalization that drive variations in labor rights, but differences in domestic political institutions, ideologies, and interest groups. While our focus is on external factors, we need to account for the possibility that domestic political factors remain key determinants of labor rights outcomes, particularly when it comes to implementation of a given set of labor laws.

We can think of domestic economic and political institutions as having both shorter- and longer-term effects. In a longer-term sense, a country's starting level of engagement with global production and commerce (as discussed in Section I) is somewhat endogenous to its past economic and political characteristics, perhaps including labor institutions. Domestic economic and political constellations affect the ways in which developing nations are integrated into the global economy. For example, democratic regimes are, all else equal, more likely to display higher levels of trade openness and, perhaps, to attract greater inflows of foreign direct investment (Jensen 2006; Milner and Kubota 2005). Furthermore, where property rights protections are stronger, firms are expected to employ direct investment, rather than subcontracting, as their preferred mode of entry (Buckley and Ghauri 2004; Henisz and Williamson 1999). In this book, I take these longer-term patterns as given: While domestic factors matter for countries' engagement with the global economy, my aim is not to explain such longer-term developments. Rather, global production and commerce are treated as largely exogenous to the process that generates labor rights outcomes.

In the short to medium term, which is the main focus of this book's analyses, domestic political and economic factors have both direct and mediating influences on collective labor rights outcomes. First, domestic conditions are likely to play a direct role in determining labor rights outcomes. We may well expect that domestic factors, taken together, are the most important determinant of collective labor rights laws and practices. Repressive political regimes are unlikely to allow their workers the rights to form independent labor unions and to engage in effective collective bargaining. Moreover, where there is a high degree of slack in the local labor market – because of a high level of unemployment or a large role for the informal sector (Abouharb and Cingranelli 2008; Flanagan 2006; Silver 2003; Visser 2003) – workers will be less likely to demand, and to achieve, protection of collective or individual rights. Conversely, when economic growth is strong and demand for workers is high, workers will be better able to effect protections of their core rights.

Recent reforms to labor law in China illustrate the fact that, even when multinational production is important to the domestic economy, governments may be motivated mostly by domestic considerations. In passing a new labor law in June 2007, the government acted over the objections of various foreign firms, which worried about the implications of the reformed law for their ability to hire and fire workers and for the power of workers vis-à-vis employers. The reformed labor law, which took effect in 2008, requires employers to provide written contracts to employees, restricts the employment of temporary workers, and allows for collective bargaining over wages and benefits. While the law was not as expansive as initially proposed, reflecting lobbying from foreign multinationals, it appears to shift the balance of power toward workers. Analyses of the reform suggest that the Chinese government was motivated by domestic considerations, namely discontent among migrant workers, which was seen as generating social unrest (Daubler and Wang 2009; Josephs 2009; Zhou 2009).[41] While the impact of the reforms remains to be seen, especially because issues of implementation loom large, this seems an instance in which domestic considerations trump, or at least partly outweigh, pressures emanating from the global economy. This also is consistent with Frenkel's study (2001) of Chinese firms in the footwear industry: Whereas those factories associated with global firms generally have better conditions for workers, their capacity to implement internationally recognized collective labor rights is limited by China's government policies regarding independent labor unions.

Second, domestic economic and political institutions may mediate the effects of global production on labor rights outcomes. This dynamic is consistent with the large body of literature demonstrating that domestic political interests and institutions affect national responses to economic globalization (e.g., Adserá and Boix 2002; Basinger and Hallerberg 2004; Brooks 2002; Garrett 1998). In some situations, domestic factors amplify pressures emanating from the global economy; in other circumstances, domestic factors mute the impact of external factors. Competitive pressures to lower labor costs, for instance, can be reinforced by right-leaning governments or historically weak union movements. The comparative political economy literature also reminds us of the distributional issues associated with global production: Whereas economic openness may promise aggregate benefits to developing nations, it is domestic interests and institutions that determine whether workers gain as much as employers (also see Vijaya and Kaltani 2007), or whether workers in some sectors gain as much as workers in other sectors.

In the international relations field more generally, recent work points to the mediating effect of domestic political institutions on governments' making of international commitments, as well as on compliance with those commitments. Beth Simmons (2009) explores the range of motivations behind governments' ratifications of human rights treaties; she notes that governments' expectations regarding the constraining effects of treaties are conditioned by domestic legal and political systems. Despite

---

[41] Also see Joseph Kahn and David Barboza, "As Unrest Rises, China Broadens Workers' Rights." _New York Times_, June 30, 2007.

signing the same treaty instrument, governments may expect to be more or less constrained, depending upon how that treaty can be used at home by courts and litigants. Hence, treaty ratifications are not merely a reflection of governments' interests, but also a product of their institutional configurations. Perhaps even more importantly, once governments have committed to various international human rights agreements, they may find themselves subject to additional domestic pressures to comply with those commitments. Simmons' logic suggests that international commitments empower social mobilization, particularly in countries with mixed and changing political regimes. Hence, the impact of external forces – in this case, treaty commitments – is an interactive one in which international obligations' effects are conditional on the domestic political climate.[42] With respect to the linkages between labor rights and trade, then, we might expect that domestic political institutions mediate the pressures emanating from the global economy.

Figure 3.1 details the causal processes linking domestic political and economic institutions with collective labor rights outcomes. The left side of the figure reminds us of the longer-run endogeneity of global production patterns to – among other things – domestic institutional influences. One set of important factors in this broad category is labor-related, potentially including the strength of organized labor, collective labor rights legislation, and the skill profile of the labor force. The next part of the figure highlights the role – both in terms of a potential positive (Hypothesis 3.1) and a potential negative (Hypothesis 3.2) effect – of global production in collective labor rights outcomes. Trade- and subcontracting-related influences work through the channel of cost pressures, whereas direct investment-related influences travel through MNCs' various incentives to adopt best practices. The middle of the figure draws attention to two types of impacts from domestic politics – as a direct determinant of labor rights outcomes (so, for instance, more democratic regimes are expected to have stronger labor rights protections) and as mediators of the forces emanating from the global economy (for example, a weak or underfunded labor inspectorate may render it easier for subcontractors to flout national labor laws in their facilities).

---

[42] In related work, Caraway (2006b) investigates the extent to which strategies of transnational labor activism are contingent on domestic political arrangements. In politically closed systems, local civil society partners are unable (or unavailable) to ally with foreign-based activists, so campaigns tend to be focused at the international (i.e., ILO complaints) or external market (i.e., U.S. trade policy) level.

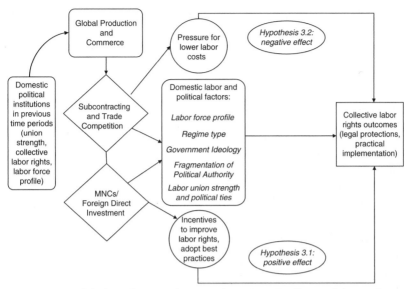

FIGURE 3.1. Global production, domestic factors, and collective labor rights outcomes.

Where mediating effects are concerned, domestic institutions may be particularly important to the implementation of (versus the passage of laws regarding) collective labor rights. A lack of political will or capacity to enforce prevailing labor laws can render such laws ineffective at the firm level. For instance, in their study of Hong Kong-owned firms in Thailand, Hewison and Chiu (2008) report that most managers found many of Thailand's (collective as well as individual) labor laws to be burdensome and unrealistic, and they expected few negative consequences for non-compliance. Hence, they were willing to flout many of these restrictions, generating a noticeable disjunction between law and practice (also see Bhagwati 2004; Schrank and Piore 2007). In other instances, national governments may have an interest in enforcement but may lack the technical or financial resources necessary; the ILO and various developed-nation governments attempt to respond to this concern by providing technical assistance (both for legal reform and for labor inspectorates; see Elliott and Freeman 2003).

We can identify several types of domestic factors that may play a direct and/or mediating role in the determination of country-level collective labor rights. Some of these are included in the statistical analyses presented in Chapter 5, while others are discussed in the context of Chapters 6 and 7, where the analyses are oriented toward qualitative methods. These domestic factors include economic conditions (including labor market conditions) as well as political institutions, such as regime type, government ideology, the dispersion of political authority, and the longer-term strength of labor unions.

A. Domestic Economic Conditions

The state of the domestic economy is directly relevant to workers' rights outcomes in several ways. First, all else equal, variation in the level of economic development should generate differences in the collective rights of workers. This reflects a more general relationship between economic development and the likelihood of democratic governance (which, in turn, also should be associated with better protections for workers), as well as a claim that higher labor standards may be a "luxury" good, the demand for and supply of which should increase as incomes rise.

Second, the state of the domestic economy in general, and the condition of the labor market specifically, will affect the demand for and supply of collective labor rights. Tight labor markets increase the appeal of labor unions, as workers are able to act collectively to exploit the mismatch between demand and supply. Success in such action heightens the incentive to join labor unions. At the same time, tight labor markets also render multinationals more likely to offer protections to their employees (Flanagan 2006; Rudra 2002) as they strive to hire and retain workers. On the other hand, if unemployment is high, workers will have less bargaining power, rendering them more likely to accept labor rights violations without complaint. A high rate of surplus labor also reduces MNCs' incentives to provide good working conditions as a means of attracting and retaining workers (Anner 2001). In low- and middle-income nations during the late 1980s and early 1990s, this effect may relate to participation in structural adjustment programs: These often were associated with increased slack in the labor market, thereby harming workers' bargaining power as well as limiting the resources of the government to implement existing laws regarding workers' rights (Abouharb and Cingranelli 2008). Additionally, in developing countries, labor market conditions entail, not only unemployment rates in the formal sector, but also the relative weight of the informal sector in the economy (Flanagan 2006): A large informal sector implies a pool of surplus labor from which firms could draw.

In the statistical analyses in Chapter 5, we assess labor market conditions using a variety of indicators. While we expect an inverse relationship between unemployment and labor rights, it also is the case that unemployment statistics are unavailable for a large proportion of the country-years in our analyses. As an alternative measure, we employ the rate of economic growth, as it correlates strongly and negatively with the unemployment rate. To further assess the direct impact of labor market conditions on collective labor rights, we also employ Rudra's (2002) "potential labor power" (PLP) measure, which is based on the ratio of skilled to unskilled workers and the presence of surplus labor in an economy. The idea behind this measure is that workers' skill profile *and* the degree of slack in the labor market combine to determine the capacity of workers to bargain vis-à-vis employers and governments. This measure also highlights the potential importance of a third feature of a nation's economy, namely its industrial structure.

Workers generally are less likely to organize in the agricultural and services sectors; but in manufacturing industries as well as in the public sector, collective action obstacles generally are less severe (Iversen and Wren 1998). Agriculture still provides many of the jobs in developing nations – especially in those nations that are also low-income (Flanagan 2006). Nations with large agricultural and service sectors, then, will experience lower levels of collective labor organization and fewer demands for respect for collective labor rights, all else equal. Within countries, this also implies that workers in the manufacturing and public sectors will be most likely to advance demands for, and take advantage of, collective labor rights. In a dynamic sense, as national production profiles shift from the agricultural to the industrial sectors (or, more recently, from the industrial to the services sector), we also may observe shifts in the demand for and supply of collective labor rights.

Moreover, the particular types of production in an economy, in terms of the demand for skilled versus unskilled workers (or, put differently, the presence of labor-intensive versus capital-intensive production) also affect the organizational capacity and bargaining power of workers. Some sectors – including much agriculture as well as lower-technology manufacturing like apparel – employ mostly unskilled labor, and their costs are largely due to wages rather than to capital equipment (Hatem 1998). Other industries (i.e., pharmaceuticals, electronics) employ a large proportion of skilled and semi-skilled workers. The latter set of industries tends toward capital- or technology-intensive production, making wage costs a lower proportion of overall production costs. The Stolper-Samuelson and Heckscher-Ohlin theorems suggest that nations in which unskilled workers are the relatively abundant factor of production will enjoy comparative advantages in sectors that use unskilled labor intensively. As a result, unskilled workers in such nations should enjoy greater real returns as the country's trade openness increases.

These results, however, assume a political situation in which workers are able (vis-à-vis their employers) to reap the benefits of trade openness. Yet, in many circumstances, unskilled workers may not have the political strength to prevent reductions in welfare state policies (Rudra 2002), to avoid a shift in the tax burden from capital to labor (Wibbels and Arce 2003), or to bargain effectively with employers (Weeks 1999). We can expect varied effects, then, of economic structure on collective labor rights outcomes: At the national level, a movement from agriculture to manufacturing, or from low-technology manufacturing to higher-technology production, could be linked with improvements in collective labor rights, as skilled workers gain from such a movement up the production ladder. However, at the same time, a shift toward trade openness could benefit the unskilled workers in low-income economies – assuming that they have the political voice necessary to reap the benefits of openness. This discussion generates several expectations regarding the impact of the domestic economy on labor rights outcomes, which can be summarized in a single hypothesis to be tested across the empirical chapters:

> *Hypothesis 3.3*: *Collective labor rights will be better protected, in law as well as in practice, where the supply of appropriate workers is more constrained, where firms' incentives to retain workers are greater, and where workers are better able – in terms of collective action factors – to organize.*

B. Political Institutions

As the discussion above highlights, the impact of economic conditions on labor rights outcomes may be straightforward; or it may depend on the constellation of political forces that prevails at a given point in time. I discuss four of these: The degree of openness of the political regime; the ideology of the government in office; the strength and political connections of organized labor; and the dispersion of authority within the political system.

Regime Type. First, consistent with a wide range of studies linking regime type with human rights protections, more democratic regimes should be more likely to guarantee and enforce collective labor rights, all else equal (Cingranelli and Tsai 2003; Neumayer and de Soysa 2006; Poe et al. 1999; Richards et al. 2001). The affinity between collective labor rights and democracy also is demonstrated by the role that organized labor has played in democratization campaigns around the developing world, including Brazil, Chile, South Africa, South Korea, and Zimbabwe (Visser 2003). In controlling for regime type in the statistical analyses, I focus on larger-scale differences in political regimes, which should correlate with the capacity of workers to demand (and to receive) protection of core labor rights. Of course, there likely also will be variation *within* autocracies, democracies, or quasi-democratic regimes (see Bueno de Mesquita et al. 2003). Within the statistical analyses in Chapter 5, I also include a measure of civil conflict, as this too has broad implications for the occurrence of repression generally and labor rights violations specifically.

Government Ideology. Even among governments with similar levels of democracy (or autocracy), we can expect that government attitudes toward workers and toward organized labor will color the conditions experienced by workers and the conditions faced by foreign multinationals. In non-democratic systems, the economic ideology of the leadership – and of the "selectorate" – is likely to influence labor-related outcomes. This may be true at a broad level, contrasting left-wing with right-wing autocracies; differences also may exist among broadly similar regimes. As an illustration of the latter, Chan and Wang (2004) find that industrial relations and working conditions are more labor friendly in Vietnam than in China – two autocratic regimes with governing Communist parties – even when holding constant sector (generally, footwear, toys, and apparel) and nationality of foreign investor.

In their comparison of Taiwanese-owned factories in China and Vietnam, they posit that the position of the host government on labor-related issues conditions the direction and degree of MNC influence on labor rights. The managers they interviewed (in 2001 and 2002) consistently remarked that, in Vietnam, they felt that they were bound to comply with the legal rules regarding labor. In China, by contrast, they viewed the government as generally less interested in compliance with such rules, and therefore unlikely to punish foreign firms for violating them.[43] Taiwanese-owned firms in Vietnam, for instance, rarely house

---

[43] Part of the explanation they offer is that the Chinese central government affords significant leeway to local governments in terms of deciding whether to enforce labor laws; Vietnam's central government has more direct control over local governments. However, on the willingness of provincial officials in Vietnam to sometimes ignore or defy national-level rules related to FDI, see Malesky (2008).

workers in factory dormitories, presumably because the Vietnamese government is averse to the round-the-clock managerial control and the potential for labor rights abuses that such arrangements facilitate (Chan and Wang 2004). They also note that workers in Vietnam were much more aware of, and much more likely to demand respect for, their legal labor rights than were workers in China. This pattern occurs despite the greater dependence of Vietnam on Taiwanese foreign direct investment. Indeed, the government of Vietnam appears to be more interested in positioning itself as a climb to the top nation; it has been keen for its factories to comply with internationally recognized labor standards. Both the national government and Vietnamese trade unions have urged local factories to apply for SA8000 certification (from Social Accountability International), certifying meeting certain standards for labor rights.[44]

In nations with competitive political systems, left-oriented parties and governments should be more inclined than their centrist or right-leaning counterparts to protect the interests of their traditional (working class, labor-related) constituents. This reasoning is consistent with research suggesting that, even in an era of neoliberal economic reforms, left-leaning governments pursue different types of policies than right-oriented ones (e.g., Brooks and Kurtz 2007). Left governments may welcome all or some forms of foreign capital,[45] particularly in the face of economic downturns; but they will attempt to do so in a way that protects the interests of their core constituents.

Along these lines, Murillo (2005) posits that, despite a broader regional trend of labor market deregulation in Latin America during the late 1980s and 1990s, some political parties used labor market policy as a means of retaining electoral support from their labor-oriented constituencies. In particular, office-holding left parties that were uncertain about their future electoral prospects supported regulatory (rather than deregulatory) labor law reforms. These reforms provided benefits to traditional left party supporters (organized formal sector workers who pay close attention to such policies), without attracting much notice from the median voter (worried more about other types of economic reform). Murillo's argument, then, is that labor regulation is a relatively cheap tool

---

[44] Certification efforts also were a requirement of the 1999 U.S.-Vietnam bilateral free trade agreement.

[45] Pinto and Pinto (2008) posit that left-leaning governments will favor FDI inflows in labor-intensive industries and that firms will respond to partisanship by increasing direct investment in these industries. Their empirical analyses employ sectoral FDI data for OECD nations.

with which to reward labor-based interest groups for their political support. This is particularly true, she suggests, for reforms affecting collective, as opposed to individual, labor rights. In the case of the latter, there are stronger economic incentives to increase wage flexibility and decrease the costs of hiring and firing. Indeed, of the collective labor law reforms that occurred in Latin America between 1985 and 1998, twelve were regulatory, while only five were deregulatory (also see Madrid 2003). I expect, therefore, that partisanship may serve as an important mediating factor between global economic pressures and collective labor rights outcomes. In the statistical analyses in Chapter 5, I test the impact of a measure of executive (or legislative) ideology. In the case study context of Chapter 7, I consider the longer-term relationship between government ideology and labor-related outcomes.

> *Hypothesis 3.4*: *All else equal, labor rights will be better protected where political regimes are democratic or where left-leaning governments hold power.*

Labor Union Strength and Political Ties. Two additional variables merit discussion in this section, although they are not addressed directly in the quantitative analyses in Chapter 5. Particularly in democratic regimes, left parties and union federations often draw upon one another, with union strength owing to past periods of left government (and policies implemented during these periods) and the left's electoral performance linked with unions' mobilization of their membership. The presence of left governments also may color workers' perception of the effectiveness of organized labor, rendering them more or less likely to participate in unions as a way of advancing their individual and collective interests (Blanchflower and Bryson 2003). Of course, not all labor unions are left-leaning, particularly in semi-authoritarian systems with largely state-sponsored industrial relations systems (Robertson 2007). In general, though, there is an ideological affinity between labor unions and left parties (Garrett 1998; Huber and Stephens 2001; Murillo 2005). Unions that are inclined to support the left also are likely to press for the observation of collective labor rights in the face of economic openness.

Conceptualizing "union political strength" is by no means straightforward (Madrid 2003), but, in general, organized labor's linkages with political parties will affect its voice in the policymaking process. In his study of social policy in OECD nations, Garrett (1998) finds that the interaction of left government with labor power (rather than either element individually) conditions the impact of economic openness on public spending. Along slightly different lines, Murillo and Schrank (2005) posit that the historical position of labor in the polity – whether it has played a role in politics or been repressed by previous governments and economic elites – affects the strategies that workers use to protect their collective rights. Moreover, Murillo (2005) points out that the strength of ties between political parties and unions has a large impact on labor law reforms: When unions have strong institutional ties with incumbent political parties, the probability of regulatory reforms to individual labor law is three times as high as the probability of *deregulatory* reforms (also see Madrid 2003; Visser 2003).[46]

As a result, where labor unions have strong ties with the governing party or parties, union members will press for the maintenance of their status quo (protected) position (e.g., Cortázar et al. 1998; Murillo 2001), even in the face of competitive pressures related to economic globalization and multinational production. Under some conditions, foreign firms could benefit from such ties if disciplined, well-organized unions facilitate more efficient tripartite bargaining among businesses, workers, and government officials. On the other hand, *if* foreign firms *do* (as some activists contend) avoid locations with highly entrenched labor unions, countries with tight union-governing party ties may participate less in global production, whereas countries in which local elites have long cooperated with multinational capital to repress labor (Evans 1979; O'Donnell 1988) will be more adept at attracting foreign investment. Unions' political strength and political affiliations, then, are likely to serve as a factor mediating the relationship between global production and labor rights outcomes. I explore this possibility empirically in Chapter 7.

Moreover, authoritarian regimes also might display differences in the treatment of organized labor, again with effects that mediate the influence of global production. Returning to the comparison of China and Vietnam, both countries have a single union structure, with all legal unions required to affiliate with the All-China Federation of Trade Unions (ACFTU) or the Vietnam General Confederation of Labor (VGCL). The VGCL operates with more autonomy from the central government than does the ACFTU: The VGCL has been allowed to participate in some international union activities, and Vietnam's labor code has been more

---

[46] In many countries, labor is organized into multiple confederations, often on the basis of sectoral divisions. Different confederations may have varying ties with political parties. This, too, may contribute to differences in labor rights within countries and across economic sectors.

detailed than China's (making violations more obvious). Hence, despite a similar overall pattern – at least on the "single union structure" element – there are differences in behavior in practice (Chan and Wang 2004; also see Visser 2003).

Dispersion of Political Authority. The final domestic political variable that I consider is the concentration or fractionalization of decision-making authority at the national government level. The possibility of changes in collective labor rights should depend somewhat on the centralization (or dispersion) of decision-making authority. The existence of a higher degree of political constraints (often operationalized as veto players and including the size of legislative coalitions; the ideological distance among coalition members; the ideological similarity between the executive and legislative branches; the political authority of sub-national units; and the number of legislative chambers) can render changes in existing laws less likely (Basinger and Hallerberg 2004; Henisz and Mansfield 2006; Tsebelis 2002). Therefore, a greater number of veto players should be associated with fewer changes to existing labor laws, all else equal. Where collective labor rights have traditionally been well-protected, their legal foundations will be difficult to change (also see Murillo and Schrank 2005).[47] However, where governments have tended to repress labor rights, it will be difficult to create legal guarantees of those rights, even where domestic interest groups, transnational advocacy networks, or MNCs press for regulatory reform.

The fragmentation of political authority also can affect labor rights through a second channel related to the implementation of laws on the books. Even with the political will to ensure labor rights, many nations have limited fiscal resources for labor law improvements. Because a large number of veto players render fiscal policy sticky, fragmented governments will be less likely to devote additional resources to implementation. Even as the demand for labor inspectors or labor courts increases (with the arrival of MNCs, the expansion of EPZs, or increased monitoring by NGOs), their supply will remain fairly constant (also see Frundt 2002). On the other hand, in systems with fewer veto players, governments are more likely – again, assuming a will to do so, which will depend on other domestic factors, such as ideology and the role of organized labor – to adjust the resources dedicated to implementation. In both cases – reforms of collective labor laws and enforcement of existing laws – the veto

---

[47] For a similar argument with respect to welfare state policies, see Huber and Stephens 2001.

player argument is about changes in, rather than levels of, collective labor rights protection. I expect that political systems with more veto players are less likely to reform collective labor laws or to change the amount of resources dedicated to their implementation. In such situations, collective labor rights outcomes will be very path dependent. Again, this expectation is a longer-run, interactive one, and, therefore, it is tested in the qualitative analysis presented in Chapter 7.

The discussion in this section suggests that domestic political and economic institutions will have both direct and mediating effects on labor rights outcomes. Where political regimes are democratic, where political parties of the left hold office, when countries are at a higher level of economic development, and where independent unions have strong ties to governing parties, collective labor rights are likely to be better protected in law as well as in practice. The climb to the top effect of multinational production should be more likely to prevail. At the same time, the centralization of political authority can reinforce either climb to the top or race to the bottom pressures, allowing for easier changes to collective labor laws and the resources dedicated to their enforcement. The fragmentation of authority, on the other hand, can render existing collective labor laws stickier despite economic globalization. Lastly, the organizational capacity of workers and their bargaining power vis-à-vis employers will affect their ability to demand – and to achieve – collective labor rights. In situations characterized by tight labor markets and a bias toward skill- and capital-intensive production, workers should be better able to achieve the rights to act collectively. This proposition also is consistent with an "industrial upgrading" view, in which developing nations experience various positive effects (economic growth, improved conditions for workers) via a shift from lower-technology to higher-technology production, effected by participation in global commodity chains (Porter 1990; also see Breznitz 2007; Gereffi 1999).

In the quantitative analyses in Chapter 5, I focus on the direct effects of domestic variables on labor rights outcomes. The reasons for this choice are both practical and substantive: In practical terms, many domestic political variables are difficult to measure in a cross-sectional, time series fashion, particularly for low- and middle-income nations. This reflects both problems of data availability (see Chapter 5 on unemployment data, for example) and data quality (i.e., how meaningful are "union density" statistics in a cross-national context?). We might expect that the subsample of country-years for which key domestic variables would be available is not a random one, thereby biasing our results in a particular direction.

More importantly, in substantive terms, some of the processes linking economic globalization with labor rights may be dynamic ones, accumulating and unfolding over the medium or long term (e.g., Huber et al. 2006). Even if operationalizing key domestic variables quantitatively were straightforward, large-N analyses would do less well at tracing the dynamic mechanisms through which some domestic influences operate. Additionally, using a case study rather than a large-N approach to gauge the impact of some domestic factors allows us to avoid an assumption of unit homogeneity, when low- and middle-income countries may exhibit a substantial degree of unit heterogeneity where domestic processes are concerned (Sambanis 2004; also see Chapter 7).

Given these concerns, I employ broad measures of domestic factors in the statistical models used in Chapter 5. These include the degree of democracy, the occurrence of civil war, and the state of the domestic economy (including the rate of unemployment as well as the level of economic development). I also check the robustness of the results to the inclusion of the political ideology of the governing party, although there are concerns about the capacity to measure ideology in a cross-national context. I reserve the examination of other domestic factors, including the historical strength of labor unions and the sectoral profile of the economy, to Chapters 6 and 7. In Chapter 6, I consider how a country's production profile conditions the effects of general economic openness on collective labor rights. I do so using a variety of qualitative and quantitative evidence intended to address some of the problems of data availability in developing nations. In Chapter 7, I use case study analysis to consider how one country's experience with collective labor rights is affected by longer-term changes in its economic structure as well as by government fractionalization, government ideology, and the longer-term role of organized labor in the polity.

III. CONCLUSION

This chapter presents the theoretical logic behind the central claim advanced in this book: That global production has the potential to affect collective labor rights in both positive and negative directions, depending on the way in which multinational production is organized and owned. Hence, pressures for *both* a race to the bottom *and* a climb to the top may be present within a given country at a particular point in time. Where countries participate heavily in global production, but do so in different ways, we can expect variation in outcomes. For instance, countries with a high degree of subcontracting but a low level of direct investment may experience greater race to the bottom pressures on collective labor rights. More generally, different elements of economic globalization are expected to affect workers' rights differently – just as they affect social policy, tax, and fiscal policy outcomes differently. In the next chapter, I describe this study's main dependent variable – collective labor rights, both in the aggregate and in terms of law versus practice. In the remainder of the book, I test this chapter's propositions empirically.

4

Conceptualizing Workers' Rights

The status of workers in developing countries involves a range of issues. For instance, are workers routinely exposed to hazardous chemicals, or are women who become pregnant subject to dismissal? Or do labor inspectors visit factories unannounced, and do their inspection findings lead to an improvement in health and safety standards? Are workers paid for overtime work, and is the length of the work week limited to a certain number of hours? Do union members and union organizers face intimidation and threats of violence? Are employees who work in export processing zones (EPZs) able to leave their factories and dormitories? Do factories routinely employ children under the age of fifteen, even when international standards and domestic law prohibit this? As we consider the empirical linkages between multinational production and workers, we could treat one or more of these as our dependent variable.

Indeed, many accounts of workers' status in developing countries – and particularly of workers employed by multinational corporations or their local subcontractors – focus on such outcomes. During the last decade, awareness-raising campaigns regarding workers in developing countries have focused on child labor in the soccer ball industry in Sialkot, Pakistan; working conditions and wages on Honduran banana plantations, especially those subcontracting for Chiquita, Dole, and Del Monte; and the right to organize of garment-sector workers in the Philippines' Cavite Export Processing Zone.[1]

[1] For representative information on these campaigns, see http://www.itcilo.it/english/ actrav/telearn/global/ilo/guide/ilosoc.htm, http://www.solidaritycenter.org/content.asp? contentid=446, and http://www.unionvoice.org/campaign/ChongWonpetition

Whereas such campaigns effectively communicate the often-dire state of working conditions in the developing world, they suffer from a common flaw. For the casual observer, or even for the socially conscious consumer or corporate shareholder, it is difficult to know how representative such cases are. It is nearly undeniable that some workers in some factories in some developing nations experience conditions that are inconsistent with widely accepted core labor standards as well as with our ideas of ethical treatment more broadly. Yet it is unclear whether the highly publicized cases of violations are the exception or the rule. To begin, large multinationals and their affiliates may be more exposed to activists' spotlight than locally owned firms or public sector workplaces (Spar 1999; Spar and Yoffie 1999). This may be particularly true in the case of branded or luxury products (i.e., Gap, Nike, or Louis Vuitton), which activists can more easily target as part of awareness raising campaigns, and which may be more likely to elicit reactions from label conscious consumers (Berger 2005; Elliott and Freeman 2003; Gereffi et al. 2005). Moreover, those who want to draw attention to a cause have every incentive to choose the most extreme cases as their public face: Repression of vulnerable groups (children, pregnant women, indigenous migrants to urban areas) strikes a deeper chord with audiences in the developed world.

For those interested in social scientific analysis of the issue, the challenge is how to situate this factory-, region-, and country-specific information in the broader context of developing country workers. When workers in developing nations face repression, is this the result mainly of working for a particular type of employer (multinationals versus subcontractors), of living in non- or quasi-democratic societies, of working in particular industries, or of laboring in nations at relatively low levels of socioeconomic development? That is, to what extent are labor rights outcomes the result of factors related to multinational production rather than to the domestic polity and the local economy?

One key to such a systematic analysis – to testing the hypotheses developed in the preceding chapter – is to employ measures of workers' rights that are comparable across countries as well as over time within a single country. Indeed, Elliott and Freeman's (2003) study argues that the lack of comparable cross-country information on compliance with international labor standards is "the greatest barrier to empirical analysis" of the globalization-labor rights nexus (p. 20; also see National Research Council 2004). While there are many qualitative studies of labor rights and conditions in particular nations or sectors, there are few comprehensive cross-national, over-time data on labor rights. In order to assess how global production affects workers, systematic data drawn from multiple, reliable sources are necessary.

A major contribution of this book is to introduce a newly generated set of measures of workers' rights, which are then used in various empirical analyses. This chapter begins by situating these data, which focus on workers' collective rights, in the broader notion of labor rights and working conditions. The collective labor rights data focuses on the formal legal rights of workers to act collectively, including the formation and operation of labor unions, collective bargaining, and strike activity; and the extent to which these rights (when present) are respected. I then discuss how our labor rights measure is constructed, with an overview of country-level labor rights scores. Finally, this chapter provides information on how this measure contrasts with, and improves upon, existing cross-national measures of labor rights.

I. LABOR RIGHTS AND CORE LABOR STANDARDS

Labor rights are a controversial issue for international institutions. For instance, while some activists have called on the World Trade Organization to consider (or to allow member states to consider) labor rights as they relate to trade policy, others – often including developing country governments – have described these calls as little more than veiled protectionist pleas, aimed at eliminating one of developing nations' few comparative advantages (Frenkel 2001; Rodrik 2007). The former view takes core labor standards as fundamental rights, the absence of which distorts resource allocation and trade (e.g., Morici and Schulz 2001). Some proponents of the latter view worry that calls for a "living wage" will simply raise costs – so that wages exceed productivity – in some nations, driving out direct investors and subcontractors. Others point out that long work weeks and suboptimal working conditions, while unfortunate, are part of the development process and were commonplace in Europe and North America less than a century ago. At the same time, even long-standing democracies vary in their respect for certain kinds of labor rights, such as the right to bargain collectively and the right to strike; in the United States, for instance, labor legislation sets clear limits on these rights.

Similarly, the main international financial institutions have varied in their attitude toward workers' rights. A series of World Bank-sponsored research reports concluded, in the 1990s and early 2000s, that core labor standards had few, if any, negative consequences for economic performance. However, while embracing internationally recognized core labor standards, the Bank also tended toward a more liberal interpretation of such standards (Caraway 2006a). Indeed, depending on the particular policy publication or initiative one analyzes, one finds a wide range of World Bank attitudes regarding labor rights. Abouharb and Cingranelli (2008) note that, in its 2006 *World Development* Report, the Bank acknowledged the importance of labor rights to the achievement of equitable economic growth. At the same time, however, the Bank's *Doing Business* initiative, which seeks to identify (and rectify) impediments to economic growth in member nations, treats labor regulations as a barrier to economic activity (and as a negative item in its country scores). Hence, it is unclear whether the Bank's position is that labor rights are good or bad for economic growth, or whether the Bank takes the view that the jury is still out on this issue.

A. Core Labor Rights Defined

Despite this ambivalence, there exists a modicum of agreement on a set of fundamental, or "core," labor rights, as promulgated by the International Labour Organization (ILO). The ILO, which operates ultimately as a United Nations specialized agency, is charged with promoting human and labor rights as well as social justice. The ILO has a relatively unique history: Created by the Treaty of Versailles in 1919, it predates most other intergovernmental organizations. Additionally, within its governing organs, member state governments, workers, and employers participate as nominally equal partners. Despite its long history, however, the ILO's direct capacity to enforce labor rights and standards is quite limited. It operates much more as a "universe" than as a club (Drezner 2007) with 179 members; and it has a very limited set of resources. The 2004–2005 ILO budget, for instance, totaled $529 million,[2] slightly less than the annual GDP of Vanuatu or Djibouti and about 75 percent of the annual budget of the International Committee of the Red Cross. By comparison, General Electric, the largest MNC, had foreign sales of $57 billion in 2004 (and total sales of $153 billion; UNCTAD 2006).

So, while the WTO would argue that intergovernmental trade organizations are second-best instruments for the enforcement of labor rights (Morici

---

[2] ILO budget information is drawn from ILO (2006). Also see the *Briefing Book on International Organizations in Geneva* (http://www.genevabriefingbook.com/).

and Schulz 2001; Stern and Terrell 2003),³ its cited first-best mechanism (the ILO) suffers its own shortcomings. The ILO has little in the way of direct enforcement mechanisms. In fact, it only once has attempted to directly enforce its standards or decisions, which was in the case of Burma and its use of forced labor. Its proponents, however, would point out that, despite its limited financial and political resources, the ILO plays a central role as a creator and promulgator of norms and standards (via its Conventions and Recommendations) and as a provider of technical assistance to both governments and labor unions in developing nations. Moreover, the ILO imposes reporting requirements on its members; these include "regular" reporting (periodic reports and reviews of working conditions in member states) and "special" reporting based on complaints about specific problems in member countries.⁴ By publicizing national problems with the observation of core labor rights, the ILO engages in a type of the "shaming" that Keck and Sikkink (1998) describe (also see Weisband 2000).

The four "core labor rights" were advanced by the International Labor Organization in 1998 via its Declaration of Fundamental Principles and Rights at Work. This declaration maintains that all ILO members, even those that have not ratified the specific conventions associated with each of the rights, are obligated to respect these fundamental principles. The core principles include the elimination of all forms of compulsory and forced labor (ILO Conventions 29 and 105);⁵ the prohibition of discrimination in employment and pay based on race, gender, ethnicity, or religion (ILO Conventions 100 and 111); the elimination of child labor (or, at least, "the worst forms of child labor;" ILO Conventions 138 and 182); and freedom of association and the right to collective bargaining (ILO Conventions 87 and 98).

B. Workers' Collective Rights

Among the four core labor standards, freedom of association and collective bargaining rights are perhaps the most controversial. The right

---

³ This argument is based on a variety of concerns, including a worry that developed-nation labor unions and firms will use "labor standards" as a veil for making protectionist demands of their national governments. See Hafner-Burton 2009.

⁴ Of course, monitoring also relies on the willingness of labor unions, governments, or NGOs to bring complaints against ILO members. Whereas such a "fire alarm" model of monitoring (Goldstein and Martin 2000; Schwartz and McCubbins 1984) is also used by other international institutions (e.g., the WTO), it does create a problem of selection: The most vulnerable groups in the least open societies may be most in need of international awareness but least able or willing to bring a complaint. Also see Moran 2002.

⁵ For a discussion of ILO conventions on forced labor, see Busse and Braun 2003.

of freedom of association is addressed in the ILO's Constitution (1919), in its Declaration of Philadelphia (1944), and in the United Nations' Universal Declaration of Human Rights (1948). ILO Convention 87, issued in 1948, establishes "the right for workers and employers to establish and join organizations of their own choosing without previous authorization." Convention 98 (1949) provides that "workers shall enjoy adequate protection against acts of anti-union discrimination," including protection of individual employees from dismissal for participation in union activities, shielding of workers' and employers' organizations from interference by each other, and provision of the right of collective bargaining (ILO 2005, 24).

Yet despite the long history of these principles, less agreement exists regarding the desirability of labor unions than does agreement regarding the importance of eliminating discrimination, forced labor, and the worst types of child labor. In some ways, the lack of consensus on collective labor rights reflects a broader debate about the relative importance of free markets in organizing societies: Some would view the elimination of discrimination and forced labor as removing impediments to freer labor markets, whereas the protection of union rights could introduce inefficiencies into local labor markets (see Caraway 2006a for a review).

Perhaps as a result of this lack of agreement, national governments' interpretations of what is and is not required by ILO core conventions are quite variable. When bilateral or regional trade agreements address labor standards, they do not always invoke the ILO-sponsored core rights. For instance, the NAFTA side agreement on labor (the NAALC) does not obligate members' national labor laws to be consistent with ILO standards, and it explicitly excludes some categories of complaints (related to collective bargaining, freedom of association, and the right to strike) from outside review by arbitrators (Hafner-Burton 2009; Moran 2002). The U.S.-Jordan Free Trade Agreement, signed in October 2000, takes a slightly different approach: It does not require either party to adopt a particular set of standards, but it mandates that each government enforce the laws on its books. In doing so, it shifts the problem of compliance from adherence to international law to enforcement of domestic law.[6]

More recently, the U.S. Trade Act of 2002 requires the executive branch to submit to Congress a Labor Rights Report for proposed new free

---

[6] On the problem of compliance in international politics generally, and on the slippage between actual behavior and compliance, see Downs et al. 1996, Mitchell 1994, and Simmons 2000.

trade agreements. (Reports on employment impact in the United States and laws governing exploitative child labor also are required).[7] These reports, which have been prepared for agreements with Chile, Morocco, Oman, and Singapore, among others, address both core labor standards and working conditions.[8] Moreover, recent agreements sometimes invoke ILO-based standards explicitly.[9] For instance, the Central American Free Trade Agreement (CAFTA-DR) retains the focus on each party's sovereign right to establish and enforce its own labor laws, but it also asks each signatory to reaffirm its commitment to the ILO's 1998 *Declaration on Fundamental Principles*. Chapter 16 of CAFTA-DR also commits the parties "not to fail to enforce labor laws" in a way that would distort trade; labor laws are defined to include, not only freedom of association and the right to bargain collectively, as well as a prohibition on forced and child labor, but also "acceptable conditions of work."[10] While it is yet to be seen whether CAFTA-DR's dispute settlement procedure will provide for an effective enforcement mechanism in the labor law arena, the specific reference to ILO-based rights may indicate a gradual change in some governments' attitudes toward collective labor rights.

Despite the controversy that sometimes accompanies freedom of association and collective bargaining rights, the ILO Conventions related to these rights have been widely ratified. As of November 2006,[11] the freedom of association convention (No. 87) had been ratified by 147 nations, while the collective bargaining convention (No. 98) had received 156 ratifications. This rate of ratification parallels that of the two child labor

---

[7] Interestingly, the definition of "internationally recognized" workers' rights found in U.S. trade law adds "acceptable conditions of work with respect to minimum wages, hours of work, occupational safety and health" (National Research Council 2004, 2; also see Caraway 2006a; Hafner-Burton 2009).

[8] Reports are prepared by the U.S. Department of Labor's Bureau of International Labor Affairs (ILAB). See http://www.dol.gov/ILAB/media/reports/usfta/main.htm for text of the reports.

[9] The U.S. government also allows for consideration of foreign labor practices via its Generalized System of Preferences, which extends preferential market access to products from some developing nations. The GSP statute states that GSP recipients must have taken or be taking measures to "afford internationally recognized workers' rights," including freedom of association and the right to bargain collectively. Interested parties that allege violations of this condition may file cases requesting the removal of a country's GSP (Office of the United States Trade Representative 2006).

[10] For details on the agreement, see http://www.ustr.gov/Trade_Agreements/Bilateral/ CAFTA/Briefing_Book/Section_Index.html

[11] Ratification information for the eight core conventions is taken from the ILOLEX database, http://www.ilo.org/ilolex/english/docs/declworld.htm, accessed November 25, 2006.

core conventions (147 ratifications for No. 138 and 162 for No. 182),[12] although it is lower than that of the forced labor treaties (170 ratifications for No. 29 and 166 ratifications for Convention 105) and of the employment discrimination conventions (163 ratifications for Convention 100 and 165 for Convention 111). Additionally, these rates of ratification are substantially higher than those for conventions related to working conditions, reflecting broader international consensus on the existence of such rights (also see Böhning 2005).

Table 4.1 offers comparative statics on the ratification rates of both core labor and other types of ILO conventions.[13] The first four rows report on Conventions that address the core labor rights areas. Ratification rates for these instruments range from 82 percent to 90 percent of the ILO's 179 members. The remaining rows report on conventions that address various elements of working conditions, including wages, working time, health and safety, and the provision of maternity benefits to women (for summaries of these rights and conventions, see ILO 2005). In all cases, the ratifications of these instruments are substantially lower than those of the core conventions, ranging from 5 percent of members (nine countries) for the Night Work Convention (aimed at protecting workers who labor during night hours) to 66 percent of member countries for the weekly rest convention, mandating that workers should enjoy a rest period of at least twenty-four consecutive hours every seven days.

In addition to being widely accepted (or, at least, ratified) by ILO members, freedom of association and collective bargaining rights are, among core labor standards, the most directly related to the general capacity of workers to improve their treatment, wages, and benefits. Standards governing workers' collective rights provide the capacity to achieve more favorable outcomes with respect to pay, overtime, and working conditions. We can conceive of these collective rights, then, as focused on the processes by which workers' interests – whatever they might be – are aggregated and represented. The existence of these rights facilitates the achievement of various outcomes for workers. These process-based rights can be distinguished from outcome standards, which refer to the actual conditions faced by workers (wage levels, working hours, or health and safety).[14]

---

[12] On child labor and globalization, see Busse and Braun (2004).

[13] For a discussion of the determinants of ratification, see Hathaway (2002) and Simmons (2009).

[14] I borrow the "process versus outcomes" typology from Barrientos and Smith (2007). Elliott and Freeman (2003) label this distinction as that between "core" and "cash"

TABLE 4.1. *Ratifications of Select ILO Conventions, 2006*

Area	Convention #	Convention	Year Established	% ILO Members Ratified
Collective Labor Rights	87	Freedom of Association	1948	82
	98	Collective Bargaining	1949	87
Child Labor	138	Minimum Age	1973	82
	182	Worst Forms of Child Labour	1999	91
Forced Labor	29	Forced Labour	1930	95
	105	Abolition of Forced Labour	1957	93
Employment Discrimination	100	Equal Remuneration	1951	91
	111	Discrimination	1958	92
Wages	95	Protection of Wages	1949	54
	131	Minimum Wage Fixing	1970	27
Working Time	1	Hours of Work in Industry	1919	29
	47	Forty Hour Work Week	1935	8
	14	Weekly Rest	1921	66
	171	Night Work	1990	5
Safety and Health	155	Occupational Safety and Health	1981	26
	161	Occupational Health Services	1985	14
Maternity Protection	183	Maternity Protection[15]	2000	7

Whereas collective labor rights may not perfectly predict actual working conditions, there is an established association between greater respect for collective labor rights and improvements in wages and working conditions (Aidt and Tzannaos 2002; Huber and

standards, where the latter represent outcomes. Rodríguez-Garavito (2005) classifies labor rights as either enabling (process) or protective (outcome).

[15] Convention 183, on maternity protection, superseded two earlier instruments: the Maternity Protection Convention (1919, No. 3, ratified by 33 ILO members) and the

Stephens 2001).[16] Along these lines, empirical analyses document the existence of a "union wage premium." These studies tend to focus, given data limitations,[17] on developed nations. For instance, in a seventeen country sample (including Brazil and Chile as well as OECD nations), Blanchflower and Bryson (2003) find evidence for a significant union wage premium in twelve of the nations analyzed. Similarly, Morici and Schulz's (2001) study of labor costs and labor rights in select developing nations suggests that "annual manufacturing labor costs per worker, after taking into account national differences in productivity, are reduced by an average of more than $6000 per year in economies where both freedom of association and child labor are not well-protected" (p. 7). Costs are reduced by $3000 per year when only freedom of association is not respected.[18] Whereas it is not clear what the magnitude of this estimate implies in countries with relatively low incomes per capita (e.g., Moran 2002), it highlights the linkage between core labor rights and wage costs.[19] Furthermore, scholars consistently find an association between the use of formal labor market institutions to set wages and the dispersion of earnings. Nations that rely on more formalized wage-setting processes, which tend to involve collective representation of labor, display significantly lower levels of wage inequality (Freeman 2007). Along these lines, recent World Bank research reports note the importance of labor regulations and workers' rights protections for the realization of equitable – in terms of

Maternity Protection Convention (Revised, 1952, No. 103, ratified by 40 countries). Each of these earlier conventions is still in force in certain countries.

[16] For research on the effects of unions on macroeconomic outcomes and on productivity, investment, and profits, see Flanagan (2006) and Metcalf (2003). The former reviews literature suggesting that a higher degree of labor coordination is associated with stronger macroeconomic performance. The latter reports mixed findings on the impact of labor unions on productivity and investment and a negative effect of unions on profits. In both cases, the analyses are focused on developed democracies.

[17] Flanagan's study (2006) uses a wide range of labor-related indicators, including measures of wages, working hours, workplace health and safety, discrimination, child labor, and forced labor. Many of his measures, however, are not available on a time series basis, and he notes issues of cross-national comparability with respect to developing country labor statistics.

[18] In their regression estimates, Morici and Schulz (2001) use the OECD's (1996) four-point scale of respect for freedom of association. The $3000 change is implied by a one-unit change in the four-point freedom of association scale (pp. 51–53).

[19] Morici and Schulz (2001) also point out, however, that the effects of restrictions of freedom of association (as opposed to limits on other core labor rights) on wages and economic growth in developing nations are likely to be mixed (pp. 39–40). In particular, the effects of such restrictions vary with the competitiveness of local labor markets.

wage and income equality – economic development (Abouharb and Cingranelli 2008).

Furthermore, by focusing our examination on workers' collective rights, we confine the analysis to what are widely (albeit not unanimously) considered to be fundamental rights, setting a minimum floor for behavior (ILO 2005; Morici and Schulz 2001). This avoids the need to define an internationally acceptable level of working hours or wages or to assess the efficiency consequences of outcomes-based standards, which are far more controversial (particularly given the linkages between productivity and wage costs and the cross-national variation in each). We also are able to avoid many of the difficulties associated with measuring wages or union density in a cross-national context, which is particularly problematic in the context of developing nations (Daude et al. 2003). Additionally, in assessing national collective labor rights outcomes, our measure differentiates between violations of labor rights on the legal side and on the practical (implementation) dimension, allowing us to address the potential for slippage between national laws and actual practices.

II. MEASURING COLLECTIVE LABOR RIGHTS

Despite the centrality of labor rights to the "race to the bottom" debate and to the study of multinational production more generally, only a few studies have examined systematically the relationship between economic globalization and the specific category of labor (versus human) rights. This stems, in large part, from a lack of cross-national, time series data regarding the existence of core labor rights (Böhning 2005; Morici and Schulz 2001).[20] Most large-N examinations of the linkages between rights and the global economy therefore have focused on human rights, defined broadly (e.g., Apodaca 2001; Blanton and Blanton 2007; de Soysa and Oneal 1999; Hafner-Burton 2005a; Poe and Tate 1994; Poe et al. 1999; Richards et al. 2001).

Such studies employ cross-national quantitative measures of human rights, usually the Political Terror Scale (PTS). The PTS focuses on personal integrity rights, which includes protection from torture, execution, forced disappearance, arbitrary imprisonment, and discrimination based on political or religious beliefs. The PTS is coded on a country-year basis, using the U.S. State Department's annual *Country Reports on Human*

---

[20] See Böhning (2005) for a discussion of potential measures of other elements of core labor standards, such as employment discrimination and child labor.

Rights Practices, as well as annual reports from Amnesty International. Possible values of the PTS range from one to five, according to the severity of physical integrity rights violations (Cingranelli and Richards 1999). An alternative human rights measure, used in some of these analyses (e.g., Richards et al. 2001), is also based on State Department reports but focuses on government respect for civil and political liberties, including openness of political participation; government control of the media or freedom from censorship; freedom of religion; freedom to travel domestically and abroad; and the freedom to unionize. This measure, ranging from zero to ten and part of the Cingranelli-Richards (CIRI) Human Rights Dataset,[21] contains one element of labor rights but is focused on civil and political rights more generally.[22]

Flanagan (2006) takes an even broader approach, operationalizing the specific concept of freedom of association using the Freedom House civil liberties index.[23] Although the civil liberties index does include the possibility of effective collective bargaining and the presence of free trade unions as component measures, it also includes several other phenomena, such as press freedom, judicial independence, and freedom of religion. As such, while the civil liberties index may provide a useful proxy for the overall degree of democratic openness in a country-year, it does not allow for a specific assessment of collective labor rights.

While measures of human rights or civil rights may correlate with the protection of collective labor rights,[24] these quantitative measures focus on broader political outcomes, which may or may not be influenced by the same global economic mechanisms as labor rights. Indeed, the precise causal linkages between broader human rights outcomes and the global economy are not always clear from, or consistent across, the empirical studies of human rights and global economics. Some studies link human rights with multinational production via the effects of direct investment on economic growth and on political development (Graham 1995; Meyer 1996, 1998; Spar 1998). According to this logic, FDI facilitates economic growth (de Soysa and Oneal 1999), and growth leads to improved living

---

[21] More information on, and the data generated by, the Cingranelli and Richard project is available at http://ciri.binghamton.edu/. Also see Abouharb and Cingranelli 2008.

[22] For a discussion of the differences across, and relationships among, human rights measures, see Milner et al. 1999.

[23] As a second indicator of freedom of association, Flanagan employs Kucera's (2002) FACB measure in cross-sectional analyses.

[24] Leary (1996) treats labor rights as a sort of leading indicator for human rights more broadly. She posits that governments that fail to respect workers' rights are less likely to respect other types of human rights.

standards, higher employment levels, increased wages, and larger expenditures for human capital formation. Economic modernization, in turn, generates demands for greater political rights (Lerner 1958; Lipset 1959). Along these lines, many studies find a positive association between the level of economic development and human rights conditions (Apodaca 2001; Meyer 1998; Mitchell and McCormick 1988; Poe and Tate 1994; Poe et al. 1999; Richards et al. 2001; Sachs and Warner 1995).[25] In other analyses, the association between FDI and human rights rests on the importance to investors of rule of law. Foreign direct investors prefer nations with a developed rule of law, which facilitates the enforcement of contracts, the assignment of property rights, and the avoidance of expropriation (Knack and Keefer 1995; Li and Resnick 2003; MIGA 2002). Most of these studies, however, use broad indicators of "human rights" as the measures of "rule of law." As a result, the direction of causality may well be reversed: It is not that FDI affects human rights, but that human rights are an "information shortcut" for foreign investors, as they indicate a stronger rule of law (Knack and Keefer 1995). For instance, the assumption that democratic governments can commit more credibly to MNC-friendly policies is said to underlie the statistical link between democracy and FDI (Jensen 2006). Similarly, democratic transitions generate uncertainty regarding the rule of law, and therefore tend to reduce FDI flows (Resnick 2001). For this reason, it also is no surprise that some studies find a negative (although insignificant) relationship between FDI and respect for personal integrity rights (Richards et al. 2001), whereas others (Apodaca 2001) find a positive relationship.

Human rights research suggests that there is still much to disentangle regarding the potential relationships between the global economy – particularly foreign direct investment – and domestic political outcomes and institutions. It also suggests, though, using more direct measures of labor rights is a more appropriate empirical strategy. During the last decade, there indeed have been some attempts to measure labor rights more directly, again in the context of large-N, cross-national research. Many of these studies (e.g., Rodrik 1996) do so on the basis of a government's ratification of core ILO conventions in a given year. Along these lines, recent OECD studies (1996, 2000) group countries into four categories, based on respect for collective labor rights. The initial assessment (OECD 1996) relied on ratifications of five core ILO conventions as well

---

[25] Poe and his co-authors are primarily interested in correlates of human rights other than international economic factors.

as on OECD staff assessments; the OECD provided these categorizations for seventy-nine nations (all OECD members, plus a select set of developing nations) at a single point in time (usually 1993). In its later study (2000), the OECD supplemented the information underlying its coding decisions with cases heard by the ILO's Committee of Experts on the Applications of Conventions and Recommendations (CEACR) during the 1989–1999 period. This revised data, for sixty-nine countries, aimed to capture more of the practical (as well as the legal) observation of collective labor rights.

In a slightly different vein, Cingranelli (2002; also Cingranelli and Tsai 2003) relies on the labor rights section of the annual U.S. State Department *Country Reports on Human Rights Practices* for the labor rights component of the CIRI human rights scale. The labor rights measure assigns country-years into one of three categories: Countries that do not provide basic respect for freedom of association and collective bargaining receive a score of zero; countries that have full respect for freedom of association and collective bargaining but some other sorts of labor problems, including the exploitation of child labor, excessive working hours, minimum wage problems, or health and safety violations, receive a score of one; and countries with no problems in either collective labor rights or individual working conditions receive a score of two. The benefit of this measure is that it addresses both collective labor rights and working conditions in a cross-national, time series fashion. At the same time, however, the scale is nominal, not ordinal: It is not clear if countries that score a zero (less than full provision of collective labor rights) have better or worse labor outcomes than those that score a one (full collective labor rights but other sorts of labor-related issues); rather, they simply display *different* types of problems in the broader area of labor rights. Additionally, this measure focuses exclusively on labor rights practices rather than on the domestic legal framework surrounding labor rights. Moreover, the CIRI labor rights measure relies on a single (and possibly biased) source, and – given its range of only three values – the measure allows for little variation over time or across countries (see Abouharb and Cingranelli 2008).

Other scholars have, however, begun to fill this empirical hole. Most notably, Kucera (2002) develops a methodology to assess and compare collective labor rights cross-nationally. Kucera's (2002) template records thirty-seven types of violations of labor rights in six categories: Freedom of association and collective bargaining-related liberties; the right to establish and join worker and union organizations; other union activities;

the right to bargain collectively; the right to strike; and rights in EPZs. In each of these broad categories, specific violations include the absence of legal rights, limitations on legal rights, and the violations of legal rights by government agents or employers. On the basis of expert assessments, Kucera's methodology assigns a weighting to each violation, with more serious violations (e.g., general prohibitions on unions) weighted more heavily than others (e.g., a requirement of previous authorization in order for a union to join a confederation of unions).

Kucera (2002) implemented his coding template to develop a cross-sectional measure – for the mid-1990s – of labor rights in a wide range of countries; he uses this measure (freedom of association and collective bargaining [FACB]) to address the linkages between labor rights and global economic factors (see Chapter 3). Similarly, Neumayer and de Soysa (2006) employ Kucera's data to test the associations between labor rights and trade as well as between FDI and labor rights. Each of these studies, however, relies on a single observation per country on the collective labor rights indicator. Cross-sectional analyses, therefore, are possible; but time series assessments are not.

This sort of measure focuses on the legal provision of collective labor rights as well as their observation in practice. There are, of course, other possible means of measuring the status of workers within societies. For instance, we might consider rates of union density (membership in labor unions) where high levels of union density would indicate sufficient protection for freedom of association. Theoretically, union density rates have a variety of determinants, many of which depend on a state's political institutions and history (as well as on the sectoral structure of its economy and the precise workings of its unemployment system) rather than on the protection of freedom of association (Huber and Stephens 2001; Iversen and Cusack 2000; Martin and Brady 2007; National Research Council 2004; Scruggs and Lange 2002). Additionally, union density data reflect both demand and supply considerations – workers' interest in joining a union and the legal and practical opportunities to do so. Given these dual influences, it is difficult to assess whether low rates of unionization are due to workers' belief that they will not gain from union membership or due to workplace or governmental impediments to union organization.

Moreover, in countries with a single union structure, such as China, Cuba, and Vietnam, union membership often is compulsory (Collier and Collier 1991). China has the highest union density rate in the world, but we would not expect the All-China Confederation of Trade Unions to act independently from the government (Chan and Senser 1997; Ngai 2005). Former Communist nations in Eastern Europe and Central Asia also tend to have high rates of union membership, owing to the historical linkages between labor unions and central governments (Martin and Brady 2007; Robertson 2007). In some nations that recently have transitioned toward democracy, "legacy unions" – state-backed unions that are a relic of the previous authoritarian regime – continue to dominate. For example, in Indonesia, the All-Indonesia Workers' Union (Serikat Pekerja Seluruh Indonesia [SPSI]) remains the strongest union (Caraway 2008).

Empirically, the quality of union density data in developing countries is particularly poor (Böhning 2005; Freeman 2007; Rudra 2002, 2008). One issue is that union membership is open only to workers in the formal sector of the economy, whereas unionization rates usually are based on a nation's total working age population. In countries with large informal sectors – which describes many low- and middle-income nations – density rates therefore may understate the level of organization of the formal sector (Brady and Martin 2007; Croucher and Cotton 2009). Another issue is that there is no standardized methodology for calculating density rates outside the OECD, making density rates difficult to compare cross-nationally. For instance, the U.S. State Department's *Country Reports on Human Rights Practices* for Costa Rica list the same rate of unionization (15 percent) for each year between 1993 and 2002, which seems unlikely, particularly given the changes in the structure of its economy during that decade (see Chapter 7).

Another alternative measure would be a count of the number of labor-related strikes and protests in a given country-year, on the grounds that strikes happen only when the right to strike is respected in practice (and, usually, in law). Again, however, strikes are driven by supply-side as well as by demand-side factors; cultural legacies, political resources, and institutional opportunities are important determinants of strike activity (Murillo 2001). Regime type also plays a role. Robertson (2007) demonstrates, for instance, that in partially liberalized regimes, the level of strike activity often is driven by elite interests or severe economic crisis rather than by the extent of union membership. Moreover, the relationship between strikes and workers' grievances is unlikely to be a direct one: A lack of strike activity could indicate a very satisfied labor force or a labor force that is too cowed by employers or by the state to engage in protest activity. Strikes, then, may not be highly correlated with the underlying level of workers' grievances; nor are strikes the only important expression of labor unrest (Silver 2003). Therefore, while such measures do provide important information about the capacity for workers to organize and to protest, they fall short on both empirical and theoretical grounds.

A. Coding Labor Rights

In order to get a better sense of the changes over time, as well as the variation across countries, in collective labor rights, we use Kucera's template (contained in the Appendix) to generate global data on collective labor rights, covering each year during the 1985–2002 period. To reduce bias, these assessments of violations of collective labor rights are drawn from three (rather than one) sources (as are Kucera's): the U.S. State Department annual *Country Reports on Human Rights Practices*; reports from the International Labor Organization's CEACR and the Committee on Freedom of Association (CFA); and the International Confederation of Free Trade Unions' (ICFTU; now ITUC) *Annual Survey of Violations of Trade Union Rights*.

The State Department's *Country Reports* have been submitted to Congress annually since 1977 (for reports covering 1976); these reports are mandated by the U.S. Foreign Assistance Act of 1961 (amended) and by the Trade Act of 1974 (amended, Section 504). The Congressional reporting requirements apply to all countries that receive U.S. foreign assistance via the two Acts, as well as all other foreign countries that are members of the United Nations. The State Department routinely includes several other nations that are not covered by the mandate so that annual country coverage is global, or nearly so. Initial drafts of the reports are prepared by embassy staff in each country on the basis of information from government officials, opposition parties, human rights activists, academics, and various others. These drafts are reviewed (and often revised) by staff of the State Department's Bureau of Democracy, Human Rights, and Labor, with further input from other State Department staff and outside experts (Poe et al. 2001). The reports have become more detailed over time; contemporary reports discuss six categories of human rights – respect for personal integrity; respect for civil liberties; respect for political rights; government attitudes regarding international or NGO investigation of alleged human rights violations; discrimination, societal abuses and trafficking in persons; and worker rights.

Various observers have criticized the State Department reports over the years; the Lawyers Committee for Human Rights, for instance, issues an annual rejoinder to the *Country Reports*. While some of its critiques concern reports on specific countries, others involve the methodology behind the reports. For instance, during the Cold War, many observers were concerned that U.S. allies were treated more favorably than Soviet allies or non-aligned countries. Others noted that, perhaps because of its bias toward protecting state sovereignty (as opposed to the rights of individuals), the State Department reports tended to treat countries more favorably than a parallel set of reports from Amnesty International, at least in the area of personal integrity rights (Poe et al. 2001; Ron et al. 2005). Another concern was that the *Country Reports* were too narrow in scope, often failing to address problems of gender discrimination, racial discrimination, and labor rights.

Empirical analyses of the *Country Reports*, however, report limited systematic evidence of bias. In their statistical examinations of the correlates of the reports' assessments (in terms of the PTS), Poe et al. (2001) find only limited evidence of bias: In some of their large-N models (covering the years 1976–1995), countries with left-leaning governments receive less favorable treatment. Poe and his colleagues report even weaker evidence that U.S. allies receive favorable treatment, all else equal. Moreover, they find that these biases are most pronounced in the early years of the *Reports*, largely disappearing by the mid-1980s. This is consistent with Innes' earlier (1992) study, which critiques the *Country Reports* for their conservative approach toward reporting violations but points out that this bias becomes less pronounced over time. Along similar lines, in 1996, the Lawyers' Committee ceased publication of its book-length critiques on the grounds that the reports had become "a more reliable and thorough guide to human rights conditions throughout the world" (Lawyers' Committee 2003, 1).[26] Moreover, on the specific topic of labor rights, observers note that, whereas information from U.S. embassy staff is not perfect, it has improved over the last decade, as the State Department has raised the professional status of its embassy labor officers (National Research Council 2004; also see Hathaway 2002).

Our second source is reports from the International Labour Organization. Both the ILO's CEACR and the CFA provide information based on regular reports from governments as well as (potentially) complaints filed by workers' organizations, employers' organizations, or

---

[26] In its 2003 Congressional testimony, however, the Lawyers' Committee also expressed a concern that a newer, more subtle type of bias might come to color the *Country Reports*: United States allies in the "war on terror" appeared, in its judgment, to receive more favorable assessments than their human rights records suggested.

other governments. The ILO mandates that governments report bienni-ally on the steps they have taken to implement any of the eight core labor rights-related conventions they have ratified.[27] These reports also are submitted to national workers' and employers' organizations, which may comment on the reports – or on their governments' application of the conventions generally (also see Böhning 2005; ILO 2005; Morici and Schulz 2001; Weisband 2000).

The CEACR was established to examine these reports; it is made up of twenty independent experts (mostly in the area of labor law) appointed by the ILO's Governing Body (its executive committee) for three-year terms. Committee members, who are drawn from a variety of geographic regions, are charged with offering technical, unbiased evaluations of gov-ernments' applications of international standards.[28] The CEACR publishes an annual report that contains general comments about member states' behavior and summarizes the Committee's observations on national applications of core labor standards. In some cases, the Committee also makes direct requests to member governments for additional information regarding their implementation of core conventions. In addition, the ILO constitution (Article 24) allows any workers' or employers' organization to bring complaints ("representations") against member states regarding their implementation of a ratified Convention. In the case of freedom of association, government ratification is not required for a complaint to be lodged. Similarly, under Article 26 of the ILO Constitution, govern-ments may bring complaints against other governments – but if and only if the complainant government has ratified the convention in question. Throughout the life of the ILO, neither Article 24 nor Article 26 has been used very frequently; during the ILO's existence, a total of eleven Commissions of Inquiry – established via Article 26 when a member has been persistently accused of committing serious violations – have been established (ILO 2005; Moran 2002; National Research Council 2004).

The CFA is more widely utilized when it comes to reporting and addressing violations of core labor standards. During the last fifty-plus years, the CFA has examined over 2,300 cases, and its annual caseload has expanded markedly since the 1980s (ILO 2005). It is a Governing

---

[27] The biennial reporting requirement also applies to the ILO's four "priority" conventions (Conventions 81, 122, 129, and 144). For other conventions, reports are required every five years.

[28] Information on the structure and mandates of ILO Committees is taken from the International Labor Organization's International Labor Standards webpage, http://www.ilo.org/public/english/standards/norm/index.htm

Body committee comprised of three representatives from governments, employers, and workers, for nine total members (plus an independent chairperson). The CFA accepts complaints regarding freedom of association violations from workers' or employers' organizations in the relevant country; from international associations of workers and employers if one of them is involved in the alleged violation; and from international organizations of employers or workers with consultative status at the ILO (Moran 2002). CFA complaints may be filed regardless of whether the targeted government has ratified Conventions 87 (freedom of association) and 98 (collective bargaining). When complaints are lodged, the CFA first decides whether to receive them; if it does so, the CFA then engages in a dialogue with the government in order to establish the facts of the case. If the CFA finds that a violation has occurred, it promulgates a report and recommends means of resolving the situation. In such cases, the CFA asks governments to report on whether and how the violation has been addressed; in some circumstances, the CFA also may propose a "direct contacts" mission to the country.

The final source of our labor rights coding is the ICFTU's (now ITUC's) annual reports. The ICFTU is the major peak association of trade unions, an international confederation of national trade union associations (Weisband and Colvin 2000). It is financed by fees from member associations as well as by ad-hoc contributions for specific projects and issues. In 2006, the ICFTU merged with the World Confederation of Labour (WCL) to form the International Trade Union Confederation (ITUC). The ITUC counts as members approximately 175 million workers in 155 countries and territories, and 311 national affiliates (also see Croucher and Cotton 2009). The ITUC runs campaigns on specific issues, such as child labor, forced labor, and health and safety standards; it also cooperates closely with the ILO and has consultative status with United Nations Educational, Scientific and Cultural Organization (UNESCO) and several specialized U.N. agencies.

Since 1984, the ICFTU (and now the ITUC) has issued an annual[29] *Survey of Violations of Trade Union Rights*, which focuses on collective labor rights, including the lack of legal rights (or many legal barriers to organization), violations of rights in practice (such as dismissals on

---

[29] ICFTU *Surveys* initially covered overlapping two-year periods (1983/1984, 1984/1985, and 1985/1986). Beginning with the fourth survey (published in 1986, covering violations in 1985), the *Surveys* reviewed violations within a single year. The ITUC has continued to publish the *Annual Survey*. Also see Colvin and Weisband 2000.

the basis of union membership), and other interference with the exercise of trade union rights (including the murder, disappearance, or detention of trade unionists).[30] The reports are based on information reported by national union centers and their local affiliates as well as by locally active NGOs. ICFTU/ITUC staff sometimes supplement this information with data from country visits (National Research Council 2004). The *Survey* has, like the State Department *Country Reports*, expanded in length over time, reflecting greater country coverage and greater attention to (if not actual violations of) trade union rights. The 2004 *Survey*, for instance, summarized violations in 134 countries for calendar year 2003.

Whereas each set of reports has potential shortcomings – for instance, ICFTU reports do not cover every country in every year, as they rely on reporting from national sources – the use of multiple sources helps to reduce bias. Single sources may vary over time in their geographic coverage and in the attention given to certain types of violations. Single sources also may be prejudiced. Likewise, we might worry that – given donor interest, access to information and local activists, and the level of political openness – transnational advocacy networks pay more attention to violations in some countries than in others (Ron et al. 2005). Although it is impossible to remove all potential biases in reports of labor rights violations, the use of multiple sources helps to reduce many of these biases.[31]

The logic behind our indicator of collective labor rights is similar to that guiding Böhning's (2005) assessments, in that it aims to derive a set of measures in a way that is methodologically transparent, that includes elements of both legal protection and actual provision of rights, and that allows for comparisons across cases (his measure covers approximately 160 countries, with annual observations for the 1985–2004 period). Böhning is ultimately interested in deriving a broader measure of core labor rights (including all four dimensions designated by the ILO), although he also discusses each of the four constituent elements. An important way in which my data departs from his, however, is its sources: Böhning eschews the use of data from national governments or non-governmental organizations "for fear that biases may be associated with them" (p. 22). He relies, instead, on information reported by the ILO. This information includes the ratification of and reporting on

---

[30] Weisband and Colvin 2000 offer a taxonomy of violations reported in ICFTU materials.

[31] Furthermore, we code information from ICFTU reports (which tend to be the most pro-labor of our sources) only when the reported violations are cited as "credible" or are confirmed by outside sources.

core ILO conventions (to measure the legal aspect of rights) as well as problems identified and investigated (direct requests, negative observations, and interim reports) by the CEACR and CFA. While Böhning's concerns about bias are justified, the use of multiple sources helps to address them. Beyond the problems with ratification-based measures of rights (see Section III, this chapter), the use of CEACR and CFA observations alone may create selection problems. If the CFA does not investigate some subset of complaints or if governments, NGOs, and labor unions elect (for reasons related to technical capacity or to domestic political considerations) not to file complaints, the set of cases generated will be biased.

When a country displays a violation of labor rights for one of the thirty-seven dimensions, we assign a score of one for that category and year. If no violation is reported for a given category and year, we assign a score of zero. We then multiply these scores by the weighting for each category; the sum of these category scores provides the annual measure of labor rights violations. If a violation is recorded more than once in a source, or in multiple sources, the maximum score per category remains one. Possible scores on the labor standards indicator, then, range from 0 to 76.5. In practice, however, no country exhibits violations in every category of labor rights, and maximum scores are in the mid-30s. Higher scores on the labor rights indicator indicate *worse* collective labor rights, and lower scores represent greater respect for such rights. Scores of zero, then, indicate no recorded violations, while scores in the mid-30s indicate the worst cases. For ease of presentation, we reverse the scale of the labor rights indicator so that higher values indicate *better* collective labor rights and lower values represent less respect for such rights. Scores of zero, then, indicate the worst cases, while scores in the mid-30s indicate few or no violations.

While the coding scheme does not distinguish between single and multiple violations within the same category, and while most of our sources focus their reporting on workers in the formal rather than the informal sector (see National Research Council 2004), our measure allows us to capture an overall picture of variations in labor rights across countries and over time. Kucera's template weights different types of violations differently, according to their severity, but these weightings have little effect on the overall scores: The correlation between the weighted scores and an index of unweighted scores (where each category of violations is assigned a weight of "one") is .89 for the global sample of countries and .87 for developing nations.

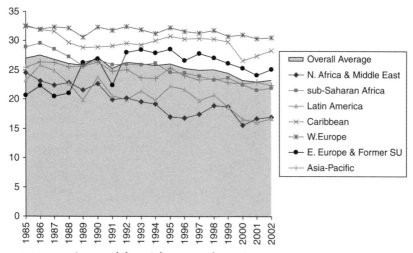

FIGURE 4.1. Average labor rights scores by region.

B. Overall Labor Rights Scores

For the 1985–2002 period, observations on the labor rights indicator range between 0 and 37 (country-years with the fewest violations), with a mean of 9.47 and a standard deviation of 7.73. Figure 4.1 summarizes the labor rights measure by geographic region and over time. On average, labor rights are most respected in Western Europe and least respected in the Middle East, North Africa, and Latin America. There also are some deteriorations over time, at least at the level of regional averages, as in Latin America and Sub-Saharan Africa. Central and Eastern Europe, on the other hand, display improvement in mean outcomes over time. Figure 4.2 presents average values of the labor rights variable for developing nations, sorted according to income decile. Among developing nations, the highest income countries display the greatest respect for collective labor rights outcomes. Note, however, that it is observations in the intermediate income deciles that are characterized by the lowest levels of respect for collective labor rights.

In Section IIA, I justify the use of multiple sources of information as a means of ameliorating the potential biases in each source. Using multiple sources also allows us to increase the amount of information available for a given country-year. For instance, if the ICFTU's affiliates pay close attention to violations in Guyana during 1997, but U.S. Embassy staff members have little information on these violations or Guyanese union affiliates lack the resources to file cases at the CFA, information from

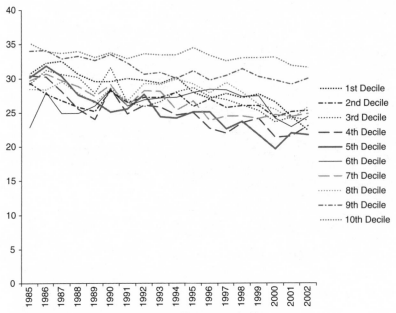

FIGURE 4.2. Labor rights, average by income decile.

the ICFTU will help to fill out the picture of labor rights violations. At the same time, though, we should be confident that the overall scores do not reflect an overwhelming influence of one source or another. Factor analyses indicate that the individual sources do, in fact, capture the same underlying dimension: When we analyze scores by source (ILO, State Department, and ICFTU), all three scores load on a single factor.[32]

Figure 4.3 summarizes changes in the collective labor rights indicator between 1985 and 2002, again by region. The bars in the figure indicate, for each region, the proportion of countries with increases in violation scores (2002 scores minus 1985 scores), with decreases in violations and with no change in violations. The solid area provides the *average* size of change in the labor rights score. For every region except Eastern Europe and the former Soviet Union, the average change is a negative one, indicating deteriorating rights; the deteriorations are largest for North Africa and Latin America and smallest for Western Europe. Moreover, the variation of the labor rights measure increases in the 1990s in developing nations, with a standard deviation of 5.8 in 1990 and 8.3 in 1999 (falling

---

[32] This remains true whether we use the entire sample (all countries), only non-OECD countries, or only non-OECD and non-Eastern European/former Soviet Union nations.

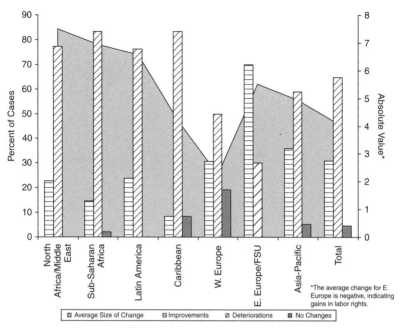

FIGURE 4.3. Changes in labor rights scores, 1985–2002.

to 7.9 in 2002), implying greater divergence as globalization intensifies. The general trend is similar to that reported in Böhning's freedom of association index, which reveals deteriorations over time (1985 to 2004) in 53 percent of countries.

The preponderance of increased violations could indicate that, at the same time economic globalization has intensified, labor rights are under siege around the world. Alternatively, this pattern could signal an increased attention by NGOs to labor rights issues, particularly in EPZs and in facilities owned or under contract with developed-country multinationals. Along these lines, Ron et al.'s (2005) analysis of the determinants of Amnesty International's publications on human rights violations finds that the level of NGO attention to violations is driven by the actual occurrence of such violations as well as by a country's significance internationally. This might lead us to expect, in the case of labor rights, greater attention to violations in China or India. The broader empirical question, though, is whether and how the trends in labor rights and multinational production are causally related to one another: Do nations with greater participation in subcontracting for global producers also display lower collective labor rights scores?

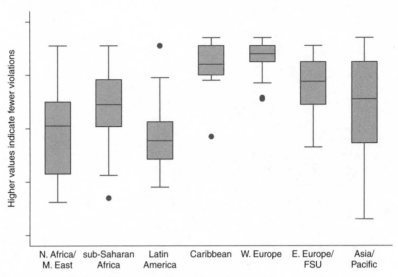

FIGURE 4.4. Labor rights scores by region, 2002.

Figure 4.4 provides additional information about the overall labor rights indicator for the most recent year in the dataset, 2002. Again, the scores displayed are averages by region. The box plot indicates the dispersion of the variable across regions. This figure suggests that cross-national variation in labor rights is particularly pronounced in North Africa and the Middle East, Sub-Saharan Africa, and Asia. Particularly in Africa and Asia, there is great cross-national variation in labor rights violations. Intra-regional variation is smallest in Western Europe (where observed violations are fewest) and the Caribbean.

C. Labor Rights by Category

The coding template used to generate the overall country-year scores also provides information regarding specific types of collective labor rights, both by subset of collective labor rights (e.g., the right to strike) and by legal rights versus practical observance of rights. In the case of the former, the six component areas (freedom of association and collective bargaining-related liberties; the right to establish and join worker and union organizations; other union activities; the right to bargain collectively; the right to strike; and rights in EPZs) are positively and often strongly correlated with one another. Factor analyses of overall labor rights scores by component indicate a strong loading on a single dimension. This pattern

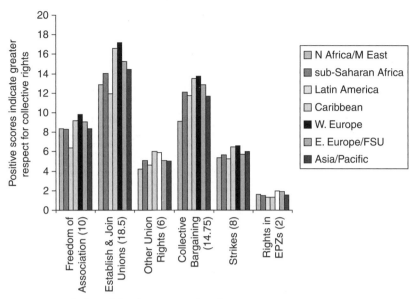

FIGURE 4.5. Labor rights by type, regional averages, 2002.

is consistent with the content and implications of each indicator: The right to collectively bargain, for instance, is difficult to realize without a right to strike.

Figure 4.5 summarizes the six categories of collective labor rights, again by geographic region and for the year 2002. The chart indicates the maximum score in each category. Again, higher scores indicate greater respect for collective labor rights; for instance, a score of ten indicates no problems with freedom of association, while a score of zero indicates a wide range of violations of rights related to freedom of association. The chart again reveals significant variation across geographic regions. It also indicates that certain types of violations are more persistent – and contribute more to overall labor rights outcomes – in some regions than in others.

Indeed, we might expect that specific categories or types of violations would be of particular interest to labor rights activists, multinational investors, and scholars of international political economy. For instance, activists often focus their attention on working conditions and collective labor rights in EPZs and on the ways in which EPZs and the legislation that creates them might be used to limit organized labor's activities. The ILO's various committees also have expressed such concerns with respect to specific countries, particularly regarding freedom of association and the right to bargain collectively in such zones (see International Labour Office Governing Body 2003). In Costa Rica's EPZs, for instance, management sometimes encourages the creation of "solidarity associations," which provide a variety of services to workers (e.g., subsidized credit and housing loans) but do not meet international standards for independent union representation (see Chapter 7).

Those who are skeptical about the effects of multinational production on workers' rights might expect that restrictions on workers' rights in EPZs will increase as foreign firms' involvement grows. Indeed, the collective labor rights data indicate that restrictions on union activities in EPZs have become more frequent over time. While only 11 percent of developing countries had restricted labor rights in EPZs in 1991 and 1992, the proportion rises to 25 percent for 2001 and 2002. Again, of course, the important question is how this trend relates to multinational production; in Chapter 5, I assess whether the component scores of the overall labor rights indicator are related to countries' involvement in multinational production.

D. Labor Rights in Law and Practice

In addition to providing overall scores and category-specific indicators of labor rights, the collective labor rights coding scheme also allows us to distinguish between rights in practice and rights in law. Some elements of the index measure whether legal rights exist (for instance, Item 6 assesses whether labor unions are permitted; Item 14 assesses whether independent labor unions are permitted; and Item 32 captures the legal right to strike). Other elements address violations of rights in practice: Do authorities interfere with union rights of assembly (Item 4); do employers dismiss workers because of their union membership (Item 10); and do authorities intervene in collective bargaining processes (Item 27)? Like Böhning (2005) and the National Research Council (2004), who differentiate between the adherence (rights in law) and implementation (rights in practice) dimensions of labor rights, we can distinguish between the content of domestic legislation and its implementation on the ground.

In this spirit, some labor rights activists suggest that, in many developing nations, it is the enforcement of rights – rather than the existence of rights – that is problematic. For instance, the Fair Labor Association (2005) argues that governments interested in taking part in a race to the bottom do not usually make explicit changes to their regulatory frameworks. Rather, they fail to enforce standards, either because of a lack of state capacity, or as a deliberate policy choice (also see American Center for International Labor Solidarity 2003; Bhagwati 2004; Moran 2002).[33] In a different vein, Greenhill et al. (2009) report that the pattern of a country's trade relationships has more pronounced effects on labor rights practices than on labor laws.

Therefore, to assess the potential differences across countries in terms of legal labor rights versus the actual enforcement of such rights, I generate two subcomponents of the labor rights measure:[34] One including the "law" elements of the coding template and the other covering the "practice" elements.[35] On average, there are more violations of the legal elements (an average violation score of 4.82, for the entire sample) than of the practical ones (an average of 4.57).[36] Interestingly, in 2002, firms in nations with higher levels of violations in practice also were more likely to report that labor regulations were a "major or very severe" obstacle to doing business.[37]

A comparison of the law and practice subcategories also hints that countries vary in the source of their overall labor rights outcomes. Country-year scores on the legal elements of labor rights are correlated positively with practice scores, but the correlations are relatively low: .27 for all countries and .23 for developing nations.[38] Figure 4.6 plots the legal and practical elements of collective rights for select developing nations for 2002. Figures 4.6 and 4.7 employ standardized values of the law and practice scores, where higher scores again indicate fewer violations (that is, the scale is again reversed, as with the main indicator).

---

[33] The CIRI labor rights indicator focuses mostly on practices – on what governments do vis-à-vis human and workers' rights – rather than on laws. See Abouharb and Cingranelli 2008.

[34] I thank Victoria Murillo for suggesting the law versus practice coding.

[35] The law indicator is the sum of labor rights template categories 6, 8, 13, 14, 15, 16, 18, 19, 20, 21, 22, 24, 25, 26, 29, 30, 32, 33, 34, 35, and 37. The practice measure is the sum of labor rights template categories 1, 2, 3, 4, 5, 7, 9, 10, 11, 12, 17, 23, 27, 28, 31, and 36.

[36] For a sample of only developing nations, the average law score is 5.67, and the average practice score is 5.04.

[37] The bivariate correlation between violations in practice and the percentage of firms surveyed by the World Bank that cite labor regulations as a serious business obstacle is .37 (n=51). See http://www.doingbusiness.org/ for information on the World Bank's *Doing Business* surveys and database. The indicator used above is from *Doing Business'* 2002 firm perceptions summary data.

[38] These correlations also vary over time: The lowest correlations are in 1986 (.14) and 1990 (.05); the highest is in 1998 (.42). For the last five years of the sample (1997–2002), the correlation between law and practice scores is .36, higher than the overall 1985–2002 period.

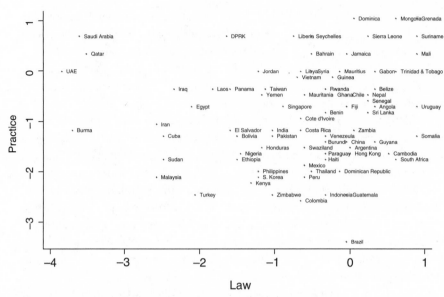

FIGURE 4.6. Collective labor rights in law and practice, select developing nations, 2002.

The figure indicates that some nations are characterized by well-protected legal rights but many violations in practice (e.g., Brazil). Others have the opposite pattern, with legal prohibitions on union activities but (or, therefore) few violations in practice (e.g., Qatar, Saudi Arabia). A third category of countries, such as Turkey, displays a mix of limited legal rights and violations in practice.

The final set of graphs displays data on collective labor rights law and practice for three separate nations – Brazil, Saudi Arabia, and El Salvador. In the case of Brazil, the plot suggests an improving legal environment in the early 1990s, then some deterioration in the late 1990s and early 2000s. At the same time, from the late 1990s, Brazil experiences a clear rise in violations of rights in practice. In Saudi Arabia, by contrast, workers' legal collective rights are never well-protected, and this becomes even more the case over time. Given this lack of legal protection for collective rights, it is not surprising that Saudi Arabia exhibits few violations in practice: If unions are not legally recognized and strikes are not allowed, then we would not expect to observe events such as dismissals for union membership. In El Salvador, the picture is more mixed: On the law side, there is an overall trend of an increase in violations during the 1985–2002 period. In terms of rights in practice, there is considerable

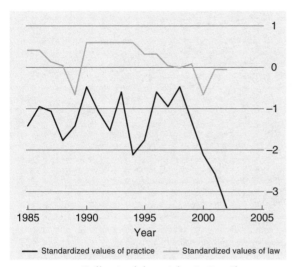

FIGURE 4.7a. Collective labor rights in Brazil.

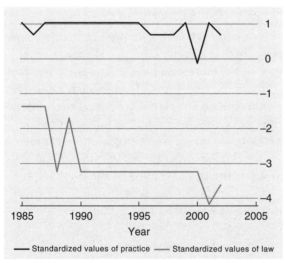

FIGURE 4.7b. Collective labor rights in Saudi Arabia.

variation over time, with some years displaying a significant number of violations and others characterized by greater practical respect for workers' rights. Given the differences both within and across nations, when I employ the labor rights measure as a dependent variable in Chapters 5 and 6, I check the robustness of the results by using different measures of labor rights (law, practice, and total collective rights violations).

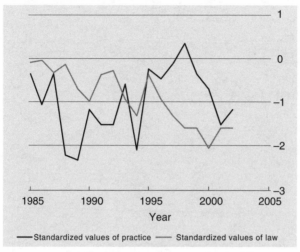

FIGURE 4.7c. Collective labor rights in El Salvador.

III. COMPARING MEASURES OF LABOR RIGHTS

In the first section of this chapter, I highlight the need for a cross-sectional time series measure that directly captures elements of labor rights rather than human rights more generally. I also point out that, whereas a few other scholars have begun to develop such indicators, they fall short in important respects. The claims are conceptual and theoretical in nature. In empirical terms, how does our indicator of collective labor rights compare with extant measures? To what extent does it convey information not contained in other measures and not conveyed by considering ratifications of treaties or reports of the ILO?

First, our index of collective labor rights is distinct analytically from conventional human rights measures. For instance, for the years (1985–2001) during which our data overlap with the "personal integrity rights"[39] measure, the overall bivariate correlation between the two measures is .18. For developing countries only (a total of 1685 country-years), the correlation is .15. Annual correlations between the measures range from .07 (1997) to .34 (1991). The relationship between our labor rights measure and the CIRI "physical integrity" measure is slightly stronger: For all nations during the 1985–2002 period, their

---

[39] This measure ranges from one to five. To calculate correlations, we use the average of the Amnesty International and State Department scores. Mark Gibney provided updated data.

bivariate correlation is .42. This is, however, somewhat driven by OECD nations: With those countries excluded, the correlation falls to .27. Interestingly, when we separate the collective labor rights measure into its legal and practical elements, the correlation is much stronger between personal integrity rights and the practical protection of workers' rights – .21 for developing countries. The legal protection of rights correlates with personal integrity rights at only .04 (developing nations). Similarly, the physical integrity rights measure is more strongly correlated with labor rights practices (.26) than with the legal protection of collective rights (.18). In all cases, however, low correlations are not surprising, given that these human rights measures focus on political repression (e.g., torture, extrajudicial killing, and political imprisonment) rather than on the specific rights and protections of organized labor and individual workers.

Second, and more importantly, our scores also are distinct from other cross-sectional time series measures of workers' rights.[40] As discussed above, the CIRI measure of workers' rights captures elements of both individual working conditions and collective labor rights, but it does so using a single data source and assigns countries to one of three categories. With respect to collective rights, however, the CIRI measure is not ordered: Those nations that do not provide basic protection for freedom of association and collective bargaining are coded zero; but scores of *either* one or two are given to countries that do respect core labor rights (but may, in the case of countries assigned a score of two, violate standards for individual working conditions). Therefore, to compare the two measures in terms of their assessments of collective rights, I recode the CIRI workers' rights variable: Country-years with a score of zero retain that score, while country-years with an original score of one or two are recoded as one ("respect basic core labor rights"). The CIRI measure, however, remains quite different from our measure: For 1985–2002, the correlation between the CIRI score and our collective labor rights score is .29. When developed nations are excluded, the correlation falls to .20.[41] In the case of the dichotomous CIRI measure, however, it is the legal protection of labor rights that correlates more strongly with the revised CIRI measure.

---

[40] I do not compare my collective labor rights indicator with Böhning's overall core labor rights indicator because he has not yet made his country-year data publicly available (Böhning 2005, xiv).

[41] The correlation between our labor rights measure and Cingranelli and Richards' original three-point workers' rights measure (1985–2002, all countries) is .41; for non-OECD nations, the correlation is .29.

Developing nations display a bivariate association of .32 between the law aspect and the CIRI score, and a correlation of .06 between the practical observation of rights and the revised CIRI measure.

Similarly, the Fraser Institute's data on labor regulations (compiled as part of their annual *Economic Freedom of the World* reports and used by studies such as Freeman 2007)[42] does not correlate highly with our collective labor rights measure. The Fraser Institute collects information related to the existence of minimum wage legislation, rules regarding hiring and firing of employees, the centralization of collective bargaining, the existence of unemployment insurance, and legal provisions for conscription. Scores for these indicators also are used to develop an overall index of labor market regulations. The correlation between the overall labor market regulation index and our overall collective labor rights indicator is −.11 for all countries and .10 for developing nations.[43] If we consider the correlations only for the year 2002, they are similarly small: −.15 for all nations (95 countries) and .04 for developing nations (58 countries). The bivariate associations between the centralized collective bargaining element of the Fraser Institute measure and our labor rights indicator are slightly higher, -.30 for all countries, indicating that country-years with more labor rights violations tend to have lower mandated levels of collective bargaining (higher levels of freedom, in the Fraser Institute's assessment). Again, though, when we limit the sample to developing nations, the bivariate association is much smaller (.04). Furthermore, the annual associations with the Fraser Institute's scores are similarly small – never above .30 and usually below .20 – when we use either the labor rights law or labor rights practice measure.

Finally, summary values of the workers' rights index suggest that skepticism regarding the linkage between ratification of ILO core conventions and actual labor rights behavior – in overall, legal, or practical terms – is well-placed.[44] Table 4.2 summarizes the collective labor rights measure, for 1985–2002, for all countries and for all developing nations, according to ratification of the two relevant ILO core conventions. The data indicate average scores on the overall, law, and practice indicators. As the table indicates, with regard to freedom of association, there is little difference in overall scores between country-years with ratification and those without.

---

[42] See http://www.freetheworld.com/

[43] These correlations include observations for the years 1985, 1990, 1995, 2000, 2001, and 2002, the six years for which the two datasets overlap.

[44] On the slippage between treaty commitments and actual behavior, see Hathaway 2002, Simmons and Elkins 2004, Simmons 2009, and von Stein 2005. Hathaway reports a

TABLE 4.2. *ILO Ratifications and Collective Labor Rights Scores*

	ILO Convention 87 Ratified (Freedom of Association)	ILO Convention 87 Not Ratified
Overall Collective Rights		
All Countries	28.22	27.22
	(n=2086)	(n=1562)
Developing Countries (excludes	26.26	26.83
OECD, E. Europe, former	(n=1326)	(n=1256)
Soviet Union)		
Labor Rights in Law		
All Countries	24.43	22.86
Developing Countries	23.43	22.49
Labor Rights in Practice		
All Countries	22.80	23.35
Developing Countries	21.84	23.34

	ILO Convention 98 Ratified (Collective Bargaining)	ILO Convention 98 Not Ratified
Overall Collective Rights		
All Countries	27.85	27.68
Developing Countries	26.18	27.15
Labor Rights in Law		
All Countries	24.26	22.86
Developing Countries	23.39	22.25
Labor Rights in Practice		
All Countries	22.60	23.82
Developing Countries	21.79	23.90

negative – and often significant – statistical relationship between treaty ratification and human rights behaviors. She posits that this is due to the dual purposes served by many international human rights treaties: States may employ treaties as binding commitment devices, as expressions of their existing norms and standards of behavior, or for both reasons. As a result, the relationship between treaty ratification and state behavior is far from straightforward. In their study of child labor and economic globalization, Busse and Braun 2004 reach a similar conclusion regarding ratification-based measures of child labor: While many of the (relatively few) extant cross-national studies employ such measures, these often do not correlate strongly with actual rates of children in the workforce or enrolled in the educational system. Indeed, Hafner-Burton and Tsutsui (2005) find that ratification is often used by repressive regimes as "window dressing," having little direct effect on government behavior. Also see Daude et al. (2003).

Country-years with ratification of ILO Convention 87 have slightly better outcomes on the legal side but slightly worse outcomes in terms of practice. This general pattern also holds when we compare ratifiers and non-ratifiers of the collective bargaining convention (Convention 98). Moreover, if we look at averages that include only developing nations, we find that country-years with ratification of Convention 87 or Convention 98 actually have *lower* levels of collective labor rights (higher numbers of violations) than non-ratification country-years.

These summary data call into question whether convention ratifications are an appropriate metric for assessing labor rights (Böhning 2005; OECD 1996). Indeed, Böhning's recent study finds a marked difference between adherence to legal commitments and implementation of such commitments in practice: While national ratifications of core ILO conventions – and freedom of association, in particular – have risen in recent years, labor rights problems related to implementation have intensified (p. 179). This also is consistent with Martin and Brady's (2007) finding regarding union membership: The number of core ILO conventions ratified by a given government has no significant effect on whether an individual in that country belongs to a union. Moreover, in another core labor standards area – forced labor – Busse and Braun (2003) report a rather low correlation (less than .2) between quantitative measures of actual forced labor usage and ratification of core ILO conventions.[45]

This chapter introduces a new set of data on collective labor rights; these data, which cover a broad set of countries over nearly two decades, are essential to our analyses of the correlates of collective labor rights outcomes. They provide information, not only on the overall state of collective labor rights in a given country-year, but also the extent to which respect for (or problems with) labor rights stem from particular types of violations, or either from a lack of legal rights or a problem with implementation of laws. These data are utilized in Chapters 5 and 6 to assess the linkages between various elements of multinational production and collective labor rights outcomes. They also will be useful for other scholars, and for policymakers, who want to assess empirically the causes and correlates of labor rights outcomes globally.

---

[45] Hathaway (2002) summarizes human rights practices (genocide, torture, fair trial, civil liberties, and women's political representation) for ratifiers versus non-ratifiers of various international human rights convention. Her data suggest a similar pattern, with little direct relationship between ratification and outcomes.

5

The Overall Picture

Economic Globalization and Workers' Rights

> The contrast between anecdotes of sweatshop labor and the actual development of labor conditions around the world is striking.
>
> (Flanagan 2006, 23).

In Chapter 3, I present several hypotheses linking labor rights outcomes with international economic and domestic political variables. The first two center upon the mixed effects of multinational production on labor rights outcomes: I predict that, all else equal, trade openness will be associated with greater violations of workers' collective rights and that foreign direct investment will be positively linked with these same rights. The remaining hypotheses developed in Chapter 3 concern domestic economic and political dynamics: I expect fewer violations of collective rights in country-years characterized by democratic political regimes and left-leaning governments. Additionally, where labor market conditions are more favorable to workers, collective rights also should be better protected.

This chapter presents statistical analyses that assess these hypotheses using quantitative indicators of key variables for approximately ninety low- and middle-income nations and relying on annual observations during the 1986–2002 time frame. The dependent variable for these analyses is the newly developed indicator of overall labor rights as well as the disaggregated measures of labor rights in law and in practice. I estimate cross-sectional time series (CSTS) models.[1] The late 1980s and 1990s are

---

[1] Observations from 1985 are omitted because of missing values on one independent variable.

periods of growing – and often high – economic openness in which the impact of globalization on labor rights should be quite pronounced; these years also provide broad coverage for key variables.[2]

I include developing nations from Africa, Latin America, Asia, and the Middle East in the analyses; I omitted country-years from these regions for which data on our independent variables are not available. I exclude developed and transition countries from our analyses, as I expect that the independent variables of interest will have different effects in these countries (Blonigen and Wang 2005). With respect to developed – wealthy, historically democratic – countries, I seek to avoid biasing our cases toward a set of nations with large amounts of trade and direct investment activity and very few reports of labor rights violations. With regard to transition nations, during the first part of the sample period, these nations were under Communist rule, and reliable data on economic indicators are usually unavailable. In the latter part of our sample period, these countries remain very different from the others in the sample (Bunce 1995). Whereas they are not necessarily exceptional in their simultaneous economic and political transitions, they are quite unique in their Communist legacy (and the attendant treatment of workers), in their degree of economic restructuring (mass privatizations and the movement away from a closed, command economy), and in the efforts of many former Communist countries to join the European Union. The list of countries included in our analyses is found in the Appendix.

The results from the quantitative analyses imply that globalization does in fact have contending effects on workers' rights: Nations with greater direct investment have better workers' rights, all else equal; however, nations with higher levels of trade openness exhibit more violations of collective labor rights. These findings are consistent with existing analyses of globalization and social outcomes, which report positive consequences of direct investment but negative effects of trade openness. The reported results also demonstrate the importance of diffusion: Labor outcomes in one country are strongly influenced by labor outcomes in neighboring nations. Domestic political institutions also play a role: The level of democracy is as important as multinational production in explaining labor outcomes. More broadly, the results support the claim that the impact of globalization on labor rights depends, not

---

[2] Also, Nunnenkamp and Spatz's (2002) study, based on twenty-eight developing nations, suggests that the determinants of FDI do not change much between the late 1980s and the early 2000s.

only on the overall level of economic openness, but also on the precise ways in which a country participates in global production networks. As "racing to the top" accounts would suggest, FDI inflows are positively and significantly related to the rights of workers. At the same time, however, trade openness is negatively associated with collective labor rights. Finally, when we distinguish between collective labor rights in law versus those in practice, we find important differences: The formal provision of labor rights is significantly linked with trade openness, whereas the actual implementation of rights appears more the result of diffusion-type factors (labor rights practices in peer nations) than of multinational production.

I. VARIABLES, MEASUREMENT, AND METHODOLOGY

In this chapter, the three indicators of collective labor rights developed and described in Chapter 4 serve as dependent variables. These include the overall measure of collective rights, which assesses the extent of collective labor rights violations in a given country-year; the "law" measure, which indicates the extent to which workers' collective rights are protected legislatively; and the "practice" indicator, which measures the extent of actual violations (or respect for legal principles) in a given country-year. Estimates of the overall labor rights score are presented in Section II, whereas the latter two indicators are the subject for Section III. The analyses reported represent departures from most extant studies (Blanton and Blanton 2007; Poe et al. 1999; Richards et al. 2001) in that they employ as a dependent variable a measure that is more narrowly focused on labor (versus human) rights. As in Chapter 4, the scale of the labor rights violations indicator is reversed so that higher values indicate *better* collective labor rights and lower values represent less respect for such rights. In the statistical analyses, a positive coefficient indicates a prediction of improvements in collective labor rights, whereas a negative coefficient connotes a prediction of deterioration. Variable descriptions and sources are included in the Appendix.

A. International Variables

The independent variables included in the statistical analyses are those identified in Chapter 3. With respect to directly owned production, Hypothesis 3.1 predicts a positive association between FDI and labor rights outcomes. This relationship stems from the causal mechanisms described in Chapter 3, including the transfer of managerial expertise to host countries and the increase in shareholder and NGO attention to MNC practices in host countries. This proposition also reflects an assumption that a dearth of labor rights in developing nations – and the more general occurrence of repression – may have less to do with the presence of MNCs than with trade openness and with internal political and economic factors. I employ two measures of foreign direct investment. One captures new flows of direct investment, whereas the other measures a country's total stock of FDI in a given year. Both direct investment variables are measured relative to the size of a country's economy (gross domestic product). Whereas it is plausible, given the causal mechanisms described in Chapter 3, that both new and total FDI have a positive impact on labor rights, I expect to observe a more pronounced effect from the flow variable. Whereas the FDI stock variable cumulates FDI from decades past as well as from more recent years, the flow variable captures the more immediate influences on labor rights outcomes. Therefore, it should better capture the many features of contemporary multinational production, such as the effort to transmit best practices to subsidiaries that have become particularly salient during the last two decades.

In terms of Hypothesis 3.2, which posits a negative relationship between arm's-length (subcontracted) production and labor rights, I employ a measure of overall trade openness. Whereas a country's openness to imports and exports does not capture directly the prevalence of subcontracting, trade serves as a reasonable proxy for such activity, particularly once I control for foreign direct investment. Because of the lack of data available on subcontracting specifically, trade openness – which includes inflows of inputs to subcontracted factories as well as exports of finished or intermediate products to other jurisdictions – allows us to assess the link between non-MNC-owned production and labor rights outcomes.[3]

Turning to some of the other international influences on labor rights discussed in Chapter 3, the statistical analyses assess whether there is a diffusion effect – specifically, a "competitive diffusion" – for labor rights. As nations compete with one another to attract and retain investment, the behavior of peer nations will influence governments' propensity to protect collective labor rights. I consider two types of peer nations – regional

---

[3] Given our focus on multinational production, an indicator of trade that captures both elements – imports and exports – is most appropriate. See Flanagan (2006) for a discussion of various indicators of trade openness. His analyses also rely on the imports plus exports/ GDP measure as well as on Sachs and Warner's index of trade openness (a dichotomous variable).

and economic. The regional variable (as in Brooks 2005; Simmons and Elkins 2004) captures the extent to which competition for FDI takes place among neighboring countries. If MNCs undertake investment because they want access to certain consumer markets, easy use of a particular set of natural resources, or low transportation costs, competition should occur within geographic regions. The regional labor rights variable is the average for a given year of the labor rights score elsewhere in the region. I expect a positive relationship between labor rights in the region and labor rights in a particular country.

The economic peer variable considers competition among nations at similar levels of economic development and with similar factor endowments. If MNCs undertake foreign production for efficiency-related reasons, locating each stage of the production process in the most productive location, then nations with similar resource endowments, skill levels, and infrastructure will be in competition with one another. For example, in the apparel sector, where firms are motivated primarily by lower labor costs, patterns of firm location and relocation often are cross-regional (Mandle 2003). The economic peer measure uses income per capita as an indicator of factor endowments. This variable is the mean of the labor rights scores in each year for all other countries in the same per capita income decile (see the Appendix). As before, I expect a positive association between respect for collective labor rights in a given country and respect for collective labor rights among that nation's economic peers.

Another element of international influence on labor rights is transnational advocacy via human and labor rights activists. Given the potential importance of both domestically and internationally based human rights advocates for labor rights outcomes (i.e., Brown et al. 2004; Caraway 2006b; Murillo and Schrank 2005), I include an indicator of human rights NGOs. Our indicator measures the total number of human rights NGOs in each country-year. Note the two possible ways in which the NGO indicator could be significantly related to labor rights violations. First, there is an observation effect: NGO activity could lead to increased reporting of labor rights violations in developing nations, generating a negative relationship.[4] Were such a mechanism at play, observed violations could increase even without any change in *actual* violations. Second, however, is an activist effect: NGOs' presence and campaigns could produce real

---

[4] For instance, today's ICFTU surveys are approximately five times as long as ICFTU surveys published in the early and mid-1980s. On a similar trend in ILO complaints, see Moran (2002).

improvements in labor rights; a greater level of NGOs, then, would be positively related to respect for collective labor rights. Given that the construction of our labor rights indicator relies on reports by governmental and non-governmental observers, we cannot rule out the possibility of an observation effect; empirically, though, we hope that our analyses will allow us to adjudicate between the two possibilities.

Furthermore, one also could imagine that the impact of human and labor rights activists on rights outcomes is contingent on the role of multinational corporations in a given location. Put differently, human rights NGOs may intensify the climb to the top effects that multinationals are expected to generate. Human rights activists may pay close attention to foreign firms' host country activities, and they may facilitate the upgrading and monitoring of labor rights in foreign subsidiaries. To test for this possibility, the analyses also include an interaction between FDI inflows and NGO activity, testing whether the impact of each is dependent on the other.

B. Domestic Variables

The main domestic-level variables included in the analyses capture the logic of Hypotheses 3.3 and 3.4. The former focuses on the condition of the domestic labor market (to what extent are workers better able to demand protections of their legal rights?), whereas the latter centers on political institutions and ideology. To assess the former, I include a measure of the growth rate of income per capita. Higher levels of economic growth should provide greater bargaining power (and political as well as economic leverage) for workers, as growth generates increased demand for employment. As the level of unemployment falls, the provision of workers' collective rights should improve; conversely, a greater degree of slack in the labor market is likely, all else equal, to be linked with less respect for workers' rights. Empirically, one could test for this effect using *either* a measure of economic growth *or* a measure of the unemployment rate. Two factors render the former more desirable: The economic growth measure has much better data coverage for many developing nations; even when available, the measure of unemployment focuses only on the formal sector (rather than the formal *and* informal sectors) of the economy. Given these concerns, the statistical models include a measure of annual growth in gross domestic product per capita. In additional specifications of the statistical models (see Section IIA below), I use Rudra's (2002) "potential labor power" (PLP) as an alternative indicator of labor market conditions. This indicator, which is available for a subset of country-years, reflects the ratio of skilled to unskilled workers as well as the presence of surplus labor in an economy. The rationale behind this measure is that it is, not only the (un)availability of workers generally, but the availability of more skilled workers specifically that enhances labor's bargaining power.

A second variable that captures socioeconomic conditions – and one that is characterized more by cross-sectional than by over-time variation – is the level of economic development. There is strong empirical support for the notion that, where levels of economic development are higher, respect for human rights is greater (Apodaca 2001; Meyer 1998; Mitchell and McCormick 1988; Poe and Tate 1994; Poe et al. 1999; Richards et al. 2001; Sachs and Warner 1995). What is less clear, however, is the causal mechanism by which this link operates (Abouharb and Cingranelli 2008). One possibility is that, given the correlation between wealth and democracy (particularly if western democracies were included in statistical analyses), the effect may be driven largely by regime type. Another possibility is that respect for human rights is, like concern with environmental issues, a luxury (or post-materialist) good, the demand for which increases as citizens' basic needs are met. In the specific case of labor-related outcomes, the level of economic development also may correlate with the structure of the economy. Countries characterized by large agricultural and/or informal sectors often – although not always – are at relatively low levels of economic development. Industrialization, urbanization, and the development of local capital markets are associated with an increase in incomes per capita as well as with a shift of employment from the rural and informal to the formal and manufacturing (and sometimes service) sectors.

If this pattern holds in the countries included in this book's analytical scope, what does it imply for the link between economic development and labor rights? On the one hand, the pressures for human rights improvement that come with development may appear, generating a positive relationship between protections of collective labor rights and incomes per capita. On the other hand, a shift from agriculture to manufacturing within an economy may be marked by *greater* challenges to collective labor rights (as well as higher visibility of problems with collective labor rights), leading to a negative relationship between income and labor rights protections.[5] The latter may be more likely, given that our

---

[5] In the robustness tests later in this chapter, I also control for the size of the manufacturing sector.

sample of countries excludes (for theoretical reasons) the high-income, democratic nations of Europe, North America, and Australasia. In any case, the statistical models include the level of economic development as an independent variable; despite previous studies that find a positive link between human rights and development, there also is reason to expect the opposite relationship in our sample.

Turning to the domestic political variables that are the focus of the final hypothesis in Chapter 3, I expect a positive association between democracy and labor rights: Where the level of democratic governance is higher, labor rights should be better protected throughout the economy (Cingranelli and Tsai 2003; Neumayer and de Soysa 2006; Poe et al. 1999; Richards et al. 2001). Including a measure of how democratic (or authoritarian) a country's government is in a given year aims to control for large-scale differences in political regimes and, therefore, in the ability of workers to demand protection. Whereas broad quantitative measures of democracy are not without their flaws, they do allow us to assess the general impact of variation in domestic political variables.

At the same time, however, we can expect that middle-range domestic factors, such as government ideology with respect to economic issues, also affect labor rights outcomes. There is a trade-off associated with including such variables in large-N analyses: Measuring ideology in a cross-national context is fraught with difficulties, particularly among lower income nations as well as democratizing and semi-democratic (or even non-democratic) regimes. I take an intermediate course: I include only democracy in the initial models of the correlates of labor rights (Section IIA) but add middle-range indicators (government ideology) in the next set of models (Section IIB). In terms of government ideology, a key distinction is that between left-oriented governments and governments with other (center or right) ideological leanings. If we expect left governments to be more labor friendly, given their historical development and their frequent labor union ties (Garrett 1998; Murillo 2001), then this measure will be linked positively with collective labor rights. In order to assess ideology in a wide range of country-years, I rely on a measure of the ideological orientation of the largest government party in the legislature, taken from the Database of Political Institutions (DPI). This legislative partisanship variable is recoded as a dummy variable, with a value of one if the largest government party is left-oriented and a value of zero otherwise. In additional specifications, I substitute a measure of executive branch ideology for the legislature-oriented indicator.

C. Additional Controls

Several additional control variables are included in the statistical analyses. The logic for including these indicators is theoretical as well as empirical, given past studies of human and labor rights. The first is the level of external debt. Where debt is high, governments are more subject to the pressures of both private international investors and international financial institutions. The structural adjustment policies suggested by these groups can have negative consequences for labor, as well as human (Abouharb and Cingranelli 2006; Richards et al. 2001), rights. One could imagine several causal pathways through which this occurs. As governments attempt to reduce spending generally, they may reduce resources for implementation of laws, including workers' rights legislation. In this way, I might observe a negative relationship between structural adjustment (or the macroeconomic predictors of structural adjustment, such as debt) and workers' rights. Alternatively, reducing the legal or practical capacity of workers to organize could be a means – depending on governments' beliefs about what attracts investors – of appealing to foreign investors, which often is consistent with structural adjustment efforts. More directly, IMF structural adjustment programs sometimes include increased labor market flexibility as one of their conditions (Anner et al. 2010), and this can be implemented in a way that limits collective labor rights. Indeed, in their analyses of the impact of World Bank and IMF structural adjustment programs on workers' rights, Abouharb and Cingranelli (2008) find that, the more years a country has been under a structural adjustment program, the worse its workers' rights outcomes (as well as its citizens' economic and social welfare outcomes and its level of respect for physical integrity rights), all else equal.[6] Higher debt, therefore, could be associated with less respect for labor rights.

Another important control is the level, if any, of violent conflict within a given nation. Civil conflict or civil war may generate violence against trade unionists as well as against other groups. For example, this has long been true in Colombia, where the murders and disappearances of trade unionists are endemic despite fairly strong legal protections of

---

[6] Their analyses employ the CIRI workers' rights measure, as described in Chapter 4, as the dependent variable. They cover country-years during the 1981–2003 time frame, for 131 developing nations. Given that some of the factors that affect workers' rights also influence participation in structural adjustment programs, Abouharb and Cingranelli employ a selection model. Interestingly, the results of the selection model (also see Abouharb and Cingranelli 2006) suggest that the Bank is more likely to enter into agreements with countries that have higher levels of respect for labor rights.

labor rights. Murders of trade unionists peaked in the mid-1990s, with local NGOs identifying 275 of these in 1996. Some observers note, however, that a significant proportion of these murders have much more to do with political violence generally than with trade union activities specifically. For example, of the eighty-seven convictions for murder of and other violence against trade unionists from 2001 to early 2008, the presiding judges found that union activity was the motive in only seventeen cases (in another sixteen cases, no motive was established). Motives in the other cases ranged from common crime to membership in a guerilla organization (Schumacher-Matos 2008). I expect, then, a negative relationship between the level of civil conflict and the protection of collective labor rights.

Another common control in quantitative studies of human rights outcomes is the size of a country's population. On the one hand, smaller populations could serve as easier targets for repression, especially of the state-sponsored variety. Were this effect to hold, smaller population sizes would be associated with less respect for collective labor rights. Another possibility, however, points in the opposite direction and is more consistent with past empirical findings: A larger population presents more opportunities for violating human and labor rights (e.g., Poe and Tate 1994; Poe et al. 1999; Richards et al. 2001). Particularly when the measures of rights rely partly on counts of violations in practice – as does our measure – this effect is expected to prevail. Table 5.1 summarizes the independent variables included in the statistical analyses as well as the expected relationship between each variable and collective labor rights.

D. Statistical Methods

I employ ordinary least squares (OLS) estimation with panel corrected standard errors, developed by Beck and Katz (1995, 2004) and widely used for cross-sectional time series data, particularly when the number of countries (N) exceeds the number of time periods (T). I assume first-order autocorrelation within panels (an AR1 process).[7] I opt against using fixed effects, given the fact that fixed effects would be collinear with time-invariant,

---

[7] Additionally, while some (e.g., Beck and Katz 2004) recommend the inclusion of a lagged dependent variable (LDV) in CSTS models, others (e.g., Achen 2000 and Plümper et al. 2005) warn against doing so. Such warnings are based on the fact that LDVs tend to dominate the regression equation, generating downwardly biased coefficient estimates on the explanatory variables as well as on the atheoretical nature of the LDV. I therefore opt to use an AR(1) process, but no LDV.

TABLE 5.1. *Independent Variables: Expectations and Summary Statistics*

Variable	Operationalization	Expected Relationship with Labor Rights	Mean (Standard Deviation)
Multinational Production			
Foreign Direct Investment – Flows	FDI inflows/GDP	Positive relationship	2.22 (2.84)
Foreign Direct Investment – Stocks	FDI stock/GDP	Positive	19.45 (18.45)
Trade Openness	Imports and Exports/GDP	Negative	67.63 (37.54)
Other International Influences			
Regional Practices	Average labor rights score for every other country in the region, by year.	Positive	23.41 (3.31)
Economic Peers' Practices	Average labor rights score for all other nations in the same income decile, by year.	Positive	23.98 (2.43)
Presence of NGOs	Total number of NGOs in a country-year (natural log)	Positive or Negative (Offsetting effects)	2.16 (1.25)
Domestic Variables			
Level of Development	Income per capita (natural log)	Positive or negative?	7.69 (0.81)
Economic Growth	Annual change in income per capita	Positive	3.39 (5.14)
Potential Labor Power	Skilled/unskilled workers × (1/surplus labor)	Positive	1.96 (2.22)
Democracy	Polity IV measure of democracy	Positive	1.41 (6.49)
Level of Development	Income per capita (natural log)	Positive or negative?	7.69 (0.81)
Government Ideology (Executive)	Left executive (left = 1; center or right = 0)	Positive	0.31 (0.46)

(continued)

TABLE 5.1 *(continued)*

Variable	Operationalization	Expected Relationship with Labor Rights	Mean (Standard Deviation)
Government Ideology (Legislative)	Left legislative party (left = 1; center or right = 0)	Positive	0.33 (0.47)
Other Controls			
Civil Conflict	Uppsala measure of civil war	Negative	0.21 (0.41)
External Debt	Total external debt/GDP	Negative	90.09 (87.19)
Population	Total population (natural log)	Positive or Negative (Offsetting effects)	16.26 (1.58)
Potential Labor Power (PLP)	Skilled/unskilled workers * 1/surplus labor	Positive	1.96 (2.22)

or largely time-invariant, regressors (Beck 2001; also see Plümper et al. 2005). Because several important independent variables (i.e., democracy, population, and income per capita) remain fairly constant across the sample period, the inclusion of fixed effects would dilute greatly the implied importance of these variables. Whereas random effects models do not suffer from this shortcoming, they do require the assumption that unit-specific errors do not correlate with the model's independent variables (see Hsaio 1986). This is likely too strong an assumption for much cross-sectional time series data, including that used in this book (however, see Blanton and Blanton 2007). The models reported in the next section assume that the disturbances across panels are heteroskedastic (variance specific to each panel) and contemporaneously correlated.[8]

II. EXPLAINING OVERALL LABOR RIGHTS OUTCOMES

A. Main Model

Table 5.2 reports results from several CSTS models, based on annual observations for ninety middle- and lower-income developing nations.

---

[8] Our results are robust to changing this assumption, e.g., with only heteroskedastic disturbances (no contemporaneous correlation across panels).

TABLE 5.2. *Correlates of Labor Rights, Cross-Sectional Time Series Analyses*

Independent Variable	(1)	(2)	(3)
FDI Inflows	0.1495*	0.6443**	0.1514*
	(0.0807)	(0.2655)	(0.0815)
FDI Stock	0.0056	−0.0181	0.0151
	(0.0138)	(0.0309)	(0.0144)
External Debt	0.0041	0.0218*	0.0050
	(0.0043)	(0.0098)	(0.0044)
Trade	−0.0169*	−0.0650***	−0.0246**
	(0.0087)	(0.0182)	(0.0100)
Regional Average, Labor Standards	0.5004***	0.5400***	0.6735***
	(0.0766)	(0.1314)	(0.1012)
Economic Peers' Labor Standards	0.1190	0.2257	0.0620
	(0.0860)	(0.1445)	(0.0832)
Human Rights NGOs	−0.4303	−0.4272	−0.3403
	(0.3060)	(0.4591)	(0.3147)
NGOs*FDI flows	−0.0621	−0.3441**	−0.0601
	(0.0408)	(0.1170)	(0.0410)
Income Per Capita	−1.5000***	0.5338	−1.1385**
	(0.3345)	(1.0954)	(0.4873)
Economic Growth	0.0435	−0.0131	0.0404
	(0.0282)	(0.0575)	(0.0282)
Population Size	−1.4492***	−1.2000***	−1.6282***
	(0.2753)	(0.4243)	(0.3446)
Democracy	0.1435***	0.1549**	0.1884***
	(0.0472)	(0.0772)	(0.0526)
Civil Conflict	−1.0203*	−2.5995**	−1.1697*
	(0.6212)	(1.0528)	(0.6285)
Potential Labor Power		0.2377	
		(0.2837)	
North Africa/Middle East			2.2566**
			(0.9153)
Caribbean			−4.2755***
			(1.3483)
Sub-Saharan Africa			0.8707
			(1.0074)
Asia-Pacific			0.8882
			(1.0983)
Constant	46.2744***	25.5915	43.1635***
	(5.9753)	(16.0772)	(7.4336)
N	1286	397	1286
Number of Countries	90	48	90
R^2	0.40	0.49	0.41
Rho	0.60	0.46	0.60
Wald Chi^2	291.93	750.23	654.95

Note: Standard errors are in parentheses. Positive coefficients imply lower levels of violations.
***p<.01, **p<.05, *p<.10.

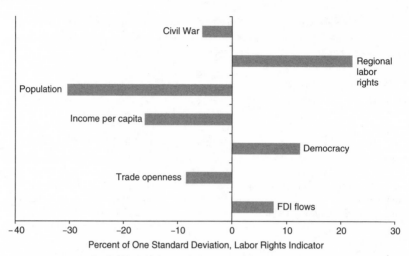

FIGURE 5.1. Implied effects of significant variables, Model 1.

Positive coefficients imply greater provision and protection of collective labor rights given the rescaling of our indicator. The correlation matrix for the cases included indicates little potential collinearity. These results lend support to the theoretical argument that variation in the form of multinational production generates differences in labor rights outcomes. The main model of the correlates of labor rights, Model 1, is summarized in the second column of Table 5.2

In order to provide a sense of the relative importance of various regressors, Figure 5.1 summarizes the substantive effects implied by the results (the coefficient*one standard deviation) for statistically significant regressors. Each of the bars represents the ratio of the implied effect of the variable to one standard deviation change in the labor rights indicator (7.51). A change of one standard deviation in trade openness, for instance, implies a reduction in labor rights that is equivalent to 8.5 percent of a standard deviation in rights, or 0.86 points on the labor rights scale. Figure 5.1 highlights the relative importance of domestic factors, such as democracy and income, to overall labor rights outcomes.

As Hypothesis 3.1 predicts, both FDI variables[9] are associated positively with collective labor rights. Only the flow variable estimate, however, is statistically significant, suggesting a more pronounced effect of recent FDI. Where inflows of FDI are higher, respect for labor rights is greater, lending

---

[9] In our sample, the correlation between FDI stocks and flows is quite small, at -0.08.

support to the climb to the top logic.[10] All coefficient signs and significances remain if the FDI stock variable is omitted from Model 1. At the same time, trade is negatively and significantly related to collective labor rights (Hypothesis 3.2). Nations with higher levels of imports and exports are less likely to treat workers well; this reflects the competitive pressures that stem from participation in global production networks.[11] This finding also is consistent with Rudra's study (2002), which reports that, where labor has little political power, trade openness is associated with a decline – rather than with an increase or a stasis as "compensation" theories of economic openness would predict – in welfare state policies (also see Kaufman and Segura-Ubiergo 2001). The substantive effect of the trade variable is just slightly greater than that of FDI flows; in overall terms, therefore, the impact of globalization on workers' rights depends upon the particular way in which a country participates in the global economy.[12] If we include an interaction between trade and growth, testing whether growth-promoting openness improves rights, the coefficient on trade openness remains as it is; the interaction term is positive but insignificant.

Turning to other international factors, the results provide some evidence for an indirect impact of economic globalization via competition. Both competition variables (regional and economic peers) are positively associated with labor rights; only the regional variable, however, is statistically significant. The implied effect of the regional variable is larger, by a factor of three, than that of FDI or trade. The impact of regional competition also is greater than that of democracy or civil war. The regional effect could be the result of shared norms (Simmons and Elkins 2004; Weyland 2003) or of the similarity in firms and industries across nations in the same region. Qualitative research into the competitive diffusion of labor rights could help to distinguish among these causal mechanisms.

The NGO variable, on its own, is negative but insignificant. Whereas the standard errors for the NGO measure are large relative to the point

---

[10] Kucera (2002) and Neumayer and de Soysa (2006)'s cross-sectional models use data from the mid-1990s; they report no significant relationship between FDI and labor rights.

[11] When Model 1 is estimated using exports as a percentage of GDP, rather than total trade, as the metric of trade openness, its coefficient is again negative. The standard errors, however, are larger, so that the exports variable falls below the conventional thresholds for statistical significance. Using exports rather than total trade does not change the sign or significances of the FDI variables.

[12] If Model 1 is estimated using random effects (requiring the assumption that error terms are uncorrelated with regressors), the effect of trade openness is similar. The coefficient on FDI remains positive; but it is the coefficient on FDI stocks, rather than on flows, that is statistically significant. Full results of the random effects model are available upon request.

estimate, the coefficient suggests that transnational advocates may help to address labor rights violations. At the same time, the statistical weakness of this variable may result from contending effects – "reporting of violations" versus "reduction of actual violations" – of NGOs. The interaction between FDI flows and national NGO activity also is statistically insignificant. In alternative specifications, I also include an interaction between trade and NGOs. The interaction term, however, is insignificant and has no impact on other results.

In terms of internal factors, the results of Model 1 suggest that domestic variables also are important influences on collective labor rights. The level of democracy is significantly and positively associated with collective labor rights; the implied effects of democracy are substantively large (0.88, compared with 0.52 for FDI inflows). This is consistent with Hypothesis 3.4. The results also are robust to using the ACLP dichotomous measure of regime type (Przeworski et al. 2000), rather than the POLITY IV indicator. Moreover, if we use a measure of veto points rather than of regime type, the results are very similar: Substituting Henisz's (2002) measure of political constraints (POLCONV) for POLITY increases the sample size slightly (n = 1306). Where political constraints are greater (a higher number of veto players), labor rights are significantly better protected. All other significant regressors remain so in such a model, and the rate of economic growth also becomes statistically significant.[13]

In Chapter 3, I discuss a potential mediating effect for domestic political institutions: They may filter the pressures on labor rights generated by directly owned and subcontracted production. To assess this possibility statistically, I add an interaction between democracy and democracy, as well as an interaction between FDI flows and democracy, to the cross-sectional time series model. Each of these indicators tests the extent to which the effect of economic openness on labor rights is conditional on the domestic political regime. These interaction terms,[14] however, are not significant predictors of labor rights, and their inclusion does not alter the results of the main model.

In terms of the conditions prevailing in the domestic labor market (Hypothesis 3.3), the annual rate of economic growth – a proxy for the

---

[13] The same pattern obtains if we use Henisz's other measure of veto players, POLCONIII. This measure is constructed in essentially the same was as POLCONV, but it does not include sub-federal entities or the judiciary as potential veto points. See Henisz 2000, 2002.

[14] I estimated models that included one interaction term (trade and democracy, or FDI and democracy) as well as both interaction terms.

demand for workers – is not related significantly to labor rights. The level of per capita income, however, is significantly and negatively associated with labor rights: Wealthier developing nations have worse labor rights practices. This result appears to contradict theories that predict improvements in rights as a result of economic development. One possible explanation for this finding is that the relationship between income and rights varies among low- and middle-income countries; the sample excludes wealthy democracies, where income and labor rights tend to be strongly and positively correlated. However, among developing countries, opportunities for violating workers' rights may be greater in more industrialized (versus agricultural) economies, which also tend to have higher incomes per capita. Industrial sectors tend toward higher unionization, lower collective action barriers, and greater demands by workers than the agriculture and services sectors. The structure of economies, then, is likely important to labor outcomes.[15]

Furthermore, the results are robust to the inclusion of a finer-grained measure of domestic labor strength. Model 2, also reported in Table 5.2, includes PLP (Rudra 2002), a measure based on the ratio of skilled to unskilled workers and the presence of surplus labor in an economy. This measure captures the capacity of workers to demand collective labor rights. The inclusion of PLP greatly reduces the number of country-years included, as the variable is available only through 1997 and only for a subset of our sample nations. PLP is not significantly associated with labor rights outcomes; the main model results on the key multinational production variables (FDI and trade) persist. In addition, the estimates on the external debt and NGO*FDI flows variables become statistically significant – albeit for a much smaller sample of country-years.

Among control variables, the external debt variable is not significantly related to labor rights outcomes. Other similar measures, including debt service as a percentage of GNP and participation in IMF or World Bank structural adjustment programs, also are not significantly associated with labor rights outcomes.[16] Second, civil war is negatively and significantly related to labor rights. Third, the coefficient on population is negative and

---

[15] When a measure of the proportion of workers in the industrial (as opposed to agricultural or services) sector is included, its coefficient is negative and significant and the income variable loses significance. This measure is available for only 40 percent of our observations (n = 487). Full results for this model are available upon request.

[16] Data on debt service and structural adjustment programs are from Abouharb and Cingranelli 2008. Additionally, when a measure of portfolio investment flows (equity investment flows as a percentage of GDP) is added to Model 1, it is not associated significantly with collective labor rights, nor does it change our overall results.

significant; larger populations appear to provide more opportunities for repression, or at least for the reporting of it.[17] Finally, our results also are robust to the inclusion of regional dummy variables, which might capture regional economic cycles, culture, or religion. Model 3 is included in the final column of Table 5.2; it includes four of five regional dummy variables, with Latin America as the reference category. All else equal, labor rights outcomes are better in countries in the Middle East and North Africa and systematically worse in the Caribbean region. These results, however, do not affect the signs or statistical significance of the various indicators discussed previously.

In sum, our cross-sectional time series models give credence to the main hypotheses presented in Chapter 3. We find support for both the race to the bottom and the climb to the top views: Trade openness augurs poorly for workers' rights, but inflows of direct investment are associated with better labor rights outcomes. We also find that national respect for labor rights is strongly related to regional labor rights outcomes. This result gives some credence to diffusion-oriented accounts of policy choice and to a potential indirect effect of FDI via regional diffusion or competition. Our results suggest that domestic factors, including the degree of democracy, are important determinants of labor rights laws and practices.

B. More on Domestic Politics

The results reported in Table 5.2 include a broad measure of political institutions (the degree of democracy or autocracy of the political regime). This measure allows for an initial assessment of Hypothesis 3.4, which predicts a positive relationship between more democratic regimes and respect for collective labor rights. The discussion in Chapter 3, though, also implies a link between the ideology of the main governing parties and workers' collective rights: Where left-leaning governments hold power, we expect workers' rights to be better provided, all else equal. Table 5.3 reports results from several statistical models that include measures of government ideology.

These ideology measures come from the Database of Political Institutions (Beck et al. 2001). Governments – either the executive or the

---

[17] When China and India (states with large populations) are excluded from the model, this result remains. The only substantive difference in such a model is the reduced statistical significance (but still approaching a 90 percent level of confidence) of the FDI inflows variable.

TABLE 5.3. *Labor Rights and Government Ideology*

Independent Variable	(4) Legislative Ideology	(5) Executive Ideology	(6) Ideology and Trade
Left Ideology	2.7934***	2.7410***	−0.2030
	(0.7464)	(0.6875)	(1.0683)
Left Ideology*Trade			0.0458***
			(0.0124)
FDI Inflows	0.0916	0.1288	0.1202
	(0.0815)	(0.0856)	(0.0833)
FDI Stock	0.0035	0.0006	−0.0048
	(0.0156)	(0.0146)	(0.0140)
External Debt	0.0007	0.0009	−0.0008
	(0.0047)	(0.0043)	(0.0041)
Trade	−0.0204**	−0.0205**	−0.0380***
	(0.0102)	(0.0093)	(0.0115)
Regional Average, Labor Standards	0.4573***	0.4311***	0.4702***
	(0.0922)	(0.0840)	(0.0910)
Economic Peers' Labor Standards	0.1031	0.1492	0.1023
	(0.0906)	(0.0951)	(0.0900)
Human Rights NGOs	−0.5410*	−0.5659*	−0.5495*
	(0.3287)	(0.3207)	(0.3169)
NGOs*FDI Flows	−0.0467	−0.0664	−0.0496
	(0.0424)	(0.0449)	(0.0403)
Income Per Capita	−1.3088**	−1.2807***	−1.3531**
	(0.5308)	(0.3775)	(0.5361)
Economic Growth	0.0264	0.0344	0.0216
	(0.0363)	(0.0329)	(0.0359)
Population Size	−1.4256***	−1.4403***	−1.3768***
	(0.2943)	(0.3000)	(0.2869)
Democracy	0.1291***	0.1459***	0.1177***
	(0.0452)	(0.0500)	(0.0444)
Civil Conflict	−1.2317*	−1.1561*	−1.4254**
	(0.6510)	(0.6701)	(0.6530)
Constant	46.2786***	45.6883***	46.9766***
	(7.5462)	(7.0712)	(7.4927)
N	1013	1070	1070
Number of Countries	87	89	89
R^2	0.46	.43	.43
Rho	.58	.57	.56
Wald Chi^2	271.03	313.83	385.15

Note: Standard errors are in parentheses. Positive coefficients imply lower levels of violations.
***p<.01, **p<.05, *p<.10.

legislative branch – are characterized on the basis of their economic policy orientations using party names, party platforms, and previous classifications by country and regional experts. Of course, classifying party ideology along a single dimension is fraught with difficulty, particularly in the context of emerging democracies and mixed regimes. Indeed, some of the country-years in the dataset are coded as "not applicable" or "missing," because their political parties do not fall along a left-right continuum.[18] In a large-N context, however, these measures provide the best means of assessing the impact of government ideology in developing nations. Another alternative, of course, is to draw on case study evidence to look more closely at the potential effects of ideology on collective labor rights outcomes, as I do in Chapter 7.

Despite the challenges associated with assessing government ideology in a cross-national, developing-country context, the statistical results reveal the expected link (Hypothesis 3.4) between left government and labor rights protections. Models 4 and 5 each add a dichotomous measure of ideology – in either the executive or legislative branch – to the main model (Model 1) estimated in Table 5.2. The variable is coded one for a left executive or legislative governing party and zero in cases of centrist or right-leaning parties. Recoding the variable so that centrist governments also receive a value of one does not change the substance or significance of the reported results.

In each model, the presence of a left-leaning government is significantly and positively linked with protection of collective labor rights. Model 4, which includes a measure of legislative partisanship, suggests that, when the largest governing party in the legislature is left-leaning, collective labor rights are 2.8 points higher, all else equal. This represents 37 percent of one standard deviation in the labor rights indicator – a substantively important effect. Similarly, Model 5, which substitutes a model of executive branch partisanship, reveals an effect of left executives equivalent to 2.7 points. Again, this effect is substantively important, and it accords with our expectations regarding the direct effects of government ideology on labor rights outcomes.

The inclusion of either ideology measure does, however, reduce the number of observations. The number of country-years included in these models is 17 to 20 percent smaller than in the main model in Table 5.2. These reductions generate two notable differences in the regression results: First, the NGO variable, which was insignificant in Model 1, is

---

[18] These country-years, then, are omitted from the models reported in Table 5.3.

statistically significant in each of the three models reported in Table 5.3. When a greater number of human rights NGOs is present in a given country-year, respect for labor rights is reduced. This is consistent with the notion that, whereas human rights activists likely create pressures for the reduction of labor rights abuses, they also facilitate the observation of such violations. Hence, there is some support in these results for the notion that reported violations of labor rights are more likely in the presence of activists or that egregious violations of workers' rights attract NGOs to certain developing nations. Second, the coefficient on the FDI inflows measure falls below the conventional thresholds for statistical significance, although the positive sign remains in all three models. Trade continues to be negatively and significantly associated with labor rights outcomes.

Models 4 and 5 highlight the existence of a direct effect of government ideology on labor rights outcomes: As a long literature in comparative politics suggests, government partisanship matters for policy outcomes. Some commentators, though, suggest that the impact of government partisanship may wane as countries become more open economically: Efforts to compete in export markets and to attract direct investment, for instance, may reduce the partisan distinctiveness of governments.[19] Alternatively, government ideology may serve to mediate the impact of global economic forces on domestic policy outcomes. Right-leaning governments may be more likely, all else equal, to allow the competitive pressures generated by openness to reduce labor rights protections, whereas left governments may attempt to couple moves toward economic liberalization with policies that protect the rights of workers.

The final model reported in Table 5.3 addresses these expectations. It includes an interaction between trade openness and (executive) ideology, testing whether the effects of trade and partisanship on labor rights are dependent on one another. The results suggest that this is indeed the case. In Model 6, the effect of trade openness remains negative and statistically significant; given the presence of the interaction effect, this implies that, when center or right executives hold office, trade is negatively related to collective labor rights outcomes (as in Model 1). In contrast to Models 4 and 5, the effect of the left-government variable on its own (when, implicitly, trade openness is zero) is not statistically significant. More importantly, the interaction between trade and left government is positive and strongly significant: Where trade openness is high and left parties

---

[19] For a review of such arguments, see Mosley 2005, Plümper et al. 2009, and Rudra 2008.

control the executive branch, labor rights are better protected. The other coefficients are largely consistent with those reported in Table 5.2, with the exception of the FDI flows variable, which remains positive but is no longer significant at conventional levels. If we substitute legislative for executive partisanship, the results are very similar: Trade openness is negatively associated with collective labor rights under center and right government but positively linked with labor rights when left parties hold the legislature.

Moreover, including the interaction between direct investment and partisanship does not produce statistically significant results, nor does it alter the other results reported in Table 5.3.[20] Whereas there is little evidence, then, that the impact of direct investment is a conditional one, these results suggest that the negative effects of trade openness, hypothesized in Chapter 3, are contingent on domestic political alignments. Left governments may serve to limit the extent to which competitive pressures related to trade and subcontracting result in diminished respect for labor rights. Although cross-sectional time series analyses do not necessary allow us to gauge the longer-term or finer-grained impact of domestic political factors on labor rights, this is an important area for future research on the globalization-labor rights nexus. I begin to explore some of these dynamics in Chapter 7.

Additional Robustness Checks. In considering the overall robustness of the statistical results, the direction of causality also is important: In addition to anticipating that multinational production affects labor rights outcomes, we might expect that labor rights outcomes influence investment decisions and trade flows (in the case of the latter, via their impact on the competitive capacity of exporters). Were this the case, the patterns reported in Table 5.2 could be due more to labor rights affecting multinational production rather than to the reverse.

This concern, however, receives little support from theoretical logic or from empirical analyses. The wide literature on the determinants of direct investment, reviewed in Chapters 2 and 3, offers few reasons to expect a systematic relationship leading from labor rights to multinationals' investment decisions. Whereas collective labor rights may affect labor costs, these effects will occur in only a subset of industries – those that are dependent on unskilled labor-intensive production rather than capital- or

---

[20] In models that include an interaction between FDI flows and partisanship, left government remains statistically significant and positive but the interaction term is statistically insignificant.

skill-intensive production. Thus, whereas some sectoral patterns of multinational production may be driven by collective labor rights law and practice, the broader set of national-level FDI and trade patterns will not be. Indeed, firm location decisions are likely influenced much more by considerations of local market size and growth (for market-seeking firms) as well as productivity, infrastructure, and the stability of legal systems.

Empirical analyses using the labor rights data confirm this expectation (Mosley 2006).[21] In both time series cross-sectional (using country-year data) and cross-sectional (using decade averages) models of the determinants of annual flows of FDI (net FDI/GDP), I find that the most important and consistently significant correlates of direct investment flows are rates of growth, country size, income per capita, and trade openness.[22] The level of democracy is sometimes associated with direct investment flows (as in Jensen 2006), but this relationship is less robust. These findings are consistent with previous econometric literature. What is not statistically significant, though, is the overall measure of collective labor rights. These results hold for models that include developing nations (as in this chapter) as well as for those that also include transition (post-Communist) economies and developed democracies. There also is no significant link between overall labor rights and FDI if the sample is truncated to include only the post-Cold War years (1990–2002); if first differences (detrended data) are used; if a time trend is included; or if the CIRI workers' rights indicator is used as an alternative measure of labor rights. Moreover, on the issue of export processing zones specifically, the occurrence of limits on collective rights in EPZs (one element of the labor rights indicator) is not associated with FDI inflows. The bottom line, then, is that it is very difficult to generate results in which labor rights in the previous period predict investment flows in the next year or in which average labor rights outcomes in the decade are linked with average levels of direct investment.

III. LABOR RIGHTS IN LAW AND IN PRACTICE

As I discuss in Chapter 3, we often observe differences between the legal provision of labor rights and their practical implementation. Governments

---

[21] See Mosley 2006 for a more detailed discussion of these findings.

[22] The CSTS models also include a lagged dependent variable, reflecting the temporal dependence of FDI flows and decisions. See Jensen 2006 and Moran 2002. All independent variables in the estimations also are lagged by one year, given that FDI has relatively long time horizons and that investment decisions often involve a long planning process.

may find it easier to change their labor code (and may receive technical assistance for doing so from the ILO and developed-country governments) than to inspect local factories to assess actual implementation of the code. Problems of compliance with laws are rife, particularly in nations that lack a well-established rule of law or the domestic regulatory capacity to oversee enforcement. Indeed, this domestic lack of regulatory capacity has been one justification for the development of private-sector-based codes of conduct and monitoring systems (Bartley 2005). Alternatively, legal protections of labor rights may be "cheap talk:" Developing-nation governments that find themselves under pressure from human rights activists or developed-country governments may improve the legal status of workers' rights while continuing to allow firms to flout such rights in practice.[23] Moreover, where there are few legal guarantees of core labor rights – typically, in very repressive political regimes – there are few incentives for workers to demand rights in practice. Hence, where labor law is very restrictive, we are unlikely to see union formation or strike attempts and therefore also unlikely to observe workers dismissed on the basis of union membership or strike activity.

Therefore, in addition to exploring the relationship between overall collective labor rights and multinational production, we ought to consider whether there are differences in the correlates of collective labor rights in law and in practice. Summary data also suggest broad differences in law and practice outcomes, both across regions and across income categories. Figures 5.2 and 5.3 summarize the practice and law scores, respectively, according to income decile. These plots, which summarize data for all developing nations in the 1985–2002 period, indicate the average score for each decile (the horizontal line in each box), the range between the 25th and 75th percentile in the decile (the top and bottom bounds of each box), and the position of outliers (the whisker lines as well as individual points beyond these lines). Figure 5.2 demonstrates that labor rights practice are, on average, worse in middle-income deciles; and there is greater variance in labor rights practices in lower- and higher-income deciles. Figure 5.3, by contrast, does not suggest clear linkages between the level of development and the legal provision of collective labor rights.

---

[23] This is consistent with Greenhill et al.'s (2009) study, which reports a significant link between a country's labor rights laws and those of its export partners but less of an effect of bilateral trade relationships on labor rights practices. If low- and middle-income countries face supply chain pressures to upgrade labor rights, they may do so in law only – indeed, domestic labor law has been the focus of much external pressure, such as that in the context of preferential trade agreement negotiations with the United States.

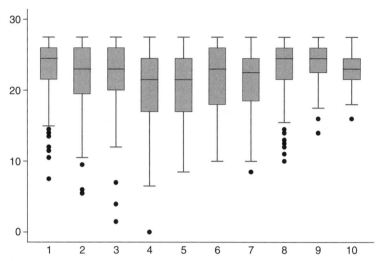

FIGURE 5.2. Average practice scores, by income decile.

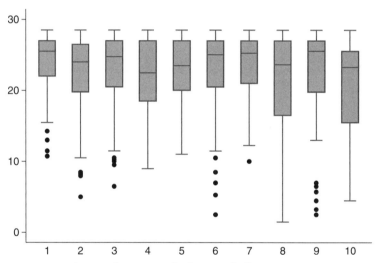

FIGURE 5.3. Average law scores, by income decile.

Considering the two figures together reveals that lower income deciles are characterized by better labor rights in law than in practice. Problems of enforcement – related either to political will or to technical capacity – may be a barrier to enforcing legal provisions of rights. The positive gap between law and practice exists in the lower seven income deciles; it is largest, on average, in the fourth (an average difference of 1.7

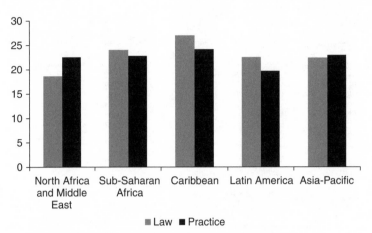

FIGURE 5.4. Average law and practice scores, by region.

points), fifth (2.5), sixth (1.7), and seventh (2.4) deciles. In the top three income categories, by contrast, labor rights practices exceed legal protections: Put differently, there are more violations of labor rights laws than there are problems with implementation. This difference is particularly pronounced in the highest income decile, where practices exceed laws by an average of 3.5 points.

We also observe differences across geographic regions, as Figure 5.4 summarizes. This figure contrasts the average law and practice scores, using annual data from 1985 through 2002. In Sub-Saharan Africa, the Caribbean, and Latin America, collective labor rights are better in law than in practice. The Caribbean is marked by the highest average legal provisions (as well as quite strong labor rights practices). The Asia-Pacific and North Africa/Middle East regions are ones in which collective labor rights are better protected in practice than in law. This is particularly pronounced in North Africa/Middle East, where the gap between legal and actual rights is greatest. The most likely reason for this pattern is that weak legal protections of rights – and, in some cases, outright prohibitions on union activities – are associated with few efforts to exercise rights in practice. In such cases, few practical violations of labor rights will be observed.

The pattern in Middle Eastern nations also suggests a potential linkage between regime type and legal protections. Indeed, if we divide the sample between democracies and dictatorships (using the dichotomous indicator from Przeworski et al. 2000), we find that democracies have noticeably better outcomes on the labor rights laws indicator (an average of 24.5) than do dictatorships (an average of 21.4). Similarly, the bivariate correlation between the POLITY measure of democracy and the labor rights law indicator is .24. Regime type, however, has less bearing on labor rights practices: The average practices score for dictatorships is 22.6, versus 22.1 for democracies; the bivariate correlation between POLITY and labor rights practices is -.21, suggesting that democracies have *more* labor rights violations in practice than do non-democracies. Of course, this may relate to the relative ease of labor mobilization in democracies: More open political systems facilitate strikes and other union activities, but such activities also generate the possibility for employers to then violate rights.

Given that labor rights laws and practices do not necessarily co-vary, we can investigate separately the correlates of each. Table 5.4 reports results from four statistical analyses, two of which model the correlates of labor rights laws and two of which model the correlates of labor rights practices. The first model for each dependent variable (Models 7 and 9) includes the independent variables used in the main model, with the exception of the interaction between FDI flows and human rights NGOs.[24] The second model for each dependent variable (Models 8 and 10) adds a measure of government ideology, as in Table 5.3. Whereas this addition reduces the number of country-years included in the model, it also allows for an assessment of another domestic political factor, one that was revealed to be an important correlate of overall labor rights outcomes.

These cross-sectional time series analyses suggest that the determinants of the legal provision of labor rights are different from those of labor rights practices. In general, the correlates of overall labor rights (Section II) are more strongly related to *laws* than to *practices*. This is particularly true of multinational production; indeed, neither trade nor FDI contributes directly to explaining variation in the actual implementation (versus the legal provision) of collective labor rights. Global production may, however, be important through an indirect channel. In both "practices" estimations, the labor rights outcomes of regional *and* economic peers are statistically significant. The regional effect is similar to that in models of overall labor rights and labor rights laws: Where nations in the same region have better labor rights, all else equal, a given country-year will be categorized by better labor rights. Where nations in the same income

---

[24] If this variable is included, it never approaches statistical significance, nor does it change the results on the FDI and NGO regressors. Excluding the variable allows for a modest increase in the number of country-years used.

TABLE 5.4. *Labor Rights Laws versus Labor Rights Practices*

Independent Variable	(7) Dependent Variable: Law	(8) Dependent Variable: Law	(9) Dependent Variable: Practices	(10) Dependent Variable: Practices
FDI Inflows	0.0028	0.0014	0.03921	0.0142
	(0.0313)	(0.0341)	(0.0306)	(0.0340)
FDI Stock	0.0139	0.0092	−0.0107	−0.0112
	(0.0101)	(0.0102)	(0.0078)	(0.0093)
External Debt	0.0016	0.0003	−0.0003	−0.0003
	(0.0031)	(0.0031)	(0.0021)	(0.0022)
Trade	−0.0163***	−0.0197***	0.0022	0.0020
	(0.0062)	(0.0071)	(0.0053)	(0.0056)
Regional Average, Labor Standards	0.2603***	0.2648***	0.1964***	0.1340**
	(0.0565)	(0.0615)	(0.0576)	(0.0630)
Economic Peers' Labor Standards	0.0512	0.0325	0.1565***	0.1809***
	(0.0506)	(0.0556)	(0.0608)	(0.0638)
Human Rights NGOs	−0.0114	0.0600	−0.7495***	−0.9324***
	(0.1813)	(0.1922)	(0.1715)	(0.1707)
Income Per Capita	−0.8377***	−0.8320**	−0.6916***	−0.4531**
	(0.2999)	(0.3308)	(0.1715)	(0.2290)
Economic Growth	0.0049	−0.0009	0.0570***	0.0554**
	(0.0165)	(0.0177)	(0.0214)	(0.0246)
Population Size	−0.9599***	−1.0745***	−0.3724**	−0.2677
	(0.1619)	(0.1724)	(0.1608)	(0.1894)
Democracy	0.1056***	0.0952***	0.0502*	0.0584*
	(0.0320)	(0.0346)	(0.0281)	(0.0316)
Civil Conflict	−0.4049	−0.5307	−0.4978	−0.4654
	(0.4315)	(0.4792)	(0.3760)	(0.3988)
Left Ideology (Executive)		1.1298***		1.6648***
		(0.3663)		(0.4263)
Constant	37.8345***	40.0130***	25.1277***	22.7210***
	(4.2721)	(4.7562)	(3.9676)	(4.5314)
N	1367	1149	1367	1149
Number of Countries	90	89	90	89
R²	0.44	0.46	0.39	0.42
rho	0.59	0.57	0.49	0.49
Wald Chi²	252.63	423.21	192.78	345.26

Note: Standard errors are in parentheses. Positive coefficients imply lower levels of violations.
***p<.01, **p<.05, *p<.10.

decile have fewer violations of collective labor rights, a given country is more likely to also be characterized by fewer violations. If peer countries have better outcomes in practice, so will a given country. Deteriorations in peers' practices, though, are implied to generate increased violations in practice at home. In other words, competitive pressures could generate *either* a lowering or a ratcheting up of standards, depending on prevailing practices among regional and economic peers.

In Models 7 and 8, by contrast, trade is negatively and significantly linked with labor rights laws. Countries that are more involved in global product markets – as domestic producers, consumers, or subcontractors – have weaker labor laws, all else equal. This effect persists when government ideology is added to the model (Model 8). Again, the implication is that competition in global product markets can generate deteriorations in workers' rights, as globalization's skeptics would predict. Foreign direct investment, however, is not significantly related to labor rights law: Whereas there remains a positive coefficient on the FDI flows variable, the standard errors are quite large. In terms of diffusion-related factors, Models 7 and 8 suggest that, when it comes to the legal elements of collective labor rights, outcomes elsewhere in the geographic region (but not those of economic peers) play an important role. Where regional peers have stronger legal protections, a country is significantly more likely also to have such protections. This is consistent with the results from the models of overall labor rights reported in Table 5.2, and it fits with the notion that pressures for improvements in labor rights may come via institutions and social learning that operate at the regional (i.e., Latin American) level.

Turning to domestic factors, the level of democracy is positively and significantly linked with labor rights laws, just as it is with overall collective labor rights. This effect holds whether the twenty-one point POLITY or dichotomous ACLP measure of democracy is used. Model 8 returns to the issue of government ideology by including a measure of left government (executive branch, in this case; results are very similar if legislative ideology is included in its place). Whereas this inclusion leads to a decrease in the number of country-years in the sample, it does not change the results on the other independent variables. Again, left-leaning governments are more likely, all else equal, to be characterized by stronger legal protections of collective labor rights. This is consistent with our theoretical expectations as well as with the results reported in Table 5.3. Lastly, in terms of control variables, the effects of income per capita and population are the same as in the overall models summarized in Table 5.2: Larger populations and higher incomes are associated with weaker legal labor rights. Civil conflict, however, is not significantly linked with labor rights laws.

Returning to labor rights in practice (Models 9 and 10), we find some additional differences in the correlates of labor rights. Both the number of human rights NGOs and the rate of economic growth are significantly linked with labor rights practices.[25] In the case of the former, a greater number of NGOs makes the existence – or, perhaps more accurately, the observation – of violations more likely. It makes intuitive sense that NGOs' presence is less important to the observation of legal protections of collective labor rights (we might expect that these are relatively easy for external actors to observe and to communicate to the ILO, the U.S. government, or the ICFTU) than to the collection of information regarding labor rights practices. In the case of the latter, where economic growth rates are higher, workers tend to experience fewer violations of labor rights in practice. Whereas economic growth may not generate variation in the legal regime for collective rights, it creates differences in the willingness of employers and governments to uphold such rights. This is consistent with Hypothesis 3.3: When economic times are good, employers will face greater pressure to treat workers well and, therefore, provide them with core labor rights. Conversely, in periods of low or negative growth, workers' bargaining power falls and violations of rights in practice increase. In terms of domestic political institutions, the results on the practice models are very similar to those on the law models: Democratic regimes and countries with left-leaning governments are more likely to experience fewer labor rights violations in practice.

The relationship between multinational production and collective labor rights, then, depends somewhat on the way in which labor rights are measured and aggregated. Formal protection of labor rights is associated with trade openness (although not with foreign direct investment), whereas actual implementation of labor rights is linked with diffusion-type factors (peers' practices) but not directly with multinational production. Factors like economic growth are important to labor rights practices

---

[25] When a measure of the size of the manufacturing sector (manufacturing/GDP) is added to the labor rights practices model, it is significantly and negatively associated with labor rights. This effect is likely driven by factors similar to that of the "employment in industry" variable (see fn. 16): More industrialized developing nations provide greater demands for the protection, and opportunities for the violation, of collective labor rights. Results of this model also are available upon request.

but not to the underlying legal framework. At the domestic political level, both democracy and government ideology play a consistent role in influencing labor rights laws and practices, regardless of levels of participation in multinational production.

IV. CONCLUSION

This chapter assesses the main expectations developed in Chapter 3, using large-N statistical analyses. These analyses reveal some support for the mixed effects of multinational production on collective labor rights. In overall terms, nations that are more involved in subcontracting and global export markets tend to have worse collective labor rights, whereas the receipt of foreign direct investment has a positive impact on those same overall collective rights. Thus, the question is not simply *whether* a given nation participates in global production networks but *how* it does so: The evidence indicates that arm's-length production has different implications for workers than directly owned production. The behavior in peer countries, particularly those in the same geographic region, is also important: Whereas multinational production generates some direct competitive pressures for countries, peers' behavior can serve as an indirect pressure in either a positive or negative direction.

At the same time, the analyses of overall labor rights outcomes reveal the importance of domestic economic and political factors. Country-years characterized by higher income levels (within the subset of developing countries) tend to have worse labor right outcomes, perhaps related to the structure of economies (agricultural versus manufacturing-oriented) and the associated ease of demanding collective labor rights and observing violations of such demands. Perhaps more importantly, more democratic political regimes are associated with better labor rights outcomes, as are left-leaning executives and legislatures.

Moreover, if we disaggregate labor rights into two key elements, law and practice, we find some important differences in the correlates of such rights. Whereas trade again has a negative linkage with legal protections of collective labor rights, there is no statistically significant relationship between labor laws and foreign direct investment. Additionally, labor rights practices appear much more the result of international peer effects (both in terms of geographic region and economic development category) and domestic conditions (specifically, economic growth) than of multinational production relationships.

These results suggest other fruitful empirical paths. Quantitative analyses may be less appropriate for exploring longer-term domestic political dynamics than are in-depth case studies, which allow the opportunity to trace the interplay of domestic politics (and economic conditions) and multinational production over a longer time period and to consider the role of the longer-running historical position of labor within a polity. Moreover, while distinguishing between trade and foreign direct investment is a starting point for unpacking multinational production, it may not go far enough. Beyond the overall effects of firms' modes of entry on labor rights outcomes, we might anticipate that different types of trade, and different types of foreign direct investment, have varying impacts on labor rights outcomes. For instance, the competitive pressures generated by global apparel markets may be quite different from those that exist in global markets for pharmaceuticals or electronics. It may be the policy actions of countries that export similar products to the same destination markets, rather than the actions of other countries generally, that determine the link between economic openness and changes in standards (see Cao and Prakash 2010). In the remaining substantive chapters (Chapters 6 and 7), I explore further the impact of multinational production on labor rights outcomes, with a focus on the heterogeneity of production within countries.

6

Varieties of Capitalists?

The Diversity of Multinational Production

In the first five chapters of this book, I advance the argument that economic globalization generally, and multinational production specifically, is a diverse phenomenon. Some low- and middle-income nations have high levels of MNC-owned production, whereas foreign direct investment plays a much more limited role in other nations. Similarly, some developing nations are highly involved in regional and global trade markets, whereas other nations maintain both legal and practical barriers to imports and exports. In some instances, high levels of trade activity coexist with low levels of FDI inflows. These cases are marked by high levels of trade competition and subcontracting activity but by little directly owned production. In other situations, multinational corporations own significant production facilities in the host nation, in which they produce goods that largely service local consumer markets – a high level of direct investment but a low level of trade openness.

These differences should generate diversity in labor rights outcomes, according to the theoretical and empirical claims advanced in Chapters 3 and 5. Trade openness tends to put negative pressures on collective labor rights, whereas foreign direct investment augurs positively for this same set of rights. As a result, *how* a given nation participates in the global economy – and how MNCs enter host economies – has important consequences for workers in that country. However, this heterogeneity captures only part of the diversity inherent in contemporary multinational production. Whereas the preceding chapters advance our understanding of the links between the global economy and workers' rights, they leave many elements of global production unexplored.

In this chapter, I explore some of these additional elements, further unpacking the diversity of global production in low- and middle-income nations. Much of this diversity is at the sector level: Developing economies vary, not only in their overall openness to trade and investment, but also in the industries in which they specialize. As a result, developing countries differ markedly in the profiles of the products they export as well as in the sectoral destinations of FDI inflows. The effects of multinational production therefore may vary across economic sectors (rather than across factors, as a Heckscher-Ohlin conception implies), as the Ricardo-Viner framework suggests (Hiscox 2002). Developing nations also vary in their investment partners: The United States is the main source of FDI for some countries, whereas European or Asian nations are the key sources for others. If MNCs bring different national "best practices" with them when they go abroad, this difference in home country locations will generate variation in labor rights. Trade partners are concerned by another element of diversity: If, like investment, trade might serve as a mechanism for the cross-national diffusion of standards and practices, then the identity of – and the practices by – a developing nation's main trade partners also is important.

Considering the effects of the "varieties of capitalists," then, is central to improving our understanding of globalization's impact in the developing world (Hall and Soskice 2001). In the first part of this chapter, I establish empirically the diversity in foreign direct investment and export activity in developing nations. I then focus on two main types of heterogeneity, sectoral and source country. I discuss, theoretically, how each type of diversity could affect labor rights outcomes. I then offer an initial empirical assessment of these propositions. I conclude with a discussion of how future research in the area of labor rights could address further the heterogeneity of global production in the developing world.

I. DIVERSITY IN GLOBAL PRODUCTION

Global production generally, and foreign direct investment specifically, features a diverse array of activities. Of the nearly 12,000 greenfield (new) FDI projects undertaken in 2006, the largest set was in manufacturing (54 percent). Among these, the industries with the greatest representation were electrical and electronic equipment (nearly 10 percent of total global projects); motor vehicles and other transportation equipment; food, beverages, and tobacco; and chemicals and chemical projects. Service-sector FDI accounted for nearly 42 percent of global projects, whereas the remaining 4 percent (492 projects) were in the primary sector, mostly related to energy (UNCTAD 2007, Annex Table A.I.2).

If we consider the global stock of FDI, which indicates all accumulated investments, rather than only new projects, we observe a shift over time away from primary-sector direct investments (accounting for less than 10 percent of inward world FDI stock in 2005, just slightly less than its share in 1990) as well as a reduction in the overall importance of manufacturing. In 1990, FDI stock in manufacturing comprised 41 percent of global FDI stock; by 2005, this had declined to 30 percent. At the same time, the role of the services sector has grown, due partly to privatization programs in various developing and transition nations (UNCTAD 2007; also see Daude et al. 2003). The services sector includes activities that are central to multinational production networks – namely, transportation, insurance, and finance (Silver 2003). Of course, the importance of various types of FDI (and subcontracting) differs across types of countries; primary-sector investment, for example, remains more important to developing and transition than to developed nations.

Among developing countries, diversity also is the rule. Even low- and middle-income nations characterized by similar levels of international economic integration can have very different production, direct investment, and export profiles. Countries with significant natural resource endowments tend to attract the bulk of their inward direct investment in the extractive sector. Chile, for which FDI stock was equivalent to nearly 70 percent of GDP in 2002, fits this pattern: In 2002, for instance, FDI inflows in the primary sector accounted for 58.3 percent of total inflows. The remainder of Chile's inward FDI was mostly (35.4 percent) in the tertiary (services) sector. Very little of Chile's inward FDI focuses on the manufacturing sector. Brazil, which had a slightly smaller stock of total FDI in 2002 (52 percent of GDP) than Chile, has a markedly different sectoral FDI profile. The secondary (manufacturing) sector comprised 33.7 percent of Brazil's FDI stock in 2000,[1] with electronics, chemicals, and motor vehicles making up the bulk of new inward FDI flows. The services (tertiary) sector also was particularly important for Brazil, at 64 percent of total FDI stock (UNCTAD 2004b). Elsewhere in the western hemisphere, El Salvador's economy underwent a significant transformation during the 1990s (as did Costa Rica's, which is discussed in Chapter 7). In 1990, El Salvador's garment assembly plants employed a mere 3,734 people. By 2000, this had grown to 69,000 workers. This shift coincided

---

[1] UNCTAD (2004b) reports Brazil's sectoral FDI data for 2000 but not for 2002.

with the decline of the coffee sector during the 1990s. By the late 1990s, the value added in *maquila* production (mostly, if not all, in textiles and clothing) surpassed the total value of coffee exports (Anner 2001).

Indeed, changes over time in production and direct investment profiles are numerous among developing nations. Some changes reflect industrial upgrading: As low- and middle-income countries improve their infrastructure, technological capacity, and labor force skills, they may transition from economies based on agriculture and natural resources to ones based on lower-technology manufactures (i.e., textiles and footwear) and perhaps eventually to economies involved largely in medium- and high-technology production (i.e., automobiles and electronics). Foreign direct investors both promote and respond to such changes. To take an example, Thailand historically has been a major recipient of FDI in Asia, second only to China.[2] The bulk of Thailand's direct investment during the last three decades has occurred in the manufacturing sector, accounting for an average of 41.8 percent of total FDI inflows during the 1970–2005 period.[3] Whereas the importance of manufacturing to overall direct investment has not changed that much over time, the specific type of manufacturing has. In the 1970s and early 1980s, direct investment in Thailand focused mostly on production for the local market and on goods such as textiles, chemicals, and automobiles. In the mid-1980s, as Thailand's policy focus shifted toward an export-oriented one, direct investment became oriented more toward labor-intensive production in lower-technology industries, such as clothing, footwear, and toys. More recently, another shift – an "industrial upgrading" – is underway, with new direct investment often aimed at electrical machinery and electronic appliances. Indeed, by the late 1990s, electrical machinery and electronic appliances accounted for over 30 percent of total manufacturing FDI in Thailand (compared with less than 15 percent in the 1970s). At the same time, the overall share of textile-sector investments fell to below 1 percent of total FDI inflows for the 2000–2005 period (Asian Development Bank 2006).

Cambodia has also experienced a shift in its FDI profile. In the early 1990s, following the government's efforts to open the country to direct investment inflows, Cambodia attracted the bulk (43 percent) of its

---

[2] In recent years, however, Vietnam has challenged Thailand in terms of FDI inflows.
[3] The percentage of FDI in manufacturing ranges from 29.9 percent of inflows (1970–1975) to 49.2 percent of inflows (1986–1990), falling more recently to 44.1 percent of total inflows (2001–2005). Asian Development Bank (2006).

foreign direct investment in the tourism sector. During the 1994–1999 period, FDI in manufacturing was slightly less important than tourism, accounting for 35 percent of direct investment. By 2005, however, a shift from services (including tourism) to manufacturing was well underway; that year, direct investment in manufacturing made up 59 percent of total direct investment (Asian Development Bank 2006). This investment was highly concentrated in the garment industry, reflecting Cambodia's level of development, its comparative advantages, and its efforts (see Chapter 3) to market itself as an "ethically conscious" apparel production location.

Vietnam offers yet another instance of changes over time in direct investment profiles as well as an illustration of the shift in focus of some FDI to export-oriented production. Since its broad *doi moi* program of economic reforms was launched in 1986 (Malesky 2008), Vietnam has witnessed significant increases in direct investment. During the 2000–2003 time frame, foreign invested enterprises accounted for nearly 20 percent of the country's industrial employment. Whereas these foreign-owned enterprises contributed 27 percent of Vietnam's exports in 1995, by 2005 their contribution had grown to 56 percent of exports. Over time, direct investment in Vietnam has shifted its orientation away from natural resources and toward manufacturing. As in Thailand, manufacturing FDI initially aimed to service the domestic market; in recent decades, though, the focus of foreign firms has been production for export. In the 1990s, much of this direct investment occurred in the garment, footwear, and furniture sectors. More recently, though, as Vietnam has experienced some improvement in infrastructure and labor force skills, foreign firms have begun to invest in the electronics sector as well (Asian Development Bank 2006). Still other changes in foreign direct investment profiles reflect shifts in the aims of MNCs in light of economic growth in host economies. In China, some foreign firms continue to use China as a production platform for exports, whereas others now aim to sell to the expanding set of Chinese consumers with substantial disposable incomes. The latter represents market-, rather than efficiency-, seeking FDI, and we would expect this shift to have consequences for labor rights as well as for the impact of foreign direct investment more broadly (also see Guthrie 1999; Santoro 2000).

If we consider developing countries' export profiles, another facet of multinational production, we observe similar diversity. In 2002, China, Ecuador, and Mexico had very similar levels of overall trade openness (ranging from 54.8 to 55.4 percent of gross domestic product). However, the products that accounted for their exports varied dramatically: 72.6 percent of Ecuador's exports were primary products, whereas resource-based manufactures accounted for a further 19.5 percent of exports. Only 7.6 percent of Ecuador's total exports were manufactured goods, and almost none of these were from high-technology sectors. By contrast, whereas approximately 17 percent of Mexico's 2002 exports were primary- and resource-related (12 percent primary products and 5 percent resource-based manufactures), a total of 82.6 percent of its exports came from the manufacturing sector. Similarly, 85.6 percent of China's exports came from its manufacturing industries.

Even China and Mexico displayed important differences in the technological content of their exports: Low-technology products (such as apparel and footwear) were the largest category of Chinese manufacturing exports, accounting for 38.7 percent of the overall 2002 exports. In Mexico, the most important export category was medium-technology products, which comprised 38.9 percent of total exports. In particular, the automotive sector contributed 17 percent of Mexico's total exports, whereas electronics and electrical parts accounted for nearly 25 percent. Electronics were similarly important to Chinese exports (26.6 percent of the 2002 total), whereas China had very few automotive sector exports (World Trade Analyzer database).[4] These examples suggest, again, that even among nations with similar levels of overall trade activity, there exists important diversity in export and production profiles. If some industries or types of productive activities are more likely to be associated with the development and protection of labor rights than others, then these differences also will have important implications for workers.

Sectoral production and investment patterns are not the only diversity we observe in low- and middle-income nations. These countries also vary in terms of *from whom* they receive investments and *with whom* they trade. Although developed nations remain the most important sources of (and destinations for) global direct investment, as well as the key trading partners of many countries, there are important differences in terms of which developed nations serve as developing nations' main trading partners. Some of these patterns reflect geography or history. Former colonies, for example, often have preferential trading relationships with colonial powers; and Latin American nations are likely to engage in

---

[4] World Trade Analyzer (WTA), produced by Statistics Canada, compiles trade data from the United Nation's COMTRADE statistics system. For information on or access to the WTA, see http://www.statcan.gc.ca/dli-ild/data-donnees/ftp/worldtrade-commerce_mondial-eng.htm

significant trade with North American countries. Other patterns reflect long-standing economic and cultural ties: Hong Kong and Taiwan's significant direct investments in mainland China, for instance, are facilitated by cultural as well as personal relationships.

Within Asia, we can observe such differences in the source countries of direct investment. The United States was the largest direct investor in Malaysia during 1999–2003, accounting for 44 percent of the country's total FDI inflows. The most important investor in Thailand during the same period (23 percent of total investment) was Japan. Half of the direct investment inflows to Cambodia for the 2001–2005 time frame came, not from a high-income nation, but from China. This also reflects the trend toward increased outward investment activities by a few large, middle-income developing nations, such as Brazil and China (see Chapter 2). Whereas many firms are truly multinational in their operations and structure, it is reasonable to expect that these differences in source countries will generate variation in the transmission of "best practices" to host countries. If such practices vary across countries (Continental Europe versus Anglo-America, or developed versus developing nations; see Berger and Dore 1996; Pauly and Reich 1997), then the diversity of investor identities will also matter for labor rights.

In analytical terms, then, there may be significant unit heterogeneity among developing nations. It is not just that some countries are more open to trade or receive more FDI than others. It also is that different countries receive different *types* of FDI, in varying economic sectors, through diverse modes of industrial organization, and at varying levels of skill intensity (Gereffi et al. 2005; Navaretti and Venables 2004). Yet, for practical reasons related largely to data availability in a low- and middle-income country context, much research – including much of what is reported in this book – treats multinational production at the national level. Such an approach requires empirical aggregation upward (to the national level) from theoretical work on direct investment, which is informed by predictions of incentives and behavior at the firm- and/or industry-level (e.g., Henisz 2000; Jensen 2006; Li 2006).[5] In this chapter, I propose ways to undo this aggregation – that is, I examine the potential consequences of sectoral and source-country diversity for collective labor rights.

---

[5] In a larger sense, very little recent literature in comparative and international political economy explicitly treats firms – versus broad sectors or categories like "trade" and "FDI" – as political actors, as did some earlier work (e.g., Bauer et al. 1963; Evans 1984; Milner 1988).

II. SECTORAL HETEROGENEITY: FDI, PRODUCTION PROFILES, AND LABOR RIGHTS

Almost by definition, low- and middle-income countries have economic structures that differ markedly from those of wealthy countries. At the aggregate level, low- and middle-income economies are oriented more toward agriculture and lower-technology manufacturing. In 2002, the last year for which the collective labor rights measure exists, manufactured goods accounted for 76.8 percent of global merchandise exports. In high-income OECD nations, manufactured goods were even more important, comprising 81 percent of merchandise exports. In middle-income nations, manufactured goods played a slightly less important role, comprising 64.4 percent of merchandise exports. However, in low-income countries, manufactures accounted for just over one third (36.7 percent) of merchandise exports. If we focus on high-technology exports, the contrast is even more pronounced: Whereas 3 percent of low-income countries' 2002 merchandise exports were comprised of high-technology products, the corresponding figure for middle-income nations was 19.3 percent (for high-income OECD nations, the figure was 22 percent).

Labor force statistics paint a similar picture: On average, over 70 percent of people in low-income nations reside in rural areas. Middle-income countries average a rural population of 54.5 percent, and high-income OECD nations average 24 percent. In 2002, a mere 3.9 percent of employment in high-income nations was accounted for the by agricultural sector, compared with 35.7 percent in middle-income nations.[6] High-income countries' labor forces were concentrated instead in the services sector (69.7 percent of total employment in 2002) as well as in industry (26.1 percent). Middle-income nations displayed a more diverse employment profile, on average, with 19.9 percent of the labor force in manufacturing and 32.6 percent in services.

Over time, many low- and middle-income countries have experienced dramatic shifts in the structure of their economies and labor forces. Some countries, particularly in southeast Asia, transitioned from a focus on agriculture to one on lower-technology consumer products and, later, on higher-technology, more capital-intensive goods. More broadly, high-technology exports accounted for only 3.4 percent of middle-income

---

[6] Corresponding data for low-income nations were not available from the World Development Indicators database.

countries' merchandise exports in 1988.[7] By 2002, 19.3 percent of these countries' merchandise exports were comprised of high-technology products. More generally, the contribution of manufactured goods to overall merchandise exports in middle-income nations more than doubled between 1984 (31.4 percent of exports) and 2002 (64.4 percent of exports). Similarly, employment in agriculture in middle-income countries last exceeded 50 percent of the labor force in 1992. Moreover, among high-income nations, employment in industry has declined steadily, albeit slowly, over time: Industry accounted for 33.6 percent of the labor force, on average, in 1980 but only 26.1 percent of the labor force in 2002.

A. Theoretical Implications

These differences among nations and the shifts over time within countries have important implications for workers' rights. In economies that are very dependent on agricultural production and exports, or on employment in small-scale, family-owned enterprises, workers' employment experiences may have little to do with multinational corporations specifically, or even with the global economy more broadly (Flanagan 2006). For such workers, domestic political and economic factors are likely to play an even greater role in determining labor force conditions. At the same time, as low- and middle-income countries undergo shifts from agriculture to manufacturing (and from rural to urban employment), the opportunities both for perpetuating (for employers and governments) and for observing (for labor rights activists) violations of workers' rights expand.[8] Of course, at the same time, workers will be more able to organize collectively under such conditions, perhaps facilitating the achievement of wage and benefit improvements.

I consider two specific causal linkages between the sectoral structure of economies and labor rights outcomes.[9] The first concerns the general structure of economies in developing countries and, as such, focuses on

---

[7] Data are from the World Development Indicators database. The year 1988 is the first year for which the aggregate measure of high-technology exports as a percentage of merchandise exports is available for middle-income countries.

[8] Recall that, in Chapter 5 I report a negative statistical relationship between the percentage of workers employed in industry and the protection of collective labor rights.

[9] There are, of course, other ways in which the structure of national economies could affect workers' rights. For instance, as Abouharb and Cingranelli (2008) point out, the sector in which a given employee works – protected previously or long-exposed to competition – will determine the impact of structural adjustment conditionality on labor rights. Those in previously exposed sectors are likely to see their fortunes remain similar or improve,

determinants of labor rights outcomes that are largely independent of multinational production. I expect that economies with a heavy focus on lower-technology, less skill-intensive production will have worse labor rights outcomes, all else equal, than economies populated by capital- and skill-intensive industries. The logic of this expectation is related both to overall levels of development (where we might consider attention to working conditions, wages, and labor rights as a "luxury good") as well as to the incentives to attract and retain the best workers in more skilled operations (and the incentives to keep employment costs low in less technology-intensive operations). This expectation has both a static and a dynamic element: In a static sense, nations with lower-technology production profiles are expected to have worse labor rights outcomes, all else equal. In a dynamic sense, as individual countries experience a process of industrial upgrading, the conditions of workers are expected to improve.

Of course, in the longer run, the structure of national economies may relate to the global economy. Industrial upgrading often has involved engagement with the global economy (export-led industrialization in Southeast Asia) or a deliberate effort to resist global economic forces (import substitution industrialization). Additionally, if we consider labor-intensive activities, we often find a variety of subcontracting relationships with foreign firms, particularly in apparel and footwear (Henderson et al. 2002). Even without the involvement of foreign economic agents, however, we can expect that differences in – and changes to – countries' sectoral production profiles will have implications for their labor rights outcomes.[10]

The second linkage between sectoral structure and labor rights relates directly to the particular type of foreign direct investment a country receives. As I describe previously, economies that receive a given amount of direct investment may nonetheless receive very different *types* of investment, either in terms of its broad sectoral profile (extractive versus manufacturing) or in terms of its specific profile within manufacturing

---

whereas those in previously protected industries are likely to lose out from the increases in trade openness that tend to accompany economic reform programs. Also see Anner et al. (2010), Haggard and Kaufman (1995), and Murillo (2001).

[10] The implications for labor rights of the broad shift from the manufacturing to the services sector are unclear. Whereas some service sector activities require highly skilled workers or are essential to contemporary global production networks, other activities (including building maintenance, retail sales, and janitorial duties) rely heavily on unskilled or semi-skilled workers.

(textiles and apparel versus pharmaceuticals). Whereas we expect directly owned production generally to have positive consequences for labor in developing countries, these consequences also may vary with firms' industrial profiles. These profiles will relate directly to firms' motivations for undertaking direct investment and, similarly, to their cost and labor-skill considerations.

In Chapter 2, I summarize the academic literature on why firms operate and invest abroad. This literature reminds us that firms vary in their motives (Leahy and Montagna 2000; Markusen 1995; Moran 2002; UNCTAD 1999). Some investors aim to extract natural resources, whereas others seek access to local markets (Graham 2000; MIGA 2000). Yet another set of foreign direct investors are efficiency-seeking (Feng 2001; Kobrin 1987; Leahy and Montagna 2000; Mutti 2003; Navaretti and Venables 2004). FDI allows efficiency-seeking firms to take advantage of economies of scale and cross-national differences in productivity, agglomeration, and various costs. Firms' strategies vis-à-vis foreign production vary in turn with their motives, as the mode of entry literature suggests. U.S.-based parent firms in the electronics and electrical equipment sector, as well as in the automobile industry, are much more likely to manufacture via directly owned foreign affiliates than are their counterparts in food processing and petroleum products (Helpman 2006). To an extent, this reflects the production processes and technologies that prevail in different sectors: Historically, greater and broader cross-national diffusion of production locations occurred in the textile than in the automobile industry. This was due, in large part, to the lower capital requirements and the broader consumer markets that characterized apparel and clothing (Silver 2003). Firms in the textile industry also could more easily rely on subcontractors, given that their designs and technologies were not considered proprietary.

The heterogeneity in firms' motivations is likely to generate diversity in attitudes toward labor rights, even within the subset of firms that engage internationally via direct ownership.[11] Efficiency-seeking MNCs likely are more concerned with labor costs than natural resource- and market-seeking affiliates. In her longitudinal study of the global automobile industry, Silver (2003) maintains that increases in labor unrest and militancy have driven global firms to relocate production, first within the United States; then to Western Europe; and later to

---

[11] On the more general heterogeneity of firm preferences regarding regulatory arrangements, see Levy and Prakash (2003).

Brazil, South Africa, and South Korea. When workers in new locations began to exercise their collective power, firms responded by looking elsewhere. The implication is that automotive firms in the contemporary era will follow this pattern, leaving locations such as Mexico and China when workers there become more able to demand better wages and conditions. Yet this argument assumes, to a large extent, that automobile manufacturers are efficiency-seeking – that they have established production in China as a means of lowering costs rather than as a strategy for gaining a foothold in a potentially enormous consumer market. To the extent that such automobile firms are market-seeking, however, their propensity to tolerate labor militancy and unrest may be greater.

Another possible distinction among MNCs is based on economic sector. Multinational firms involved in labor-intensive production should be more concerned with labor costs than multinationals involved in capital- or technology-intensive sectors (Hatem 1998; Nunnenkamp and Spatz 2002). In the former set of industries, firms are likely more focused on minimizing labor costs and less attentive to protecting workers' rights. Labor costs are a larger part of these firms' overall expenditures, creating greater incentives for repression (Elliott and Freeman 2001; Herzenberg 1996).[12] Exit also is easier in such sectors; firms may move repeatedly, seeking out those locations with lower labor costs and less stringent regulations (Mandle 2003; Mutti 2003). To the extent that slack labor markets exist, they often occur at the lower end of the spectrum, so that a large pool of surplus workers reduces the bargaining power of labor in unskilled production activities.

In capital-intensive sectors, by contrast, labor costs are a relatively small portion of firms' overall costs, and it is important for employers to attract and retain skilled labor. Firms also have larger sunk costs (rendering them less likely to credibly threaten exit *ex post*). Foreign direct investment from technology- and skill-intensive firms should have better consequences for workers, all else equal, than investment from firms in labor-intensive industries. Moreover, as the sectoral composition of FDI varies (in a cross-national sense) or changes over time within a particular

---

[12] There also is some (limited) evidence that FDI is more likely to lead to lower wages for female (versus male) manufacturing workers (Vijaya and Kaltani 2007). This likely stems, at least in part, from sectoral differences in employment: Textile and apparel firms tend to have largely female work forces (and often express a preference for hiring young female workers, as they are assumed to be more docile), whereas the work forces of capital-intensive firms tend to be largely male.

country, labor rights outcomes also should change.[13] Furthermore, this sectoral distinction often correlates with differences in firm motivations. Many market-seeking MNCs are involved in the production of high-technology, skill-intensive commodities (Moran 2002; UNCTAD 2002). Efficiency-seeking, high-technology firms often have microeconomic incentives to keep production in-house (via FDI) rather than to subcontract.

This logic, then, generates two hypotheses linking sectoral production patterns with labor rights:

> *Hypothesis 6.1*: *Developing nations with a greater focus on higher-technology, skill-intensive production will have better labor rights outcomes, all else equal.*

> *Hypothesis 6.2*: *Greater foreign participation in labor-intensive, unskilled sectors will be associated negatively with collective labor rights, whereas greater foreign participation in capital-intensive, skilled labor-oriented sectors will be associated positively with collective labor rights.*

Recent studies linking human rights with multinational investment offer some support for these propositions.[14] Santoro's (2000) analysis of foreign firms and human rights in China draws a contrast between firms that aim for low-cost production for export, via a "sweatshop model," and firms attempting to access the growing domestic market, which focus on training and retaining highly motivated, highly skilled workers. Gallagher's (2005) more recent study of China's foreign-invested sector reveals a similar pattern, with resulting differences in the treatment of workers.[15]

---

[13] Silver's longitudinal analysis makes a similar claim on a global scale. As the identity of the leading industries changes, so does the bargaining power of workers. The shift from textiles to automobiles as the key global industry, for instance, implied an increase in labor's structural bargaining power. See Silver (2003) and Chapter 3.

[14] Alfaro (2003) investigates the varying effects, by sector, of FDI on economic growth. Brady and Wallace (2000) analyze the impact of employment in foreign-owned affiliates on various labor outcomes, such as unionization, worker dissent, and compensation in U.S. states during 1978–1996. Their results suggest that FDI in manufacturing has fewer consequences – and sometimes positive consequences – for labor than non-manufacturing FDI. The latter is negatively and significantly related to worker grievances, victories in union elections, and union organization efforts. Like Javorcik and Spartaneau's analysis, however, their empirical assessments do not differentiate among types of manufacturing – labor versus capital intensive, for instance.

[15] Similarly, in her analysis of European firms' preferences over social insurance, Mares (2003) finds that smaller firms and firms in lower-risk sectors tend to worry about the

Blanton and Blanton (2009) examine a different causal pathway, asking whether the impact of human rights on U.S. firms' investment location decisions varies by economic sector. They measure accumulated investment by U.S. firms in twenty-eight developing nations during the 1990–2004 period. They find some, albeit mixed, support for the theoretical claim that human rights is a significant (and positive) determinant of direct investment in industries that employ highly skilled labor or in industries that aim for high levels of integration with the host economy. Of the ten industrial sectors they analyze, they find a significant and positive linkage in four – chemical manufacturing, financial services, electrical manufacturing, and fabricated metals. They classify the first three of these as dependent on highly skilled labor; fabricated metals are a sector in which the labor employed tends to be low-skill but in which integration with the host economy often is a goal, given the market-seeking nature of the enterprises. In the remaining six industrial sectors, including petroleum, mining, and food, Blanton and Blanton report no statistically significant linkage between FDI and human rights. Whereas their analysis suffers from the limited availability of data (representing outflows only from the United States and to a fairly limited set of destinations) as well as from the difficulty of linking firm motivations with industrial sectors (a given sector may include a mix of market- and resource-seeking firms, for instance), it also supports the claim of sectoral heterogeneity among MNCs.

A 2008 *New York Times* report contrasting two locally owned firms in China offers anecdotal evidence regarding how widely conditions vary across industries, even in the same general location. One firm (Shanghai Jinjue Fashion Company), a locally owned clothing factory, manufactures apparel as a subcontractor for various European firms. Its owners and managers were very concerned about the effect on costs of the 2008 reforms to China's labor law as well as about cost competition from Mexico and Vietnam. By contrast, the second firm (Renesola) manufactures silicon wafers for solar panels. When it was founded in 2001, Renesola was a subcontractor for foreign firms, completing assembly of solar panels. In the mid-2000s, the firm shifted to higher value-added activities, making its own solar wafers and competing directly with German and Japanese firms. The firm, which completed an initial public offering on the New York Stock Exchange in January 2008, was among

costs of various social insurance programs, whereas larger firms and those in higher-skilled sectors prefer a high degree of employer discretion in social insurance programs.

the top five global suppliers of solar wafers in early 2008. Renesola's workers are well-paid relative to others in China, and they operate complicated machinery, which accounts for at least as much of the firm's production costs as do wages. Managers' concern there is with improving productivity rather than with reducing labor costs.

Beyond these case examples, how well are the expectations of Hypotheses 6.1 and 6.2 borne out by empirical evidence? Existing studies provide some support for the linkages between economic structure and labor rights outcomes. Moran (2002) presents case studies of export processing zones in Costa Rica, the Dominican Republic, and the Philippines. He considers which factors explain within-country variation, as well as changes over time, in conditions in the EPZs. He finds that the movement from lower- to higher-skill operations tends to bring with it an "extensive institutional transformation" in the treatment of workers. Whereas foreign firms might generally want to hire at the top end of the labor market (hiring the best workers for a given skill or wage level), the incentives to do so are particularly pronounced in skill-intensive industries. Foreign investors in labor-intensive operations (such as apparel in Mauritius and Madagascar), then, are very sensitive to changes in relative wage levels, as these directly affect their global competitiveness (also see Romero 1995). By contrast, companies involved in exporting higher-technology products, such as electronics, are very focused on attracting and retaining the most skilled workers because this serves to maintain firms' productivity. Indeed, many jobs in EPZs, which tend to include a fair proportion of higher-technology operations, pay higher than close equivalents elsewhere in a given country. As a result, the low rates of unionization that often are observed in EPZs could be less about supply and more about demand: If workers in EPZs, especially in more skill-intensive firms, experience better wages and working conditions than workers elsewhere in the economy, they may be less interested in forming or joining unions. Low rates of unionization, then, could indicate a *lack* of problems rather than a problem in and of themselves (Elliott and Freeman 2003; also see Boyenge 2007).

Similarly, in its 2005 annual report, the Fair Labor Association (FLA) notes that "race to the bottom" concerns are particularly important in labor-intensive sectors, "where labor costs may represent as much as 25 percent of the total [production] cost and, more importantly, the most malleable of the cost factors" (FLA 2005, 8–9). Indeed, many of the NGOs that aim to identify labor rights abuses are focused on labor-intensive sectors, particularly apparel and textiles. In some part, this relates to the potential for mobilizing consumer attention to labor rights violations in the production of branded apparel products. It also suggests that such sectors are the most likely locations for the identification of labor rights violations. For example, in its report for the 2006 calendar year, the FLA summarizes assessments carried out at 147 FLA-accredited factories worldwide. At these factories, in the apparel and footwear sectors, FLA-accredited monitors identified 2,511 instances of non-compliance with international labor standards. Forty-six percent of these instances involved health and safety issues, and 17 percent concerned wages and benefits. Only 4 percent were related to freedom of association and collective bargaining. These assessments were carried out in countries ranging from China, Vietnam, and Indonesia to Mexico, Guatemala, and Brazil as well as Bulgaria, Turkey, and India (FLA 2007). Whereas the FLA does not operate a comparable assessment program for other (capital-intensive) sectors (allowing us to compare the extent of violations identified across sectors), its annual reports suggest that labor-related issues are a particular challenge in the apparel and footwear industries.[16] Many such operations, of course, do involve the global economy, particularly in terms of local subcontractors producing for foreign-based firms (Elliot and Freeman 2003); but the broader point is that competition on the basis of cost tends to augur poorly for workers.[17]

Moreover, Morici and Schulz (2001) report a statistical relationship between low respect for freedom of association rights (based on the OECD's index) and high levels of textile exports. The policy implication, then, is that industrial upgrading – a transition away from labor-intensive production – may offer the best hope for improving labor rights in low- and middle-income countries.[18] Of course, such a transformation is neither inevitable nor easy, but it does suggest (as do some of the analyses in

---

[16] Locke et al.'s (2007) study of Nike supplier factories, though, highlights variation between footwear and apparel factories. Footwear factories tend to be larger and more capital-intensive, whereas apparel factories are smaller and much more labor-intensive. Even within the same broad industry, and even within a single large firm in the industry, we might observe variation in capital intensity and labor intensity and, therefore, in workers' rights outcomes.

[17] This is, of course, not inevitable. As I discuss in Chapter 3, a few countries, such as Cambodia, have attempted to distinguish themselves from other textile producers by promising "sweatshop free" products.

[18] Javorcik and Spatarneanu's (2005) analysis of firm location decisions in nineteen Western and Eastern European nations also reveals broad sectoral differences. Labor market flexibility appears to matter more to investors in services sectors than for those in manufacturing.

Chapter 5) that developed-nation governments' and transnational activists' attention to internal development issues may be more effective than a focus on the behavior of foreign firms.

B. Empirical Assessment

What is the most appropriate empirical strategy for evaluating Hypotheses 6.1 and 6.2? The former suggests that the relevant indicators to consider are a nation's export profile and overall sectoral orientation during a given year. Nations with intensive export involvement in low-skill industries are expected to have worse outcomes than nations with exports weighted toward high-skill industries. In some of the analyses in this chapter, I employ data from UNCTAD, as well as some measures based on Statistics Canada's *World Trade Analyzer* database, to measure a country's trade profile by broad commodity group. I also use more general indicators of the economy's structure to test the sectoral argument. All else equal, country-years marked by a concentration in capital-intensive, higher-technology production should have better collective labor rights outcomes.

In terms of evaluating Hypothesis 6.2, one possibility would be to classify multinationals (or portions of multinationals' operations) as resource-seeking, efficiency-seeking, or market-seeking. We could then investigate whether there are more violations of labor rights reported in efficiency-seeking firms or whether economies with a bias toward efficiency-seeking direct investment have worse labor rights, all else equal. Of course, this empirical strategy requires separating FDI flows according to motivation, which likely requires firm-level surveys or interviews. In addition, we could investigate whether labor rights violations are more likely to occur – or, at least, more likely to be reported – in certain firms or industries. We also could ask whether firms in labor-intensive sectors have different attitudes regarding labor costs and labor laws than do firms in other sectors. Firm-level empirical studies may be an ideal tool,[19] but they are beyond the scope of this book.

In the short run, a more tractable strategy is to consider whether there is a relationship between labor rights outcomes and the distribution of direct investment by sector. Before considering this evidence, it is important to

---

[19] Brady and Wallace (2000), however, question the use of micro-level (firm or industry) data on workers' outcomes; if foreign participation changes norms and practices regarding labor throughout the economy, as they argue, it is reasonable to focus the analysis on country-level outcomes.

note that the labor rights indicators introduced in Chapter 4 measure the overall respect for collective labor rights in a nation rather than collective rights at the sectoral (or at the subcontractor versus foreign-owned) level. They offer a picture of the pattern of collective labor rights in a given country, and how this evolves over time, but they do not indicate whether violations occur more frequently in labor-intensive sectors, export-oriented industries, or subcontractor-owned firms. The hypotheses introduced in this chapter, though, suggest that violations may well cluster in particular sectors (or in facilities owned by particular source countries).

If, for instance, we consider the information (from the State Department, ILO, and ICFTU) used to generate the labor rights indicator for Thailand, we find that of the thirty-seven violations of rights in practice reported in the 1993–2002 period, 51 percent (nineteen violations) occurred in the textile sector. Among these thirty-seven violations, six of the firms were foreign-owned, and another eleven were subcontractors for foreign corporations; of the remaining firms, six were identified as export-oriented producers. In total, then, 62 percent of firms with violations were involved in global production, albeit in different ways. Similarly, for collective labor rights violations reported in Mexico,[20] six of eighteen occurred in foreign-owned firms that subcontract for MNCs, and another seven of eighteen occurred in MNC-owned subsidiaries or operations. Only five of the violations for which details were reported occurred in the public sector, or in Mexican-owned firms. At the sectoral level, the most common locations of violations were automobiles and automotive parts (five of eighteen) and electronics (four of eighteen), with two violations occurring in the textile sector.

Whereas the collection of firm- and sectoral-level labor rights data is left as a task for future research, we can assess whether country-years marked by a greater specialization in capital- and technology-intensive activities also are characterized by greater protections of collective labor rights. If our expectations are correct, we should observe a correlation between specialization in high-technology exports and labor rights protections and, conversely, a relationship between a focus on low-technology exports and labor rights violations. Figure 6.1 divides the country-years in our sample into four quartiles, based on the percentage of manufactured exports accounted for by high-technology products.[21] This figure includes average labor rights outcomes both for developing countries and

---

[20] In this case, from 1992–2006, and drawn largely from ICFTU reports.
[21] Data for this figure come from Statistics Canada's *World Trade Analyzer* database.

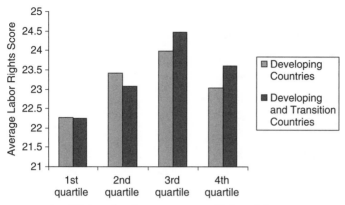

FIGURE 6.1. High-technology exports and labor rights outcomes.

for developing *plus* transition economies. For both groups, a similar pattern holds: Collective labor rights protections are lowest among those countries in the first quartile (an average labor rights score of 22.3 in developing nations and 22.2 in developing plus transition economies). The average level of labor rights protections increases for country-years in the second and third quartiles of high-technology exports. Interestingly, nations in the fourth quartile display average labor rights scores that are lower than those in the third quartile. The most pronounced difference (and the one that is statistically most significant among developing nations), though, is between those country-years in the first quartile of high-technology exports and those in all other quartiles.

Figure 6.2 also divides our sample into quartiles, in this case according to the percentage of low-technology products that comprise a given country-year's exports. The low-technology category includes goods such as apparel and footwear and therefore captures the notion that a specialization in labor-intensive production is linked with labor rights violations. Figure 6.2 reports overall average labor rights scores as well as the average scores for the practical and legal elements of the collective labor rights indicator. Country-years with the lowest reliance on low-technology exports have the highest average respect for collective labor rights (an average score of 24.5; when transition nations are included, the average score is 24.2). Country-years falling in the second quartile of low-technology exports have slightly lower average scores (23.7), as do those in the third quartile (22.7). The lowest labor rights scores characterize those country-years with the highest (fourth quartile) dependence on low-technology export products (an average of 21.5 in developing

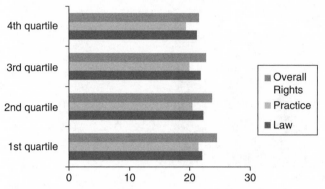

FIGURE 6.2. Low-technology exports and labor rights outcomes, developing nations.

nations and a mean of 21.8 when transition economies are included). The averages for the first and fourth quartiles are significantly different, at a 95 percent confidence level, from the remainder of the country-years in the sample. Turning to labor rights in practice, it also is those country-years in the fourth quartile of low-technology exports that have significantly lower scores. The average "labor rights practice" score for the first quartile of country-years is 21.4, compared with a mean of 19.4 for the fourth quartile country-years. In general, then, these graphs imply that country-years with more capital-intensive exports have better labor rights outcomes, on average, whereas country-years with greater labor-intensive exports have worse labor rights outcomes.

For a more systematic analysis of the impact of a country's production profile on its labor rights outcomes, we can include measures of economic structure in our estimations of labor rights outcomes (as developed and presented in Chapter 5). The most relevant indicators for testing Hypothesis 6.1 – the "structure of economies" proposition – are those that provide information about an economy's overall industrial orientation, as well as the types of industries and products on which a nation's exports are based. When we add such indicators to the main statistical models presented in Chapter 5, a mixed picture emerges.[22] Many indicators of economic structure are *not* significantly related to labor rights outcomes. These include the size (as a percentage of GDP) of the agricultural sector (n = 1236); the size of the manufacturing sector (n = 1205);

[22] To avoid problems of collinearity and to maximize the number of observations included in each estimation, the economic structure indicators are added one at a time to the overall model (Model 1) reported in Chapter 5.

and the percentage of manufacturing exports in the high-technology sector (n = 522).

At the same time, however, there appears to be a significant and positive relationship between extractive industry-related variables and labor rights outcomes.[23] Indeed, the positive and significant effect of these variables exists, not only for the overall labor rights indicator, but also for the separate measure of labor rights practices. This result lends some support to the positive effects of capital-intensive production. Natural resource extraction tends to be very capital-intensive; and given that natural resource endowments exist in some countries but not in others, multinationals are less able to threaten exit as they might do in manufacturing (also see Kobrin 1987). Several multinational oil companies, including British Petroleum, Royal Dutch Shell, and Total, also have come under the spotlight of transnational human rights activists, perhaps generating additional incentives to improve workers' rights. The link between extractive-sector production and labor rights also is interesting in light of research linking natural resource wealth with lower rates of economic growth (Sachs and Warner 2001) as well as with lower levels of democratic development (Ross 2001, 2008).

Perhaps even more interestingly, from the perspective of Hypothesis 6.1, is the relationship among production in textiles, trade, and labor rights outcomes. In the first model (Model 1) reported in Table 6.1, a measure of the importance of textile and apparel production to the economy (again, as a percentage of GDP), as well as an interaction between textiles and trade openness, are added to the model of overall labor rights outcomes. Given the centrality of textile production to recent consumer awareness and corporate social responsibility campaigns (see Chapter 3), the effect of the textile sector's size on labor rights may be contingent on a country's level of integration (trade) with the global economy.

Indeed, the results suggest a negative relationship between the size of the textile sector and labor rights outcomes, just as Hypothesis 6.1 anticipates. In country-years with very low (or no) trade openness, a

---

[23] The results using extractive industries as a percentage of GDP are based on 1,205 country-years (eighty-eight nations). The trade coefficient remains negative and significant, while the FDI flows coefficient becomes statistically insignificant but still positively signed. The model that includes extractive sector exports (as a percentage of total exports) includes 755 country-years (seventy-five nations). The trade and FDI flow coefficients remain statistically significant (negative and positive, respectively). Furthermore, if an alternative "percentage of exports of ores and metals" measure is used, the results are very similar (n = 889). In all three cases, results on other variables remain, as in the main model reported in Chapter 5. These results are available on request.

TABLE 6.1. *Labor Rights, Sectoral Profiles, and FDI Source Country*

Independent Variable	Model 1	Model 2	Model 3	Model 4
FDI Inflows	0.1978	0.2694	0.1546	0.1526
	(0.2258)	(0.2067)	(0.0986)	(0.0969)
FDI Stock	0.0163	−0.0012	0.0056	0.0073
	(0.0221)	(0.0123)	(0.0157)	(0.0158)
External Debt	−0.0040	0.0004	0.0043	0.0042
	(0.0124)	(0.0053)	(0.0054)	(0.0054)
Trade	−0.0763***	−0.0198*	−0.0255**	−0.0262*
	(0.0194)	(0.0121)	(0.0132)	(0.0140)
Regional Average, Labor Standards	0.4338***	0.4420***	0.4063***	0.4082***
	(0.0888)	(0.0877)	(0.0866)	(0.0852)
Economic Peers' Labor Standards	0.1161	0.2300**	0.1394	0.0712
	(0.1048)	(0.1038)	(0.1129)	(0.1143)
Human Rights NGOs	−0.1504	−0.3949	−0.5373	−0.5469
	(0.3265)	(0.3739)	(0.4783)	(0.4582)
NGOs*FDI Flows	−0.1498*	−0.1146	−0.0731	−0.0746
	(0.0856)	(0.0820)	(0.0546)	(0.0498)
Income Per Capita	−0.5715	−1.5027***	−1.0510**	−0.9441**
	(0.8191)	(0.3922)	(0.0132)	(0.4259)
Economic Growth	0.0601	0.0552	0.0902**	0.0827*
	(0.0442)	(0.0456)	(0.0443)	(0.0427)
Population Size	−1.5975***	−1.4227***	−1.4186***	−1.3022
	(0.4032)	(0.3073)	(0.3604)	(0.3889)
Democracy	0.0933	0.1772***	0.1885***	0.1844***
	(0.0685)	(0.0475)	(0.0625)	(0.0601)
Civil Conflict	−2.2979**	−2.0016***	−1.5183*	−1.5830*
	(0.9495)	(0.7102)	(0.9034)	(0.9026)
Textiles/GDP	−0.9169*			
	(0.4942)			
Textiles*Trade	0.0094*			
	(0.0050)			
Chemical Products Exports		0.0812*		
		(0.0457)		
FDI Stock in Transportation Manufacturing			0.1859***	
			(0.0705)	
FDI Stock from U.S. (Percent)				−0.0322***
				(0.0119)
Constant	47.8314***	44.6030***	44.1784***	46.2070***
	(9.3715)	(7.0468)	(8.6713)	(9.3874)
N	623	899	696	763
Number of Countries	65	80	79	79
R²	0.47	0.46	0.44	0.46
Rho	0.58	0.56	0.55	0.56
Wald Chi²	257.44	359.14	205.75	206.78

Note: Standard errors are in parentheses. Positive coefficients imply lower levels of violations. ***p<.01, **p<.05, *p<.10.

specialization in textile production augurs poorly for labor rights. As in the models reported in Chapter 5, trade openness on its own (where, given the interaction term, textile production is zero) is negatively and significantly related to labor rights outcomes. At the same time, however, the significant result on the interaction term (trade openness*textiles) suggests a joint *positive* impact on workers' rights. Country-years characterized by larger textile sectors and higher degrees of trade openness have better, not worse, labor rights outcomes. Comparable results, in terms of signs and significance, obtain if we use an alternate measure of the textile sector: textiles as a percentage of total manufactures. In addition, a similar set of results emerges if we use labor rights laws, rather than the overall labor rights indicator, as the dependent variable.[24] The implied effect of a one standard deviation change in the size of the textile sector on labor rights is greater than that of the textiles*trade interaction (−1.85 versus 1.35).[25] Whereas these results are based on a smaller number of countries and country-years than the main statistical model, this result suggests that engagement with the global economy can mitigate, rather than intensify, the effects of specialization in labor-intensive production. Perhaps, then, recent NGO-backed efforts at corporate social responsibility and consumer labeling can be a fruitful means of improving workers' rights in developing nations.

Turning to data on export profiles, I assess the impact on labor rights of the percentage of a country's exports in various broad sectors, for which UNCTAD reports export profile information. These include food products; agricultural raw materials; fuels; ores and metals; manufactured goods; chemical products; machinery and transport equipment; and other manufactures. In terms of our hypotheses, we expect a positive impact of machinery and transport on labor rights; given the results regarding the extractive sector, a positive relationship also could exist between labor rights and ores and metals as well as fuels. The effect of manufactured goods on labor rights, however, may not be straightforward: UNCTAD's manufacturing category includes industries that are labor-intensive (such as textiles) as well as those that tend to be capital-intensive.

In fact, adding each of the export profile indicators to the model (again, one indicator at a time) generates very mixed support for Hypothesis 6.1.

---

[24] There is, however, no significant relationship between the size of the textile sector or the interaction between the size of the textile sector and trade openness, on the one hand, and collective labor rights practices, on the other.

[25] Note that an interaction between FDI and the size of the textile sector, when included, is not associated significantly with labor rights outcomes.

There are no statistically significant associations between agricultural raw materials, fuels, (all) manufactured goods, or machinery and transport equipment, on the one hand, and collective labor rights, on the other. At the same time, the analyses reveal positive and statistically significant relationships between export shares in ores and metals and labor rights as well as between the share of exports in chemical products (which includes pharmaceuticals) and labor rights. If both ores/metals and chemicals are considered capital-intensive sectors, these results are consistent with Hypothesis 6.1. The latter estimation is reported as Model 2 in Table 6.1. Again, despite the decline in the number of country-years included, the overall negative and significant effect of trade on labor rights outcomes remains. The result on overall FDI inflows, however, is less robust to the inclusion of the sectoral variable: The coefficient remains positive, but falls far below conventional levels of statistical significance. A similar pattern of results – including a significant and positive coefficient on the chemical products variable – also emerges when collective labor rights laws are used as the dependent variable.

By contrast, there are negative and significant associations between export share in food products, and export share in other manufactures (including all goods other than chemicals and transport equipment), and collective labor rights. Given that the latter category combines both labor- and capital-intensive industries, it is difficult to draw a connection between this result and our first hypothesis. More broadly, each of these categories of export profile data combines several sectors and products. This allows for consistency of measurement across countries (given that national statistical offices often use slightly different industry classifications), but it limits our ability to evaluate the sectoral effects of production profiles.

Finally, when a measure of the ratio of low-technology exports (or, specifically, of textile exports) to total exports, as in Figure 6.2, is added to the main statistical model, it is significantly and negatively associated with labor rights; in a multivariate context, there is again a connection between low-technology exports and labor rights outcomes. Adding this variable, though, leads the main multinational production variables (trade and direct investment) to become statistically insignificant, and it reduces the number of country-years in the estimations by more than half. Overall, these results are only suggestive: Multinational production and production for export may well vary in their effects on workers' rights, but in complicated ways.

The data limitations for cross-sectional time series evaluations are even more pronounced for measures related to Hypothesis 6.2. Most developing nations collect data on aggregate flows and stocks of foreign direct investment. However – while improving in recent years[26] – data on the sectoral (and source country; see Section III) breakdowns are few and far between. Whereas a few nations (Chile, Thailand, some countries in central Europe) have sector and/or source country FDI statistics dating to the 1980s or early 1990s, many others have begun to collect sectoral FDI data only since the mid-2000s. UNCTAD compiles national-level data as part of its *World Investment Directory*, but, for most countries, the data are not available annually; UNCTAD publishes data for each region on a rotating basis.[27] Each volume contains several years, so it is possible to construct time series, but these series are plagued by missing data and interruptions. Data on the amount of direct investment in various sectors (such as mining, textiles, and transportation manufacturing) are available for fewer than twenty developing countries for each year since 1990.

Another possibility for measuring by sector is to employ national statistics that record outward direct investment. Despite the recent growth in outward direct investment from, as well as some high-profile acquisitions by, a few middle-income nations (including Brazil, China, and Mexico), the bulk of FDI continues to originate in wealthy nations. Many home countries require domestically based firms to report on their foreign mergers, acquisitions, and greenfield direct investments.[28] By collecting these data for a variety of source countries, covering a significant portion of direct investment outflows, it is possible to build a dataset of FDI flows by sector to individual developing nations.[29]

In the analyses that follow, I utilize FDI data from government agencies of the three largest outward direct investors: the United States, the

---

[26] For instance, in generating statistics regarding sectoral patterns of FDI for its 2007 *World Investment Report*, UNCTAD relies on sectoral data that cover a total of fifty-four nations (high- as well as low- and middle-income) in 1990 and eighty-two countries in 2005.

[27] The Latin American volume, for instance, was published in 1994 and again in 2004.

[28] Note an additional problem with sectoral FDI data, either from host or home countries: In many cases, a firm's main production activities are focused on one sector (automobile manufacturing), but the firm outsources other types of operations (finance, accounting, and advertising) to foreign entities in other sectors. Many national measures of sectoral direct investment classify firms by their main industry so that the sectoral element of such transactions may be misclassified (WTO 2005).

[29] France, Germany, Italy, Japan, Norway, Spain, Sweden, the United Kingdom, and the United States collect outflow data by sector and source country, at annual or other

United Kingdom, and Japan. These three nations account for a considerable proportion of FDI to developing nations.[30] Unfortunately, the number of years for which all three source countries' data on FDI (especially FDI flows) are available is relatively small.[31] Data are available for several (but not all) economic sectors, including textiles and apparel, construction, transportation manufacturing, and electrical machinery. The data coverage is somewhat better for stocks (total accumulations) than for flows (investment in a given year) of direct investment; in both cases, though, the inclusion of sectoral variables in the statistical models dramatically reduces the number of country-years in the analyses.

Using these data, I conduct an initial evaluation of Hypothesis 6.2.[32] When the percentage of direct investment stock in textiles and apparel[33] is included in the regression analysis, it is not significantly related to collective labor rights. The textiles data are available for only a very small subset of country-years (n = 184, covering thirty-one nations), but they offer scant support for the claim that FDI in labor-intensive sectors has different effects than FDI overall.[34] On the other hand, when we add a measure of FDI stock in transportation manufacturing (the automobile sector) to the main model, that variable is positively and significantly related to labor rights outcomes. Data for direct investment in the automobile sector also are more widely available, allowing the inclusion of nearly 700 country-years (and seventy-nine countries). This estimation (Model 3) is reported in Table 6.1. The results provide some support for the notion that FDI in capital-intensive sectors has positive consequences – and different consequences than other types of FDI – for labor rights.[35] The coefficient estimate for the transportation manufacturing FDI variable

regular intervals. These nine countries accounted for 66 percent of OECD FDI outflows during the 1995–2004 period (OECD 2005). These data can be combined (with appropriate currency conversions) to create estimates of the dollar value of direct investment in developing countries. For a summary of national sources of FDI outflow data (often based on surveys of domestic firms), see Falzoni (2000).

[30] The correlation between the total stock of FDI from Japan, the United Kingdom, and the United States, on the one hand, and a country's overall stock of FDI is .55.

[31] A third potential source of data on sectoral FDI is the *World Investment Directory*, which provides data on FDI by sector for some countries and years. Its coverage, however, is even more limited.

[32] To avoid problems of collinearity and to maximize the number of observations, the sectoral FDI indicators are added one at a time to the overall model.

[33] The national FDI data treat textiles, apparel, and wood as a single category.

[34] When labor rights law or practice is used as a dependent variable, the relationship between textiles FDI and labor rights also is statistically insignificant.

[35] In a model that uses labor rights laws as the dependent variable, the transportation manufacturing FDI indicator also is positively and significantly linked with labor rights

implies a 0.80 point improvement in labor rights with a one standard deviation increase in that sector's FDI. This compares with a 0.96 deterioration in labor rights that is implied by the trade variable's coefficient estimate. The result for FDI in the automobile sector may reflect the relatively minor role that labor costs play in capital-intensive sectors as well as the demand for highly skilled (and, therefore, better-treated) workers in that industry (also see Silver 2003).[36]

In Model 3, overall trade remains negatively related to labor rights, whereas overall FDI flows (and stocks) are positively linked with rights. Only trade, however, remains statistically significant at conventional levels. Indeed, this is a more general pattern in the analyses that include sectoral and FDI profile variables: Overall FDI tends to be less robust to the inclusion of these measures than is trade, lending support to the notion that, whereas overall FDI may matter for labor rights, the specific type of direct investment may be even more important causally. All other coefficient estimates retain the signs and significances reported in Chapter 5; the rate of economic growth also becomes statistically significant.

Turning to another capital-intensive sector, the stock of direct investment in metals-related industries also is significantly and positively linked with collective labor rights.[37] This result obtains whether the dependent variable is overall labor rights, labor rights law, or labor rights practices. This result also is consistent with the notion of better labor rights protections in sectors with capital-intensive multinational investments. Further analyses suggest that nations with a higher percentage of FDI stock in electrical machinery manufacturing and those with greater FDI in construction also have better labor rights outcomes, all else equal. These estimates, however, are based on a very small number of observations and are not statistically significant at conventional confidence levels. These initial results therefore offer very modest support for the notion that FDI's effects on labor rights vary across economic sectors. Labor-intensive FDI may well have different effects than capital-intensive FDI.[38] Collection of better indicators of the sectoral composition of FDI

outcomes. It is not, however, a statistically significant correlate when we model labor rights practices.

[36] Silver's analysis of longer-run trends in the global automobile industry suggests a mixed impact of multinational production on workers. MNCs responded to various waves of labor unrest by moving production to new locations. Workers in the original locations suffered as a result, whereas workers in new locations benefited.

[37] These results are not reported but are available on request. The model includes 653 country-years and seventy-nine countries.

[38] On differences in firm strategies, based on capital intensity, see Helpman et al. (2004).

(via an expanded set of source country data, supplementing that from the United States, the United Kingdom, and Japan; or, for more recent years, from national sources) would allow us to evaluate Hypothesis 6.2 more systematically.

Another body of empirical evidence employs firm-level surveys to assess whether there is variation, based on industrial sector, export activities, and foreign ownership, in business views regarding labor-related issues. Are firms in skill-intensive industries less concerned about labor costs and labor regulations than firms in unskilled sectors, as Hypothesis 6.1 implies? Are firms that are more export-dependent more concerned with labor-related issues? Through its Enterprise Surveys program, the World Bank conducts opinion analyses of firms in various developing and transition economies.[39] The surveys were first conducted in 2002; as of December 2008, surveys had been conducted in a total of 106 nations, covering nearly 85,000 firms.[40] Some countries (particularly post-Communist nations) have had two or three waves of surveys, while others have had only one. The surveys usually are weighted toward firms in specific economic sectors, often those with ties to the global economy, such as textiles, electronics, and pharmaceuticals. Survey methodologies and questions vary somewhat across nations (although more recent survey instruments have tended to include a standardized set, or subset, of questions). Respondents provide general information about the firm (size, sector, main products, and export markets); employment and labor costs (total employment and wage costs, with some distinctions between skilled and unskilled labor); and the extent to which various factors create impediments to doing business. The latter usually includes at least one survey item dealing with labor laws and regulations.[41]

---

[39] These include the Investment Climate Surveys, conducted in Latin America, Asia, and Sub-Saharan Africa, as well as the Business Environment and Enterprise Surveys, conducted jointly with the European Bank for Reconstruction and Development (EBRD) in transition economies. Firm survey data and questionnaires are available through the World Bank's Enterprise Survey Portal, https://www.enterprisesurveys.org/portal/Default. aspx. The core firm survey is available at http://www.enterprisesurveys.org/documents/ Manufacturing_Sector_Module_coded.pdf. The World Bank makes these data available, with prior consent, by individual country survey (for some nations, surveys have been conducted in multiple years) or for the entire set of firms that use the standardized survey module.

[40] For a summary of overall firm characteristics, by survey country and year, see https:// www.enterprisesurveys.org/documents/datadetails.xls

[41] A notable exception is China, where the 2003 survey did not ask firms to report their views on government policies, including labor issues.

In order to assess the extent to which attitudes regarding labor-related issues vary among firms, I assemble data from the first round of surveys (2002 to 2004, which most closely parallels the time period of the collective labor rights data), covering five Asian nations – Bangladesh, Cambodia, India, the Philippines, and Sri Lanka. These nations produce multinationally in a variety of product categories, including electronics and textiles. Indeed, the surveys tend to focus on firms in such sectors: More than half of respondent firms in Bangladesh are in the garment (306 firms of the 1,001 total firms) or textile (262 firms) industries. In India, 282 firms (from a total of 1,827 respondent firms) are in the electronics sector, whereas 380 firms are active in chemicals and pharmaceuticals.

These five surveys provide data on 4,500 firms in total. Approximately 35 percent of respondent firms employ 20 or fewer workers; 27 percent of firms employ 20 to 100 workers; and a further 32 percent have more than 100 employees.[42] Approximately one-quarter of firms are identified as exporters, whereas just slightly less than 10 percent of firms are foreign-owned (versus domestically owned). By examining firm views on labor regulations,[43] as well as rates of union activity, we can gain additional insight into how the effects of global production on labor might vary across sectors.

Summary statistics suggest that, in general, firms that are involved in the global economy differ – often significantly – from domestically oriented firms. First, firms with foreign ownership are more likely to report that labor regulations present an obstacle to their operation and growth. The average "labor rights as an obstacle" score for firms with more than 10 percent foreign ownership is 1.44 (n = 393), on a four-point scale, compared with an average of 1.16 (n = 3768) for other firms.[44] If the cutoff for foreign ownership is raised to 25 percent, this difference persists. Both foreign- and domestically owned firms,[45] however, report very similar views

---

[42] Percentages do not sum to 100 percent because a few firms did not provide data on descriptive indicators.

[43] Respondents were asked to indicate whether various factors pose obstacles to their firm's growth and operation. Possible answers ranged from zero ("no obstacle") to four ("very severe obstacle"). Most national surveys include among the set of possible obstacles "labor regulations" and "skills and education of available workers" as well as items dealing with infrastructure, taxation, and the macroeconomy.

[44] Firms were asked whether competing firms avoid labor and social security regulations. Responses ranged from zero ("not at all") to four ("to a great degree"). This question was included in Bangladesh and Cambodia. Firms that export their main product averaged a score of 2.14 (n = 70); the average score for other firms was 1.47 (n = 394).

[45] Unfortunately, firms are not asked the nationality of their foreign owners; such information would be useful for assessing Hypotheses 6.3 and 6.4.

(averaging 1.13 for both sets) on the extent to which the skills and education of available workers are obstacles to business operations.

Second, firms that produce for export express greater concerns about labor regulations. The average level of concern about labor regulations is 1.51 among firms (n = 837) whose main product is exported, compared with an average of 1.06 among firms who do not export their main product (n = 2131). The former set of entrepreneurs also worries more, on average, that competing firms fail to enforce labor regulations. Among firms with a majority of sales accounted for by exports, the average level of concern with labor regulations is 1.43 (n = 1046); firms with less than 50 percent of total sales as exports average 1.10 (n = 2970) on the labor regulations item. Again, such firms also are more likely to report that competing firms avoid enforcing labor regulations. Similarly, firms that use EPZs for part or all of their production report a greater degree of concern about labor market regulations, as well as about minimum wage laws, than do other firms. EPZ-involved firms, of course, are focused mostly on the global economy, with an average of 68 percent of their sales accounted for by exports.[46]

Third, dividing firms by sector also reveals differences in attitudes and labor practices. Table 6.2 classifies firms by sector – textiles and apparel, electronics, and all other firms.[47] Firms in electronics and textiles participate in export markets at a higher rate (21 percent of total sales among electronics firms are exports; exports account for 46 percent of sales by textiles firms). Such firms also report higher rates of foreign ownership (17.3 percent, on average, in electronics; 9.5 percent in textiles; and 2.8 percent in firms overall). Firms in the textile sector do, in fact, report higher labor costs than other firms: Labor costs average 23 percent of total costs in textiles, compared with 20 percent in electronics and 19 percent in other firms. Hence, textile firms might experience greater temptation to repress collective labor rights. Firms in the textile and apparel sector also report greater concern with labor regulations than do nontextile firms (1.27 versus 1.08, in terms of the "obstacle" measure). Interestingly, firms in the electronics sector – a less labor-intensive sector – also report a higher degree of concern with labor market regulations (1.33). Both electronics and textiles firms are more likely than other firms (means of

---

[46] Firms were asked whether they use EPZs on the Bangladesh and India surveys. Among firms that do not use EPZs, exports account for 28.5 percent of total sales on average.

[47] Because of cross-national differences in survey items, the number of respondent firms varies by question.

TABLE 6.2. *Firm Responses and Characteristics, by Sector*

	Textiles & Apparel	Electronics	All Other Firms
Labor Costs, as % of Total Costs	23.35% (n = 1063)	19.78% (n = 226)	19.34% (n = 832)
Labor Regulations as Obstacle (0 to 4)	1.27 (n = 1529)	1.33 (n = 369)	1.08 (n = 2055)
Competitors Avoid Labor Regulations (0 to 4)	1.81 (n = 211)	1.91 (n = 70)	1.33 (n = 471)
Is Your Plant's Workforce Unionized? (% Yes)	50% (n = 1340)	63% (n = 352)	39% (n = 1768)
If Unionized, % Workers Who are Union Members	9.82% (n = 1596)	4.82% (n = 397)	8.56% (n = 2153)
Days Lost to Strikes by Employees at Firm, Previous Year	1.35 (n = 159)	1.2 (n = 5)	0.18 (n = 513)
Exports as Percent of Total Sales	46.2% (n = 1598)	20.5% (n = 393)	9.4% (n = 2118)
Percent of Firm That is Foreign-Owned	9.54% (n = 1655)	17.34% (n = 387)	2.83% (n = 2177)

1.81 and 1.91, versus 1.33 for other firms) to suggest that competing firms avoid enforcing labor and social security regulations.

In terms of unionization within their production facilities, firms in both electronics and textiles sectors are more likely to have a union presence than other firms; 50 percent of firms in textiles and 63 percent of firms in electronics report that their workforce is unionized. Thirty-nine percent of other firms are unionized. In textile firms with unions, a higher percentage of workers (9.82 percent, on average) are union members than in electronics (4.82 percent) or in other firms (8.56 percent). Moreover, firms in textiles and electronics are more likely than others to lose employee working days to strikes. So, despite the possibility that textile firms will have greater incentives to repress labor rights, unions often are able to operate in such firms. One possible explanation for this pattern is that internationally oriented firms – either those with significant foreign ownership or those with significant export activities – are more likely to allow labor organization, given the "spotlight" that accompanies global production.[48] In fact, as the final two rows of Table 6.2 indicate,

[48] Another possibility is that some unions are employer-dominated entities, which do not provide real representation to workers. See FLA (2005), Moran (2002), Robertson (2007), as well as Chapter 7.

foreign ownership and involvement in foreign markets (via export) are markedly more common for textiles and electronics firms than they are for other types of firms sampled.

In the sample generally, both foreign ownership and participation in export markets are associated with greater levels of firm unionization as well as with higher levels of union activity. Strike days, for instance, are greater among firms that use EPZs (0.45 per year, versus 0.21 per year in other firms); they also are greater in firms with significant foreign ownership and in those with higher participation in export markets. In terms of unionization, 55 percent of export-oriented firms are unionized, compared with 43 percent of other firms. Among firms with labor unions, the rate of union membership also is higher in export-oriented firms (15.1 percent versus 8.8 percent in other firms). These patterns may reflect the fact that foreign-oriented firms – be they owned by domestic firms or by multinationals – permit greater collective labor mobilization than do domestically owned firms. Were this true, it would suggest that multinational production, regardless of the mode of entry, can be a boon to workers in developing nations. Alternatively, this pattern could reflect demand for labor representation: If workers in foreign-oriented firms have more complaints than their domestic counterparts, they may be more likely to strike and to unionize.

These surveys, then, suggest that participation in the global economy – either via foreign ownership or by export sales – is linked with greater firm concerns about labor market regulations, but also associated with a greater extent of organized labor activity. The key factor for workers may be whether their plant participates in any form in the global economy rather than whether their plant is foreign-owned or a domestically owned subcontractor. An optimistic reading would suggest that global participation is more likely to bring an upgrading of labor rights practices rather than a competitive lowering of standards.

The evidence presented in this section offers modest support for the claim that the linkages between collective labor rights, on the one hand, and global production, on the other, vary according to economic sector. Foreign direct investment in textiles and apparel may, for instance, have different implications for workers than does direct investment in pharmaceuticals or extractive industries (also see Silver 2003). Additionally, the broad sector profile of a country's economy may be just as important to workers' capacity to achieve collective rights as a country's degree and type of overall economic openness.

A more complete evaluation of these claims, however, requires additional empirical analyses, ideally using higher-quality and more broadly-available data on production profiles and foreign direct investment by sector. As low- and middle-income nations increasingly collect and report such data, the opportunities for such cross-sectional time series studies will improve. Moreover, at the individual country level, a subset of governments now collect and publish inward direct investment data that are sorted by country of origin (source) and industrial sector (usually corresponding to two-digit SITC codes). The advantage of these measures is that they require little manipulation or conversion; the disadvantages are that the methodology for collecting them often varies across countries and that data often are unavailable prior to the mid- to late 1990s. Such country-level data may be most appropriate to use in country case studies, allowing us to assess whether changes in collective labor rights laws and practices follow from changes in direct investment profiles (also see Chapter 7). Future research also would do well to measure labor rights outcomes, not only at the national level, but also at the sectoral level.

Additionally, even *within* broad industrial sectors, the motivations of foreign firms may vary. For instance, different types of extractive-sector firms may have different reasons for investing abroad. Those involved in exploration and mining are driven by the search for resources. Other extractive-sector firms, particularly those involved in processing or early-stage manufacturing, could be motivated more by efficiency and cost considerations. Of course, recent foreign investments in extractive industries by state-owned companies suggest yet another motivation related to the strategic control of natural resources (UNCTAD 2007).

Moreover, returning to the mode of entry literature discussed in Chapter 3, firms' characteristics and motivations vary among firms within the same sector. Some of this variation generates differences in firms' propensity to operate abroad. Models of monopolistic competition and heterogeneous firms, for instance, posit a relationship between firms' degree of productivity and their international strategies (Melitz 2003). High productivity firms find it profitable to engage with foreign markets, whereas lower productivity firms do not. The most productive firms serve foreign markets via subsidiary sales (and, therefore, direct investment relationships); lower productivity firms serve foreign markets using exports; and the lowest productivity firms serve only the domestic market. The implication, then, is that MNCs are more productive, across sectors, than exporters that are not multinationals; and exporters are more productive than firms that serve only domestic markets (also see Antràs 2005; Helpman 2006; Helpman et al. 2004). Hence, within the same sector, foreign-owned firms are different from domestic-owned ones. Foreign firms tend to be more capital- and technology-intensive in their production processes; this often means that they also employ more skilled workers than their domestic counterparts (Jensen and Rosas 2007).

Such differences among firms may extend to cost- and labor-related considerations, leading to firm-level diversity in implications for collective labor rights. Again, this task – unpacking multinational and exporting firms and treating them as political actors at the firm as well as industrial level – is an important subject for future comparative political economy research. In the remainder of this chapter, however, I examine another dimension of broad-range heterogeneity in global production, one based on differences in source (home) countries.

III. SOURCE COUNTRY VARIATION: BEST PRACTICES AND NATIONAL FIRMS

A second axis for variation within global production is firms' nationality. In Chapters 2 and 3, I suggest that foreign-owned firms may act differently, in terms of concerns regarding labor rights and in terms of the tendency to bring best practices with them, than domestically owned firms. Just as foreign firms may vary according to economic sector, they also may differ on the basis of their nationality. Variation in national "corporate cultures" (Hall and Soskice 2001; Kreps 1990) can include diverse views regarding workers' rights. Host economies attract FDI from an array of home countries; source country investment patterns often are the result of long-standing economic, political, and cultural ties (i.e., Bandelj 2008). Therefore, these differences in home country practices can have important consequences for labor rights.

A. Theoretical Implications

Despite the increasing integration of the global economy and the multinational nature of many firms, there remains room for "national models" of capitalism and for corporate practices that vary across countries (Berger and Dore 1996; Doremus et al. 1999; Gourevitch and Shinn 2005).[49] Recent literature in comparative political economy takes as a

---

[49] Doremus et al. (1999) argue that, despite increased financial globalization, multinational firms retain many of their distinct national characteristics; these generate differences in

starting point the existence of two broad models of economic organization among wealthy countries – a "liberal market economy" model and a "coordinated market economy model" (i.e., Hall and Soskice 2001; Mares 2003). Each model is taken to embody a different constellation of institutions as well as a different function for governments and markets. In short, the assumption is that the coordinated market economies of Continental Europe tend to be more attuned to the provision of labor rights, ranging from social security benefits to the freedom of association. Attention to labor issues provides incentives for workers to acquire firm- and industry-specific skills, thereby benefiting employers. On the other hand, the Anglo-American liberal market economies provide high degrees of labor market flexibility, which allows firms to make changes easily to their production strategies and to keep their labor costs relatively low. In such economies, attention to labor rights and to labor organization, is much more muted.[50]

These differences may persist when firms operate abroad. For example, Garcia-Johnson's (2000) study of U.S. chemical firm affiliates in Mexico and Brazil finds that firms take home-country environmental practices with them rather than adopting (sometimes cheaper) host-country practices. Consistent with this logic is a 2001 MIGA survey, which asked firms to rank the most important factors in their selection of investment sites (MIGA 2002). Whereas this and other surveys of MNCs tend not to differentiate by industry, they do differentiate by firm headquarters location. North American firms were more likely than their European and Asian counterparts to cite reductions in costs as an important motive for overseas investment. Moreover, North American and Asian firms reported higher levels of concern with information about labor costs, as well as with labor relations and regulations, than their European counterparts.[51] Furthermore, in a quantitative, cross-national study, Prakash and Potoski (2007) find that the national identity of a country's FDI partners affects host country adoption of environmental standards (ISO 14001). The higher the rate of adoption in home countries (that is, the higher the

corporate governance, intrafirm trade, and research and development. On the extent to which Japanese multinationals operate differently from other MNCs, see Brady and Wallace (2000).

[50] Of course, as patterns of corporate ownership become more international, the impact of "national" firms may become less important. For instance, Colonomos and Santiso (2005) report that, of the 120 French firms that make up the Societe Bourses Francaise (SBF) 120 index, Anglo-American shareholders are relatively significant in about 25 percent of firms.

[51] MIGA (2002), 16, 30, Appendix 2. Hatem (1998, 159) reports a similar finding.

"bilateral FDI context" score), the higher the rate of adoption in the host country.[52]

We might expect, then, that FDI from different source countries will affect labor rights outcomes differently. Whereas drawing broad distinctions runs the risk of oversimplification, firms from continental European countries should, all else equal, demonstrate a greater concern for protecting collective labor rights. Firms from the United States and the United Kingdom should, on the other hand, be less concerned with providing and protecting such rights.

> *Hypothesis 6.3*: *Developing nations that attract a higher proportion of direct investment flows from continental European nations (versus from Anglo-American and Asian sources) will have better labor rights, all else equal.*

Certainly, there are other mechanisms that may lead to variation, by home country, in firms' attitudes abroad. If a nation's firms have a long experience operating in a particular country, such firms may experience lower levels of economic uncertainty and higher levels of information. They will be less deterred by political risk. Accordingly, Meyer's (2001) survey of European firms finds that German MNCs have better information about and deeper contacts with Eastern European nations, rendering them more likely to opt for direct ownership (rather than subcontracting) in transition-country markets. Another possibility, drawing on the literature linking security considerations with economic interchange, is that MNCs are more likely, all else equal, to invest in countries with which their government has a military alliance (Gowa 1994), or that such firms will be less concerned with shorter-term political instability in the host country. I leave these possibilities as topics for future research.

A second broad way in which I distinguish among source countries is to contrast high-income with low- and middle-income home countries. Most FDI to date – and global production generally – has occurred among developed nations, as firms in the United States invest in Europe and Japan, or vice versa. Even in terms of FDI to developing nations, the bulk of investment continues to originate in wealthy nations. However, the proportion of direct investment originating in developing countries has grown over time (UNCTAD 2009). In particular, middle-income developing nations such as Brazil, China, India, and Mexico increasingly

---

[52] At the same time, a country's overall level of FDI stock is *not* significantly related to its rate of ISO adoption.

serve as sources of, as well as destinations for, FDI. Given the general contrast between the protection of labor rights in developing countries and that in developed nations, as highlighted in Chapter 4 (the variation within each group notwithstanding), this trend may have implications for collective labor rights outcomes. That is, developing country MNCs might take different sets of best practices to new production locations (also see Greenhill et al. 2009):

> **Hypothesis 6.4**: *Developing nations that attract a higher proportion of direct investment flows from other developing nations (versus from developed-country sources) will have worse labor rights, all else equal.*

B. Empirical Assessment

As one means of evaluating Hypothesis 6.3, I use the U.K., U.S., and Japanese national data on FDI outflows, described above. Again, data coverage is much better for accumulated stocks of FDI than for annual flows. Model 4, reported in Table 6.1, addresses the question of whether nations with greater FDI shares from the United States (versus from the United Kingdom and Japan, implicitly) differ significantly in their collective labor rights outcomes. The results indicate that this is, in fact, the case: There is a significant and negative relationship between the proportion of a country's FDI stock from U.S. sources and its collective labor rights outcomes. The coefficient on the trade openness variable remains negative and statistically significant, whereas those on the overall FDI variables are still positive but not statistically significant. The significant relationship between FDI shares from the U.S. and labor rights also appears in estimations that use collective labor rights law, or collective labor rights practices, as the dependent variable. If we replace the U.S. FDI measure with a measure of direct investment shares from Japan, we find a significant relationship in the opposite direction: Developing nations that attract more investment from Japan have better labor rights outcomes, all else equal. There is no statistically significant relationship between direct investment from the United Kingdom and labor rights outcomes.[53] Although data from Japan, the United Kingdom, and the United States provide better country-year coverage than do inflow data from

---

[53] Results of these additional cross-sectional time series models are available on request.

low- and middle-income countries, they (obviously) include measures for only three source nations.

Another possibility, then, is to use FDI outflow data from the OECD's *International Direct Investment Statistics*. This database provides information on outflows from OECD members to a relatively small set of developing nations. Using these data, we can measure the percentage of a nation's direct investment from Germany, from continental Europe, or from various other individual developed nations. Given that OECD membership now includes countries such as Mexico, South Korea, and Turkey, we also can generate a (very limited) measure of a country's direct investment from middle-income nations (relevant to Hypothesis 6.4). The drawback, however, is that these data are available for a very small number of country-years, generally 150 to 275, and for a limited number of host countries (seventeen to twenty nations). This greatly dilutes confidence that the results from these estimations represent effects in developing nations generally or that the pattern of missing data is random.

When these measures are added to the main cross-sectional time series model, there is a positive and significant relationship between direct investment flows from Germany and labor rights outcomes, something a "varieties of capitalism" account would anticipate.[54] When FDI from Continental Europe as a whole is included in the statistical analyses, however, the estimate is significant only for labor rights laws and not for overall collective labor rights or for labor rights practices. In terms of direct investment from middle-income nations (Hypothesis 6.4), there is no significant association between the proportion of flows from developing nations (in the OECD data, Mexico, South Korea, and Turkey) and overall labor rights outcomes.[55] A negative and significant association between labor rights *laws* and the proportion of a country's direct investment flows from Mexico, South Korea, and Turkey exists; again, however, this result is based on a very limited number of observations.

Given the constraints of FDI statistics, a more appropriate strategy for evaluating Hypotheses 6.3 and 6.4 could be to employ case studies of foreign-owned production in particular developing nations. Where time series data on FDI by source country is available – as it is for a few developing nations – we could investigate whether labor rights outcomes

[54] This result is based on 184 country-years and seventeen nations. When labor rights practices are used as the dependent variable, a similar relationship obtains.
[55] Similarly, there is no relationship between FDI from the individual nations – Mexico, South Korea, and Turkey – and overall labor rights outcomes.

change as the sources of FDI shift. When FDI comes from Korean textile firms rather than from U.S. textile firms, for instance, does El Salvador's labor rights situation change? Does reliance on FDI from other developing nations – rather than from high-income nations – lead to worse labor rights outcomes?

Indeed, several recent case studies focus on the behavior abroad of MNCs based in developing nations. Moran's (2002) multi-country study reports that workers are more likely to be treated poorly in plants that are owned by non-OECD investors.[56] Gallagher (2005) notes that overseas ethnic Chinese investors (based in Hong Kong and elsewhere) are the most egregious violators of labor rights in mainland China. Similarly, others find that, in their operations abroad, Hong Kong-based investors tend to be particularly hostile to organized labor (Chiu 2007; Hewison and Chiu 2008). Similarly, a recent ILO (2007) study discusses the implications of the recent growth in South-South direct investment flows for employment and labor rights in Southeast Asia. The ILO study concludes that, relative to developed-nation MNCs, developing-country MNCs tend to use more labor-intensive production processes (even when holding constant the industrial sector),[57] which could generate more employment in host countries. At the same time, though, "many Northern MNEs bring with them higher labour standards as part of their corporate social-responsibility practices, but these practices may not be as widely implemented by Southern MNEs" (ILO 2007, 47).

Turning to more specific examples, in their study of labor conditions in Taiwanese-owned factories in China and Vietnam, Chan and Wang (2005) observe that even in directly owned (versus subcontractor) factories, Korean and Taiwanese managers are renowned for their disciplinarian approach to workers. These managers have reputations for harsh treatment of employees, not only in Asia, but also in Central America and Southern Africa. Similarly, Won's (2007) interview-based study considers labor conditions in Korean-owned facilities in China. Most of the factories included in his analyses are involved in the production of

[56] He also finds that workers are likely to be treated poorly in plants that are older or smaller; that require the lowest level of skills; that produce non-branded products; and that are located in isolated or poverty-stricken areas.

[57] In a different vein, Malesky (2008) describes differences between MNCs from Southeast Asia and those from the United States and Europe in terms of how they managed their investments in Vietnam in the 1990s and early 2000s. Asian investors generally worried less about political institutions and property rights than their American and European counterparts. Instead, Asian-based MNCs were more likely to rely on relationships with provincial government officials to address problems.

labor-intensive commodities. Workers in these facilities tend to be young and female, often migrants from rural areas; turnover in these factories is very high. Won reports that workers and middle managers in China would rather work for U.S., European, or Japanese firms, as they view Korean-owned enterprises as treating workers less well. (This is substantiated by a study he reports, conducted by the Chinese Development Research Center at the State Council in 2004, which asked employees, experts, and journalists to provide their overall views of foreign-owned businesses; South Korean and Taiwanese firms were rated lowest.) In terms of collective labor rights, Won finds that Korean firms tend to discourage or avoid labor unions – even the Chinese government-controlled ACFTU – because unions "are the very reason they fled Korea for China" (Won 2007, 312).[58] In terms of individual working conditions, Won details a litany of violations in Korean-owned factories, including sexual harassment, mandatory overtime, and the use of intimidation.[59]

There is, of course, also a correlation between nationality of firm owners and the sector of production. Given their own economic structures, the outward investments of middle-income countries tend toward labor-intensive (or, sometimes, extractive) sectors. Some of the problems observed in non-OECD-owned factories may relate more to industrial sector (i.e., apparel) than to source country identity. For example, in Central America and the Caribbean, most of the direct investment from middle-income nations (often, Hong Kong and South Korea) is in apparel and textile factories. Similarly, over 80 percent of Korean-owned enterprises in China are involved in labor-intensive manufacturing, and most of these are small and medium-sized firms (Won 2007). These firms are focused largely on reducing labor costs. Won compares such enterprises with larger, more capital-intensive Korean firms that also have Chinese operations, such as Hyundai and Samsung. Whereas there are fewer such firms, they tend to provide relatively good working conditions as well as

[58] Won argues, however, that the union avoidance strategy can be self-defeating for Korean managers because unions provide workers with an institutionalized mechanism for venting their complaints and therefore help to resolve tensions between workers and management.

[59] Also see Frenkel's (2001) study of athletic footwear manufacturing in China, which contrasts – in terms of personnel management practices and the treatment of workers – plants owned by Korean and Taiwanese with those owned by Americans and Europeans. Ngai (2005) examines two apparel factories in China, one owned by Hong Kong nationals and another owned by Taiwanese nationals. He reports that labor conditions in the factories are far from those prescribed by the codes of conduct of the U.S. and European MNCs for which the Chinese firms serve as suppliers and subcontractors.

extensive skills training to their employees – consistent with Hypothesis 6.2. A manager at Hyundai, for instance, boasts that Chinese workers there receive wages that are more than twice what Chinese state enterprises pay. Such firms are motivated much less by labor costs and more by accessing China's expanding domestic consumer market.[60]

This brief empirical exploration of Hypotheses 6.3 and 6.4 suggests, as does Section II before it, valuable questions for future research centered on the potential impact of firm nationality on the transmission of collective labor rights laws and practices. Particularly as the contribution of middle-income developing nations to global direct investment outflows increases, such effects are likely to become more pronounced.

IV. VARIETIES OF CAPITALISTS: DIRECTIONS FOR THE FUTURE

This chapter explores two axes of variation within multinational production – industrial sector and source country. Each of the four hypotheses is based on the notion that multinational production has a range of effects in developing countries, even within the broad categories of FDI and subcontracting. Although it is clear that developing countries are integrated differently into the global economy, extant empirical analyses have done little to account for heterogeneity within direct investment, or within multinational production more generally. Doing so allows for a more accurate – albeit a more complicated – picture of the causal relationships between economic openness and collective labor rights.

The initial empirical analyses in this chapter buttress the claim that the precise nature of a country's multinational production has implications for labor rights outcomes. For instance, nations with larger extractive sectors, or those with more direct investment in the automobile sector, tend to have better labor rights outcomes, all else equal. Moreover, nations with a high share of trade activity in the chemicals sector are characterized by better labor rights. In other cases, however, statistical analyses do not reveal evidence of systematic sectoral effects. Similarly, there is initial evidence that FDI from some countries may have different effects from direct investment from other countries. Again, though, the ability to evaluate statistically the "source country" hypothesis is limited

---

[60] Even among such firms, though, individual working conditions may differ from collective labor rights. Samsung (routinely rated as the best Korean company for which to work in China) does not allow any independent union activities at its factories in China. However, the company shares profits with local universities and high schools, providing fellowships and donating equipment (Won 2007).

at this point – particularly with respect to the impact of developed versus developing nations.

Sector and source country are just two of the distinctions to be drawn regarding multinational production. Another possible distinction concerns the nature of a country's bilateral trade relationships, and specifically, prevailing labor rights conditions in export partners. Greenhill, Mosley, and Prakash (2009) claim that it may be important, not only how open a country is to trade, or what sorts of goods an economy produces, but also *with which countries* the bulk of trade occurs.[61] If bilateral trade relationships promote the diffusion of standards, including those for workers, then the prevailing labor practices in a country's main trading partners are another important factor to consider. They propose that a "California effect" (Vogel 1995, 2009; also see Prakash and Potosi 2006) maintains, in which economic exchange facilitates an expansion in the scope and stringency of regulatory standards in exporting economies. More specifically, developing countries that export to destinations with strong labor rights protections are more likely, all else equal, to experience improvements in their labor rights. This trade-based diffusion occurs through a variety of mechanisms, including importing firms' concerns with labor issues throughout their supply chains as well as the diffusion of partner countries' best practices. Indeed, high labor standards found among a country's export destinations are associated with improvements in the labor laws of the exporting country in subsequent years. The effects are particularly pronounced for labor laws (rather than for labor rights practices), demonstrating again the potential differences between legislated and implemented collective labor rights. For those governments and activists who want to use trade as a means for promoting improvements in labor rights, these results imply that engagement (encouraging trade with nations that have strong protections of workers' rights) is far preferable to sanctioning (restricting trade when developing nations violate workers' rights).

Of course, the direction of change in labor practices (improvement or deterioration) is dependent on labor practices in major export destinations. As such, the implications of the California effect would be less

---

[61] Cao and Prakash (2010) offer an alternative means of disaggregating countries' trade relationships: They measure the "structural equivalence" of countries in the global trade network by considering the extent to which countries export the same products and the degree to which they export to the same importing countries. They find that trade competition is associated significantly with environmental outcomes, especially in terms of a competitive lowering of standards, among structurally equivalent countries.

sanguine if countries showing disregard for labor rights absorbed the bulk of world imports. Under such conditions, a "China effect" instead of a California effect might rule the day; this, of course, suggests a common logic between arguments regarding trade-based diffusion and those regarding the importance of FDI source countries. It also predicts that, as patterns of bilateral trade change, we might observe changes in the process of labor rights diffusion. Again, then, further disaggregating the concept of multinational production is a promising avenue both for scholars and for policymakers.

The task for the future, then, is to develop new means of measuring the various ways in which developing nations participate in global production. One possibility, as I suggest in Section II, is to consider firm-level attitudes and patterns. Through analysis of a larger set of firm-level survey data, or through development of a firm-level survey geared at multinationals and/or subcontractors, we might gain a better sense of the extent to which certain types of firms are likely to pressure governments for changes in labor law, or the extent to which firms view collective labor rights as an impediment to their competitiveness.[62] Moreover, finer-grained data on export profiles and on direct investment by sector and source would allow for more comprehensive quantitative analyses. Finally, analysts should consider the location of labor rights violations: When violations are observed, do they occur in foreign-owned firms, in subcontracting firms, or in domestic-owned and domestic-oriented businesses? Are violations of rights simply more common in internationally oriented firms, or is it more the case that we (and the sources on which the labor rights measure is based) are more likely to observe them in those sectors? Improving our empirical grasp on multinational production in developing nations, then, will allow us to test further our theoretical claims regarding how the global economy affects workers' rights.

---

[62] We also might find differences between firms within the same sector, stemming from variation in ownership or in the types of products manufactured (e.g., branded vs. non-branded). Spar and Yoffie (1999), for instance, predict that race to the bottom pressures are more likely among firms with homogeneous products, where competition is mostly on the basis of costs. Firms with differentiated or branded products are less likely to focus solely on costs. Gereffi's older distinction (see Gibbon et al. 2008) between buyer-driven and producer-driven commodity chains is another useful way that future research on this subject could draw distinctions – and varying predictions regarding labor rights – among firms and industries.

7

Labor Rights, Economic Development, and Domestic Politics

A Case Study

The systematic, cross-national assessment of collective labor rights outcomes, and their causal determinants, is the central aim of this book. As such, much of the evidence presented is quantitative in nature, and it is cast at the country level of analysis. Whereas I discuss the importance of domestic economic and political variables as independent and intervening variables in Chapters 3 and 5, the explanations advanced focus on the impact (or lack thereof) of the global economy on national-level labor rights outcomes. Yet, despite the need (both from the point of view of international political economy *and* that of economic policymakers) for systematic, large-N treatments of the linkages between global production and labor rights, such an analytical approach also has limitations. Some of these are identified in the preceding chapter, which highlights problems of data availability among low- and middle-income nations.

Another drawback relates to the difficulty of gaining a sense of the longer-term (and often domestically driven) processes linking the global economy, domestic politics and institutions, and the rights of workers. Such causal processes often unfold over many years, and they may unfold in a path-dependent fashion. This longer-term dynamic process may relate to the hypotheses introduced in Chapter 3 as well as to the sector and source arguments discussed in the previous chapter. As the nature of a country's engagement in global production networks changes (in terms of the extent of its involvement, the sectors in which it is involved, or the developed nations from which investment and subcontracting come), labor rights outcomes also should change. Such changes, though, may happen over several years or even decades, making their impact easier to trace in qualitative analyses. Qualitative analyses not only facilitate the consideration of longer-term processes; they also allow for the possibility of unit heterogeneity (Sambanis 2004). That is, the medium- and longer-term processes linking labor rights, domestic politics, and the global economy may vary across units. Given these considerations, it is useful to complement quantitatively based approaches to understanding collective labor rights with qualitative analyses, either by industry (i.e., Silver 2003) or by country and region (i.e., Murillo 2001). By investigating a single case or set of cases over a longer period of time, we can assess the ways in which external variables (here, multinational production) are linked with outcome variables (labor rights) via various domestic political and economic institutions.

In the case of the hypotheses introduced in Chapter 3, we can gauge the longer-term direct impact, as well as the mediating effects, of economic structure, government fractionalization, government ideology, and the role of organized labor in the domestic policy. When the longer-term case study succeeds in identifying the mechanisms hypothesized to link globalization with labor rights outcomes, our confidence in the causal nature of these processes is increased (Mahoney 2007). Of course, large-N work also provides some advantages, such as the ability to consider the correlates of labor rights outcomes (assuming appropriate measures of those outcomes) across countries and over time and the capacity to control for the effects – both independent and interactive – of contending causal factors. As such, this analysis should be seen as a complement, rather than a competitor, to statistically oriented work on labor rights.

In this chapter, I consider Costa Rica's experience with multinational production and labor rights. During the last two decades, Costa Rica has become more involved in global production and commerce: The importance of both exports and foreign direct investment to the country's economy has expanded markedly. On the basis of the theoretical arguments advanced in the preceding chapters, these changes should generate both positive and negative pressures on collective labor rights. Foreign direct investment, on the one hand, could be associated with increased respect for workers' rights, especially as firms shift from labor- to technology-intensive production. At the same time, however, increased trade competition can place downward pressures on the provision and implementation of collective labor rights. However, each set of pressures occur in the context of a specific domestic political climate. The key question, then, is *how* and *to what extent* this set of pressures is mediated by domestic political institutions and histories. Given the occurrence of industrial upgrading and the shift toward higher-technology industries, Costa Rica may represent a "most likely" case for the claim that participation in multinational production will have positive consequences for labor rights.

Yet Costa Rica's experience indicates that, even when a process of industrial upgrading accompanies the growth of multinational production, domestic factors can counteract the positive effects of global production and reinforce the negative pressures of trade competition on workers' collective rights. Put differently, this case suggests that the appearance of positive consequences of multinational production on collective labor rights is contingent. When domestic political institutions and histories counteract the effects of global economic forces, and where participation in high-technology industries is limited to a small portion of the labor force, the broad positive impact of multinational production does not necessarily obtain. In the next section, I summarize briefly the expectations regarding collective rights outcomes generated in Chapter 3, particularly as they apply to the effect of various domestic factors on longer-run outcomes. I then discuss the rationale for selecting Costa Rica for an in-depth analysis. The remainder of the chapter explores the longer-run development and evolution of collective labor rights outcomes in Costa Rica as a whole as well as in specific sectors of the economy.

I. COLLECTIVE LABOR RIGHTS OVER THE LONGER RUN

Chapter 3 discusses the various determinants of collective labor rights outcomes with a focus on those related to the global economy. Despite this book's focus on multinational production, there remains a substantial role for domestic politics, both as direct determinants of labor rights outcomes (consider, for instance, the link between regime type and labor rights, evidenced in Chapter 5) and as mediators of the forces emanating from the global economy. The latter, mediating role of domestic politics may be particularly important for the implementation of collective labor rights laws, but it also may play a role in the earlier passage of domestic laws that protect (or fail to protect) workers' core labor rights.

In particular, a range of domestic factors are hypothesized to affect labor rights outcomes (Hypotheses 3.3 and 3.4). These include the structure of the economy and labor market (for instance, the degree of slack in the labor market as well as the skill intensity of industrial production); the ideology of the governing party; and the strength of connections between organized labor and governing political parties. The quantitative analyses in Chapters 5 and 6 establish the importance of a subset of these factors – the nature of the economy, the type of political regime, and government ideology – as significant correlates of collective labor rights outcomes. The quantitative analyses, however, are not an appropriate means of assessing the longer-run impact of these domestic factors, nor are they particularly useful in measuring and gauging the role of other domestic factors. For instance, where labor unions have strong ties to governing political parties, collective labor rights protections will be stronger, all else equal. Such ties are difficult to measure in a cross-national context, however. Moreover, turning to the structure of the domestic economy and the sectoral allocation of FDI, the cross-national data employed in Chapter 6 are somewhat limited. Whereas we may expect that countries that experience a process of industrial upgrading are, all else equal, also more likely to experience improvements in collective labor rights, our capacity to measure the degree or nature of such upgrading (specifically, as it relates to export profiles and foreign direct investment activity) in a large-N context is limited. Again, the case study format affords another opportunity to assess the expectations developed in Chapter 6.

This chapter, therefore, examines the experience of Costa Rica. Focusing on the last two decades, I consider how domestic factors mediate influences from the global economy, in a static as well as dynamic sense. The within-case analysis (see Mahoney 2007) limits the empirical domain, but it also complements the cross-sectional time series analyses. The case study allows us to assess the potential mediating or interactive role that domestic politics play, in conjunction with FDI and trade. If the case analysis reveals the hypothesized mediating effects, our confidence in this book's hypothesized causal linkages (as identified in Figure 3.1) is enhanced. For instance, if a high number of veto players contribute to the path dependence of collective labor laws, we gain confidence that domestic institutions play a central causal role, despite pressures from the global economy. Moreover, by treating the conjunctural nature of causation as given, case analyses may avoid the problems associated with specifying and interpreting interaction effects in a statistical context (Braumoeller 2004). Furthermore, the processes linking economic globalization with labor rights may accumulate and unfold over the medium or long term (Huber et al. 2006; Mahoney 2007). Even if operationalizing important domestic variables quantitatively were straightforward, large-N analyses would do less well at tracing the dynamic mechanisms through which they operate.

A case study approach can reveal further information about the longer-run linkages among domestic institutions, the global economy, and collective labor rights. Given that the case study is employed here to explore and illustrate causal connections, rather than to provide a definitive test of various hypotheses, I elect to focus on a middle-income country that faces contending pressures from the global economy – those involving trade-based competition, as well as those related to a surge in directly owned production, which is concentrated largely in the high-technology sector. Costa Rica's exports have grown relative to the size of the country's economy, from a starting level that was typical for developing nations, to one that is markedly higher. If trade competition leads to downward pressures on labor rights, this change should augur poorly for workers' rights. At the same time, though, Costa Rica has experienced a marked increase in the importance of foreign direct investment to its domestic economy. Additionally, new direct investment is different from older multinational activity, as it has been concentrated in high-technology, skill-intensive industries. In terms of direct investment, then, extant research would predict positive trends in collective labor rights. This expectation also is consistent with an "industrial upgrading" view of the benefits for developing nations of integrating into global production networks. In the face of these contending global pressures, then, the mediating role of domestic political institutions and histories is critical.

II. COSTA RICA: PROFILE, EXPECTATIONS, AND INDEPENDENT VARIABLES

A. Costa Rica's Economy

Costa Rica's economic profile and political history may render it better able than many other developing nations to reap the benefits of global economic integration. Costa Rica's income per capita was $4,370 in 1986, compared with $3,385 elsewhere in Latin America, and $2,972 elsewhere in the developing world. By 2002, Costa Rica's income per capita was almost $9,000, nearly 50 percent greater than that elsewhere in Latin America and over 70 percent more than the average in other developing regions. Costa Rica also has been distinguished by a very high level of literacy (Rodríguez-Clare 2001; Schrank and Piore 2007). Perhaps most important in comparison to its closest geographic neighbors, Costa Rica was a long-standing democracy, unmarked by the post–World War II experience of civil war, and viewed by potential investors as having a well-developed rule of law. It has long had a well-developed social security system and a large public sector (Wilson 1999).

In terms of economic policy changes, however, Costa Rica's experience is more typical: Costa Rica experienced negative or very low rates of growth during the first half of the 1980s. In the early 1980s, it shifted away from an import substitution model of industrialization and toward economic openness via the creation of EPZs, the liberalization of trade, and participation in the Caribbean Basin Economic Recovery Act (CBI), the latter providing increased access to the U.S. market (Rodríguez-Clare 2001). In Costa Rica, these efforts were very successful: During the mid-1980s, Costa Rica's exports were equivalent to 31.3 percent of its gross domestic product, very close to the mean level of exports (31.0 percent of GDP) for developing (non-OECD, non-Soviet bloc) nations. Similarly, Costa Rica's accumulated stock of direct investment was 23 percent of GDP in 1986, compared with 21.1 percent for developing nations.[1] By 2002, Costa Rica's export openness, at 42.4 percent of national income, had surpassed the mean level (37.4 percent) in other developing nations. Direct investment also grew in relative importance to Costa Rica's economy, with FDI inflows in 2003 representing 17 percent of gross fixed capital formation, compared with 10.3 percent elsewhere in Latin America and the Caribbean, and 9.8 percent in the developing world generally (UNCTAD 2006). Moreover, the absolute amounts of these flows increased markedly, more than tripling (in U.S. dollar terms) between the beginning and the end of the 1990s.[2]

At the sectoral level, Costa Rica experienced a dramatic shift during the 1980s and 1990s. Whereas agriculture accounted for approximately 20 percent of value added economy-wide in the late 1980s and early 1990s, its contribution had fallen to less than 10 percent by the year 2000.[3] Similarly, in 1992, half of FDI inflows were in the agricultural sector. By the late 1990s, FDI in agriculture accounted for less than 10 percent of annual inflows; in 2002 and 2003, FDI in this sector was negative, indicating the prevalence of divestment in agriculture. Much of the decline in agriculture was paralleled by a growth in the importance of the services sector, including tourism as well as financial services and data processing. While the contribution of manufacturing to Costa Rica's economy remained largely constant throughout the 1980s and 1990s,

---

[1] These statistics are based on data employed in the statistical analyses in Chapter 5 and described in the Data Appendix.
[2] Based on data from UNCTAD's Foreign Direct Investment Country Profile for Costa Rica.
[3] Data from *World Development Indicators*, Agriculture, value added as a percentage of GDP.

at between 20 and 25 percent of GDP each year, the types of products manufactured changed markedly. This shift also is reflected in employment data. In 1985, 27 percent of workers were employed in agriculture; 21 percent in industry (which includes manufacturing, extractive activities, and public utilities), and 51 percent in services (public and private sector). By 2003, employment in agriculture had fallen to 15 percent of the total, while employment in services had expanded to 62 percent. Employment in industry remained fairly constant, at 22 percent. The size of the national labor force also increased during this period, from just under 1 million workers in 1985 to 1.8 million in 2003.[4]

Figure 7.1 summarizes the role of five intermediate categories of products in Costa Rica's total exports – primary products (including the agricultural sector), resource-based manufactures, low-technology manufactures, medium-technology manufactures, and high-technology manufactured goods.[5] Two trends feature prominently: the relative decline of agricultural exports (mostly coffee and bananas), and the rise of high-tech manufacturing, particularly after the mid-1990s. Similarly, data on export profiles by two-digit SITC code reveals that, in 1986, the two most important categories of exports were coffee (SITC category 07, accounting for 37 percent of exports) and fruit (SITC 5, representing 24 percent). By 2002, coffee had fallen to 3.7 percent of exports, while fruit (bananas and pineapples) remained the second-largest export category (nearly 18 percent of exports). As a result, Costa Rica's largest export category in 2002 was office machines and data processing equipment (SITC 75). Other top-five export categories included apparel and clothing (8 percent of exports) as well as electrical machinery and appliances (SITC 77) and professional and scientific instruments (SITC 87), with each of the latter accounting for 7.6 percent of total exports.

The changes in Costa Rica's export profile reflect, not only the pressures generated by falling global coffee prices in the 1980s, but also a deliberate change in the strategy of the country's privately run export promotion agency, Coalicíon Costarricense de Inícitivas para el Desarrollo (CINDE). During its first decade of existence (the 1980s), CINDE focused on agricultural activities and unskilled labor-intensive *maquilas*, such as apparel assembly (Clark 1997). In the early 1990s, motivated by competition

---

[4] These statistics are drawn from the ILO's Key Indicators of the Labour Market database.
[5] Based on data from the COMTRADE database, using the classifications developed in Lall (2000). Data calculated and provided by Gary Thompson.

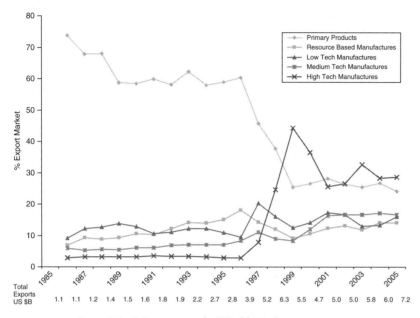

FIGURE 7.1. Costa Rica's Exports to the World Market.

from other economies in the region (particularly Mexico) *and* by a desire to exploit Costa Rica's endowment of relatively skilled workers (Buitelaar and Perez 2000), CINDE changed course. Its new strategy, aimed at service as well as high-technology manufacturing activities, included the development of an EPZ system, with exemptions from corporate taxation and free repatriation of profits. The free trade zones (*zona franca*) contained 109 firms in 1992 and 227 firms in 2005. By 2005–2006, these EPZ firms, in sectors including textiles, electrical machinery, and pharmaceuticals, accounted for 36,000 jobs (a relatively small fraction of the labor force), but 52 percent of the country's total exports (Boyenge 2007). The *zona franca* were home to 42 percent of the country's direct investment in 2005, a near doubling from 1997 (PROCOMER 2006). The majority of firms in the EPZ are U.S.-based[6]; in the service sector, they include Procter and Gamble and Western Union, both of which established call centers in Costa Rica in the 1990s (Rodríguez-Clare 2001).

Foreign direct investment in manufacturing (rather than in other sectors) grew from less than one-quarter of total FDI inflows in 1992 to

---

[6] Based on data from UNCTAD's Foreign Direct Investment Country Profile for Costa Rica. Also see Buitelaar and Perez 2000.

more than two-thirds of total flows in 2002. Foreign MNCs include Remec, Sawtek, Conair, Abbott, and Baxter, all involved in electronics and medical devices. Perhaps the most visible success in Costa Rica's export promotion efforts was Intel Corporation's 1996 decision to build a microchip assembly and inspection plant there; strikingly, Costa Rica's main competitors for the Intel plant were not other Central American nations but several emerging market economies in Asia and Europe (Moran 2002; Spar 1998b; World Bank 2006). Whereas Intel was not the first MNC to site a high-technology manufacturing operation in Costa Rica, its investment was large and visible: Between 1997 and 1999, it invested $390 million, equivalent to approximately 3 percent of Costa Rica's GDP. In 1999, Intel alone accounted for nearly 40 percent of Costa Rica's total exports (Rodríguez-Clare 2001). The assembly and testing facilities in Costa Rica also were significant relative to Intel: By 2003, the products assembled and tested in Costa Rica accounted for approximately one-fourth of the company's total sales.

Indeed, after Intel's arrival, Costa Rica's national statistical agency began to calculate two sets of economic statistics, one with Intel and one without, a reflection of Intel's size relative to the national economy. In 1999, for instance, real GDP growth was 8.4 percent in total but only 3 percent "without Intel." However in 2001, reflecting the global economic downturn and subsequent fall in demand for Intel's products, the Intel contribution was much smaller. The rate of real GDP growth was 4.6 percent with the company and 4.1 percent excluding Intel (World Bank 2006). By 2005, Intel's total investment in Costa Rica was $770 million, and their facilities employed 2,900 workers directly; observers estimated that Intel also was responsible for an additional 2,000 jobs indirectly. In 2006, the electronics "cluster" in Costa Rica (as promoted by CINDE) included fifty-five firms, forty-two of which were foreign; these firms employed a total of 12,000 workers (World Bank 2006).

Many observers point to Intel's investment and subsequent economic impact as evidence that – building on the appeal of the EPZ system, its offer of vocational training for local workers, and targeted efforts by CINDE – Costa Rica was able to pursue (and to benefit from) an industrial upgrading strategy. Indeed, if workers' situations do not improve with the arrival of high-skilled, capital-intensive FDI, then the statistical finding that directly owned production generally has positive consequences for collective labor rights (Chapter 5) needs to be placed more deeply in the context of domestic politics and institutions.

B. Domestic Factors

Turning from international economic variables to domestic ones, what do Costa Rica's domestic political institutions and interests lead us to expect regarding labor rights outcomes? First, Hypothesis 3.4 posits an impact of government partisanship – specifically, of left party representation, in either the executive or legislative branch – on collective labor rights, and we report large-N evidence for this relationship in Chapter 5. Like most Latin American nations, Costa Rica's executive system is presidential, although its president is weak relative to presidents elsewhere in Latin America (Wilson 1994). Direct presidential and legislative elections are held every four years. For many years, the party system was dominated by two main parties, the National Liberation Party (PLN) and the Social Christian Unity Party (PUSC); in the 1980s and 1990s, electoral volatility was low, especially in comparison to the rest of the region (Roberts and Wibbels 1999). Within Costa Rica's centrist party system, the PLN leans to the social democratic left, whereas the PUSC is inclined toward the Christian democratic right (Coppedge 1998). Owing largely to term limits on both presidents and legislators, party discipline among legislators is low (Wilson 1999).

In the 1982 and 1986 elections, the left-leaning PLN won both the presidency and a majority of seats in the assembly. During this time, there was some disagreement within the PLN regarding the need for economic policy reform in the face of economic crisis (Clark 1997; Wilson 1994). In 1990, PUSC candidates were elected both to the presidency and to a majority of legislative seats. The parties alternated power again in 1994, although the PLN won only twenty-eight (of fifty-seven) assembly seats, leaving it without a majority. During this time, the PLN presided over economic reform (Wilson 1999), despite sometimes-strong opposition from Costa Rican labor unions. The 1998 election brought the return of a right-leaning president, with the largest share of legislative seats (twenty-seven) won by the PUSC. The PUSC candidate again won the presidency in 2002, although legislative elections resulted in nineteen seats for the PUSC, seventeen PLN seats, and thirteen seats for the newly formed populist PAC. As Costa Rica became more engaged in the global economy, then, its governments alternated between left and right. During much of the last decade, though – when competitive pressures from economic globalization were likely most severe – right-leaning parties held office. On this basis, Hypothesis 3.4 would predict few improvements to collective labor rights, all else equal.

Second, as discussed at the end of Chapter 3 and tested in Chapter 5, we also expect political fragmentation (a high number of veto players) to limit changes – in either direction – in collective labor rights. Indeed, the pattern of political fragmentation in Costa Rica predicts a marked degree of path dependence in labor rights. Throughout the last two decades, ruling political parties' legislative majorities were often thin. By the mid-1990s, they had become nonexistent.[7] The trend toward legislative fractionalization intensified in 2002. While the presidency remained in the hands of the PUSC, the Citizens' Action Party (PAC), a populist party founded in 2000 on an anti-corruption platform and opposition to neoliberal reforms, received a substantial number of votes in both the presidential and legislative elections. Even with the political will to pass laws altering collective labor rights, then, governments in such a fractionalized system would have difficulty enacting legal changes. Moreover, right-leaning politicians have electoral incentives to promote market liberalization – and labor market deregulation – as a means to spurring economic growth and gaining the support of the "winners" from globalization (skilled workers and owners of small and medium enterprises with potential linkages to MNCs). Again, then, the domestic degree of fractionalization leads us to expect few changes to Costa Rica's labor legislation, as well as few changes to the level of enforcement of existing laws, in the 1990s.

The discussion of domestic political institutions in Chapter 3 also highlights the importance of national labor unions to collective labor rights outcomes. Specifically, when organized labor is strong *and* well-connected to governing political parties, the provision of collective labor rights should be higher, all else equal. Whereas unions' domestic strength and political connections are somewhat endogenous to collective labor rights outcomes in earlier eras, the development over time of labor union strength helps to predict the ease (or difficulty) with which governments will repress (or promote) labor rights in the wake of growing multinational production. Moreover, if left-leaning political parties face increased electoral uncertainty (as the PLN did in the 1990s), they may have greater incentives to appeal to labor-based constituencies (through expanded provision and enforcement of collective rights; e.g., Murillo 2005), assuming that the labor movement is organized sufficiently to deliver votes to the PLN.

---

[7] Seligson (2002) examines the roots of this fractionalization, in terms of voters' assessments of political system legitimacy.

Rates of unionization in Costa Rica are low by regional standards, and they have remained low throughout recent decades.[8] In 1985, 22.9 percent of Costa Rica's non-agricultural labor force (and 29.1 percent of wage and salary earners) were union members.[9] McGuire (2005) reports that, by 1995, this figure had declined to 13.1 percent, compared with 14.8 percent in developing countries generally. Data for 2000 indicate that 12 percent of all Costa Rican workers were unionized. Unionization rates also vary markedly between the public and private sectors: 53 percent of public sector workers are unionized, although public sector unions generally lack the right to bargain collectively. In the private sector, only 5.2 percent of workers belong to unions; if unions of small agricultural producers are excluded, the rate falls to 2.3 percent of private-sector workers.[10] Given that Costa Rica's unions are unable to claim a broad-based, private-sector membership, they are likely to play less of a role in mediating between pressures from the global economy and government policy decisions.

Indeed, Costa Rica is characterized by weak labor mobilization: In recent decades, labor unions have not enjoyed tight linkages with the main political parties or with presidents and legislative leaders. Whereas organized labor was politically influential prior to the 1948 civil war, post-war governments tended to repress labor unions (Wilson and Rodríguez 2006), often with the cooperation of local agricultural oligarchs (Murillo and Schrank 2005; Schrank and Piore 2007). In terms of ties with political parties, the social democratic-oriented PLN, formed in 1952, is rooted in the elite and upper middle class levels of society, rather than among working classes; many of the party's early founders were university-affiliated elites who joined with conservative factions of the oligarchy to oppose President Calderón's populist reforms and labor mobilization (Roberts 2002). The 1943 Labor Code imposed broad limits on the right to strike, and later governments – even those led by the left-leaning PLN – sometimes used labor-related laws to repress labor and to resist external

---

[8] As I note in Chapter 4, union density data are notoriously inaccurate and difficult to compare cross-nationally in developing countries. The U.S. State Department's *Country Reports on Human Rights Practices* list the same rate of unionization for Costa Rica for each year between 1993 and 2002, which seems unlikely.

[9] Schrank and Piore (2007) report a lower rate of union density for Costa Rica in the early 1980s – 14 percent. They point out that this is below both the Central American (16 percent) and Latin American (21 percent) means.

[10] Data for 2000 are reported by AFL-CIO 2001. In its 2005 *Country Report on Human Rights Practices*, the State Department noted that 9 percent of Costa Rica's workers were unionized, a decline from the 12 percent it reported in 2003.

actors' (especially the ILO's) calls for reform. As a result, whereas Costa Rica had the most active labor movement in Central America at the start of the 1940s (Rueschemeyer et al. 1992), organized labor was not a key political actor later in the twentieth century. By the 1980s, low rates of union membership and concentration[11] rendered organized labor unable to play a strong role in the development of economic and social policies. In terms of union political strength, then, we would expect little impact of the labor movement on Costa Rica's collective labor rights outcomes. The low rate of unionization, particularly in the private sector (where pressures from trade competition are greatest), suggests that unions may not play a key role in resisting downward competitive pressures or in pressing for improvements that might come with greater directly owned production.

Lastly, Hypothesis 3.3 highlights the influence of labor market conditions and structures on workers' capacity to demand protections of collective labor rights as well as on firms' incentives to provide such rights. In terms of labor market conditions, Costa Rica's unemployment rate has ranged from a low of 4.1 percent in 1992 and 1993 to a high of 6.8 percent in 1985, again reaching 6 percent during the first half of the 2000s. Costa Rica has a small informal sector compared to other countries in the region. Schneider (2006) estimates the informal sector as accounting for 26.2 percent of GDP in 1999–2000, 27 percent in 2001–2002, and 27.8 percent in 2002–2003.[12] This compares with a 2002 average of 43.4 percent of GDP throughout the Latin American region; shadow economies accounted for 34 percent of GDP in the Dominican Republic, 48 percent in Nicaragua, and 52 percent in Guatemala. The smaller informal sector suggests less slack in the labor market, which should place Costa Rica's workers in a relatively strong bargaining position vis-à-vis employers.

The characteristics of workers in Costa Rica's formal sector also imply, on economic grounds, a relatively strong bargaining position vis-à-vis employers, especially for skilled workers. In 1985, 9 percent of Costa Rica's workforce was categorized as working in professional and technical occupations. In 1999, 15.7 percent of workers were employed as

---

[11] Roberts (2002) reports a peak rate of union density (in the 1970–1995 period) of 15.4 percent, compared with 31.9 percent in Latin American "labor mobilizing" political systems. He categorizes Costa Rica's union concentration – the percentage of unionized workers belonging to the largest labor union – as low.

[12] Schrank and Piore (2007) suggest that the informal sector has become less important over time. In the early 1980s, 52 percent of Costa Rica's workforce labored in the informal sector.

managers, professionals, and technicians; by 2004, the proportion of professional workers had increased to 23.4 percent.[13] Similarly, Rudra's (2002) measure of potential labor power (PLP), which is comprised of the ratio of skilled to unskilled workers, multiplied by the inverse of a measure of surplus labor, predicts a greater voice for labor over time. The ratio increases from 0.85 in 1985 to 1.44 in 1997, the last year for which the measure is available. The sectoral shift among Costa Rica's labor force also should have implications for workers' bargaining power. Agriculture – which, from the point of view of labor unions, is notoriously difficult to organize – accounted for 27 percent of employment in 1985 but only 16 percent in 2002.[14]

At the same time, however, employment growth has occurred largely in services (over 60 percent of the economically active population in 2002), which includes both the sheltered public services as well as tourism, call centers, and financial services.[15] Tourism and call centers tend to be labor-intensive activities which employ low- or semi-skilled workers; often, unions have difficulty mobilizing workers in such enterprises. Within the manufacturing sector, however, there have been some employment shifts toward more skill-intensive industries, particularly in the EPZs. PROCOMER (2006) reports, for instance, that workers in EPZ textile-oriented firms accounted for nearly 50 percent of total EPZ workers in 1997. By 2005, the largest proportion of EPZ workers was in electronic and electrical equipment (23 percent) and services (22 percent). Textiles accounted for only 19 percent of employment, while medical equipment firms employed 13 percent of EPZ workers.

We might expect, then, that – given their bargaining power vis-à-vis MNCs, as identified by Hypothesis 3.3 – these skilled workers would be offered expanded collective labor rights. At the same time, though, this

[13] Calculated from data on economically active population by occupation and status, ILO LABORSTA database, Table 1D. Through 1998, these data use the ISCO-1968 classification of employees (categories 0 and 1 cover professional and technical workers). From 1999, the ISCO-88 classification is used. I treat professional workers as categories 1, 2, and 3 in the newer classification.

[14] Rural population declined from over 50 percent in the mid-1980s; but, with 38 percent of the country's population still residing in rural areas in 2005, there remains a significant portion of the labor force in such locations. In Central America as a whole, the rural population accounted for 32 percent of total population in the mid-1980s and 23 percent in 2005.

[15] Data are taken from the *World Development Indicators* database, unemployment, employment in agriculture, employment in manufacturing, and employment in services. Similar data, on employment by broad sectors, also are found in the ILO's LABORSTA database, Table 1C.

segment (skilled workers employed by foreign-owned firms) of the labor market is very small – approximately 0.02 percent of the total labor force. Indeed, in 2002, the MNCs with the most employees in Costa Rica were Conair Costa Rica (finance sector, 2,100 employees) and Intel (2,000 employees).[16] Given the very small size of this segment of the labor force, such positive "industrial upgrading" effects on collective labor rights may be experienced very narrowly.

Taken together, then, the values on key domestic variables suggest that collective labor rights will be difficult to achieve and/or reform in Costa Rica, despite the country's engagement with directly owned multinational production. Whereas labor market conditions suggest some bargaining power for workers, especially those in skilled, capital-intensive industries, labor unions' lack of organizational strength and political party ties does not bode well for collective labor rights. More broadly, Costa Rica's historical tendency to exclude organized labor from the political process – a tendency with roots in a post-World War II agriculture-based economy – means that the arrival of MNCs in skilled sectors will not lead necessarily to a "climb to the top" in collective labor rights. Indeed, some observers suggest that the exclusion of labor unions, and government support for employer-backed *solidarismo* organizations, has helped Costa Rica to attract multinationals. I explore this possibility in the next section.

III. ASSESSING COLLECTIVE LABOR RIGHTS IN COSTA RICA

The hypotheses generated in Chapter 3 identify several domestic factors that may mediate the impact of economic globalization on labor rights. Ideally, we would isolate the independent impact of each factor (as Figure 3.1 suggests), allowing us to test each hypothesis separately. In reality, though, the effects of government ideology, the fragmentation of political authority, labor unions' political strength, and the nature of the labor force likely are conjunctural and therefore difficult to disentangle, particularly with a single (albeit multifaceted) dependent variable. Instead, then, we can ask whether the pattern of collective labor rights changes in Costa Rica is consistent with the "mediating factors" logic that informs our expectations regarding each of these independent variables. In other words, how are the effects of increases in FDI in Costa Rica moderated by a political system that lacks strong left party union ties, and in which organized labor is historically weak? How does Costa Rica's tight labor

---

[16] UNCTAD, Foreign Direct Investment Country Profile, Costa Rica.

market and its (modest) shift toward more highly skilled employment affect the capacity of workers to achieve the rights to organize, bargain collectively, and strike?

The overall picture is mixed: The observation of collective labor rights in Costa Rica has improved during the last two decades, although many (both legal and practical) impediments to the full observation of these rights remain. In terms of the legal elements of collective labor rights, Costa Rica's 1949 constitution recognizes freedom of association and the right to organize; the right to voluntary collective bargaining; and the right to strike. Additionally, Costa Rica has ratified the eight ILO core conventions, including those related to freedom of association and collective bargaining.[17] The 1943 Labor Code, however, imposes limitations on some elements of freedom of association and collective bargaining, as various ILO bodies and non-governmental activists, as well as the U.S. State Department (in its annual *Country Reports on Human Rights Practices*), have noted repeatedly. Over time, Costa Rica's governments have eliminated some of these restrictions, particularly with the 1993 reform of the Labor Code, carried out under a right-leaning PUSC government (Murillo and Schrank 2005). In some instances, the Supreme Court – its own role in policymaking reformed in the late 1980s – played a key part in the expansion of collective rights (see Rodríguez and Wilson 2006).

Table 7.1 identifies the main criticisms of collective labor rights in Costa Rica; where relevant, it notes changes that have addressed the problem as well as the economic sector in which the problem occurs. This table reveals a pattern of improvements over time, but with notable violations remaining. First, Costa Rican law prohibits non-nationals from holding trade union office. In Costa Rica, this is most relevant in the sugar and banana industries, in which many workers are from Nicaragua. The ILO has repeatedly criticized this law as contravening freedom of association, but legislation to repeal it had not been enacted as of 2010. Second, the 1943 Labor Code falls short in terms of protecting workers from anti-union discrimination and particularly dismissals on the basis of union membership. The 1993 reforms made more explicit the prohibition, elaborating the right of union leaders to special protections from retaliatory dismissal (*fuero sindical*). In this case, the ILO and others have expressed

---

[17] Additionally, the Supreme Court has ruled that, when protections to fundamental rights (including core labor rights) are higher in international norms than in domestic law, international standards should prevail (Vice Ministers 2005).

TABLE 7.1. *Collective Labor Rights Violations in Costa Rica, Legal Elements*

Labor Rights Issue	Summary and Legal Basis	Economic Sector	ILO Findings	Relevant Changes
Trade Union Office	Non-nationals may not hold trade union office. LC, Sect. 345 C, Art. 60	All	CEACR reports from 1994.	Draft legislation in 1996, 1998, 2002, 2003, 2005; not passed.
Anti-Union Discrimination	Concern that 1943 Labor Code does not adequately specify protection and remedies; complaints are investigated slowly; rein-statement provision of 1993 law not well enforced.	All	CEACR and CFA reports from early 1990s. These request effective protec-tion against all types of anti-union discrimination and note problems with addressing complaints.	1993 LC reform (Act 7360): prohibits anti-union discrimination; protects union officials from dismissal. 1999: Constitutional Court rules that labor inspectorate must comply with 2-month time limit for investigations. 2003: draft bill 14676.
Solidarity Associations (SA)	Concern that SAs interfere with collective bargaining. Number of direct agreements vs. collective bargaining contracts. Trade unions require 20 members; SAs require 12.	Private	CFA, 1990 and 1991: Inequalities of treatment between SAs and unions; concern about SA involvement in collective bargaining. CEACR: Continued concerns, 2001–2006	1993 LC modifications (Act 7360): prohibits SAs from engaging in collective bargai-ning; trade unions may be formed with a minimum of 12 members. 2000 Workers' Protection Act
Collective Bargaining	Prohibited for all public sec-tor employees with statutory employment status (Public Administration Act of 1978). Supreme Court rulings, 2000	Public sector	1998: violates Convention 98 2001: Task Force reports serious deficiencies. 1995–2006 CEACR	1994: Bill introduced to guarantee CB in public sector, but not passed. 2001 decree adopted (Assembly approves rule allowing).

Official Intervention in Collective Bargaining	Terms of agreements require authorities' approval for "proportionality and rationality."	Public sector (case: RECOPE oil refinery, 2000).	CEACR 2001 and after.	
Right to Strike	Requires 60 percent of workers in enterprise to approve. (LC 373)	All	CEACR: 1993 and after.	Draft legislation 2005 (Bill 13475); not passed.
Right to Strike	Broad definition of essential services, including transport. (LC 376)	Public	CEACR: 1993 and after.	Scope of prohibitions narrowed in 2003, but ILO still critical on transport. Draft legislation 2005 (Bill 13475); not passed.
Right to Strike	Prohibited in public sector and agriculture (LC 375 and 376); essential services are defined to include activities like coffee and sugar cane.	All	CEACR 1991–1998	1998: Supreme Court rules that public sector workers do have a right to strike.

Abbreviations: LC = Labor Code; C = Constitution; CEACR = ILO Committee of Experts on the Application of Conventions and Recommendations; CFA = ILO Committee on Freedom of Association satisfaction with legal reforms but also worry about their practical implementation. For instance, in response to long delays in the adjudication of workers' complaints, the constitutional court ruled in 1999 that the labor inspectorate was required to investigate allegations of discrimination within two months. As recently as 2008, however, the International Trade Union Confederation (the ICFTU's successor) reported that the national labor inspectorate (DNIT) usually takes more than two months to certify a violation and that cases that go to trial tend not to reach a verdict for several years.

Perhaps the most frequent criticism of collective labor rights in Costa Rica, though, concerns solidarity associations and, specifically, the extent to which such associations prevent effective and independent interest representation. *Solidarismo* associations, in which membership is supposed to be voluntary, provide members with benefits like access to credit. Employers (and, often, the government) point out that these associations offer a variety of services to employees, but that they do not aim to replace labor unions. Some EPZ firms instead argue that, by providing various services as well as relatively good working conditions, they eliminate workers' need for unions (Moran 2002). However, some employees and many labor rights activists long have alleged that solidarity associations represent an attempt by employers to undermine collective organization and bargaining by concluding direct agreements at the firm (rather than at the industry or national) level. *Solidarismo* has its roots in Costa Rica's banana plantations, but solidarity associations now exist throughout the economy: Castro (2003) reports that, in the 1996–2003 period, solidarity associations outnumbered unions by a factor of four or five. In 2002, there were 219 active unions and 1,074 active solidarity associations; solidarity associations were estimated to have 330,000 workers as members.[18]

For over a decade, the ILO's Committee of Experts on the Applications of Conventions and Recommendations (CEACR) noted that solidarity associations interfere with freedom of association. Whereas solidarity associations continue to dominate the private sector, the Costa Rican government has made changes to the laws governing them, as Table 7.1 notes. In 1993, a new chapter (Act 7360) was added to the Labor Code; it

---

[18] Membership estimate is taken from the 2004 U.S. State Department *Country Report on Human Rights Practices* for Costa Rica, Section 6. The 2007 State Department report estimated the number of solidarity association members at 225,000. In its 2008 annual report, the ITUC estimated that solidarity associations continue to outnumber labor unions in Costa Rica by a factor of four to one.

prohibits solidarity associations from undermining trade unions by signing labor-related collective agreements. The reforms also reduced (from twenty to twelve) the number of workers needed to form a union, putting unions on par with solidarity associations.[19] In another reform related to solidarity associations, the Workers' Protection Act of 2000 allows unions to administer occupational deposit funds and pension funds, a task often performed by solidarity associations (Vice Ministers 2005).

The next items in Table 7.1 concern additional elements of collective bargaining. Historically, Costa Rica restricted the use of collective bargaining by many public sector employees and, where collective bargaining contracts were allowed, required administrative approval of collective pacts. In 2001, however, following a 2000 Supreme Court ruling, the parliament adopted a decree allowing collective bargaining by a broader set of public employees. Administrative approval of public-sector collective contracts remains a requirement, despite some promises of reform. Lastly, workers' right to strike has been restricted, in terms of the sectors in which strikes are allowed and the requirements for a legal strike. The former, which has been subject to judicial as well as legislative modifications, prohibited strikes in sectors that went beyond the internationally accepted set of "essential" sectors (AFL-CIO 2001). In 1998, the Supreme Court ruled that most public sector workers *do* have the right to strike, and legislative action in 2003 narrowed the definition of "essential." The government continued to define a legal strike, however, as one that is approved by at least 60 percent of an enterprise's workers, a requirement deemed onerous by the ILO.

In purely legal terms, then, we could note that the existence of a relatively tight and somewhat formalized labor market, along with the shift toward higher-technology production, has been accompanied by improvements over time in collective labor rights. Most observers agree that, with a few exceptions, Costa Rica's collective labor legislation is in line with core international standards (Murillo 2005; Vice Ministers 2005). Observers also note, though, that enforcement of these standards is sometimes problematic (ILO 2003; U.S. State Department, various years). Of the ninety-four violations that the ILO's Trade Union Freedom Committee substantiated in Costa Rica during 1990–2006, the offending

---

[19] Some labor rights activists continue to criticize the requirement of more than twelve members for the formation of a union. They argue that this requirement renders a union presence difficult to realize in small businesses. See, for instance, the ITUC's 2008 survey on violations of trade union rights.

parties complied fully in ten cases, partially in thirty instances, and not at all in fifty-four cases – a high rate of non-compliance.[20]

Such problems are most evident in dismissals related to union activities. Whereas the 1993 reforms clarified workers' legal rights in such cases, they did not specify procedures to be followed should employers refuse to reinstate wrongfully dismissed workers. There are many outstanding rulings for reinstatement, particularly in the private sector (U.S. State Department 2002; Castro 2003). Additionally, the judicial process for addressing acts of anti-union discrimination has remained slow (ILO 2003; Vice Ministers 2005). On a positive note, the government created specialized labor courts in the late 1990s, reducing its backlog of outstanding cases related to union rights from over 16,000 in 1998 to fewer than 8,000 in the year 2000 (U.S. State Department 2003). The backlog, however, began to grow after 2002; the government then prepared, but delayed passing, legislation to reform the labor court system further. Given the degree of political polarization and the dispersion of political authority in Costa Rica during the first half of the 2000s, the lack of legislative action to further guarantee labor rights is not surprising, despite international pressure.

A related enforcement issue concerns the labor inspectorate: A lack of resources devoted to inspections is likely to lead to a disjuncture between the legal and practical observation of collective labor rights. Throughout much of the 1990s, the U.S. State Department's annual reports noted that Costa Rica had one labor inspector for every 30,000 workers. Inspectors tend to focus on urban areas, leading to the possibility of worse collective labor rights practices in the agriculture sector, and in manufacturing firms located in more rural areas (AFL-CIO 2001). Relative to the region, Costa Rica has far fewer inspectors than Chile (19.25 inspectors per 100,000 workers), but more than Mexico (1.72 inspectors) or Ecuador (0.57; Schrank and Piore 2007).

The shortage of inspectors could be particularly troubling in the private sector, where concerns about the effects of *solidarismo* on the opportunities for union organization and activities are particularly pronounced. For instance, there are very few private-sector strikes in Costa Rica. Without effective monitoring, it is difficult to know if this is the result of repression (where workers would prefer to strike, but employers suppress such efforts) *or* the consequence of a satisfied work force.

---

[20] Information taken from the QVILIS database, http://www.oit.org.pe/qvilis_world/, accessed April 23, 2007.

Likewise, all Costa Rican labor laws apply in the EPZs, but it is unclear whether they are followed in practice and whether adherence to them varies across types of firms (as Hypotheses 6.1 implies). Similarly, the limited availability of inspectors in EPZs renders it difficult to determine whether the prevalence of direct arrangements over collective contracts, and of solidarity associations rather than unions, reflects a denial in practice of collective labor rights (e.g., Moran 2002).[21] Recently, however, Costa Rica has joined other Latin American nations in renewing its enforcement efforts; in 2002, it introduced a plan to reorganize and expand its labor inspectorate. Between 2002 and 2005, the Labor Ministry's budget increased by 25 percent, and its compliance budget doubled.[22]

Both Hypothesis 3.3 and Hypothesis 6.1 suggest that collective labor rights outcomes will vary across economic sectors. In particular, in sectors that employ fewer skilled workers, employers will have greater opportunities for the repression of labor rights, both collective and individual. If workers also face slack labor markets, or are migrant workers (who may worry about their legal status and, therefore, be less likely to complain about their treatment), this possibility is even more pronounced. Moreover, in terms of the spotlight that may accompany multinational-owned firms, enterprises located in rural areas also are less likely to be monitored by NGOs and activists, again increasing the likelihood that employers with preferences for repressing labor will follow through on such inclinations.

Indeed, in Costa Rica, reported violations of workers' rights appear most severe in the agricultural sector, where labor union organization is typically weak and where labor costs are a central concern. Of the 129 denunciations for union persecution registered with the Labor

---

[21] The ICFTU (1995) reports that, in the early 1990s, approximately 90 percent of U.S. MNCs in EPZs dealt solely with solidarity associations. The ICFTU (1993) also has alleged that CINDE openly promotes *solidarismo* as an alternative to trade unions. A recent marketing presentation from CINDE touts the "non-existent unions in the private sector" as well as the flexibility of Costa Rica's labor law in comparison with other Latin American nations. See http://www.cinde.org/UserFiles/File/CINDEpercent2oGeneral percent2oPresentationpercent2oEN.pps#35.

[22] Schrank and Piore (2007) note, however, that reforms of the labor inspectorate may be easiest to achieve under left-leaning governments and with left-leaning governments in office in the United States. By the time Costa Rica's labor ministry decided to embark on reforms of the inspectorate, the right-leaning Rodríguez was in office, and there was little pressure from the U.S. government. The number of Costa Rican labor inspectors declined in real terms, relative to the work force, in the early years of this decade. Locke et al. (2009a) discuss the issue of under-resourced inspectors and auditors with regard to the implementation of voluntary, private-sector-based codes of labor conduct.

Ministry and originating in the private sector from 1993 to 2000, 52 percent were from banana plantations. Specific incidents mentioned in the ICFTU's annual surveys are overwhelmingly from the agricultural sector. Violations identified by the ICFTU involve both multinational and Costa Rican firms (ITUC 2007; also see Frundt 2002). Moreover, the bias toward direct accords and away from collectively bargained agreements is most pronounced in agriculture: In the 1998–2003 period, there were 311 direct accords in agriculture (and 9 collective bargaining agreements); in non-agriculture private-sector enterprises, there were 51 direct accords and 18 collective bargaining agreements (Castro 2003).

The banana industry also has attracted attention from labor rights activists; their campaigns are linked toward the movement toward "fair trade" bananas in this sector as well as to the visibility of bananas as a consumer product throughout the developed world. Given this combination of activist interest and opportunities for violation, reports on labor rights issues in Costa Rica tend to highlight problems in this sector (whereas it is very difficult to find similar reports for the electronics sector). For instance, a 2007 report from ActionAid (a UK-based NGO) highlights a variety of labor rights violations, both collective and individual, in Costa Rica. This report is based largely on approximately 170 interviews with workers on sixteen Costa Rica banana plantations, conducted in late 2006. The report points out that price competition among banana producers (and among supermarkets) is fierce; given that fixed costs (such as pesticides) account for the majority of firms' costs, labor costs (estimated at 15 to 20 percent of firms' total expenses) tend to be the focus of efforts to reduce production costs. Reported violations include a shift from hourly wage rates to piece rates, which require laborers to work for twelve to fifteen hours per day in order to earn a salary that equates to the statutory minimum wage; exposures to pesticides and other hazardous chemicals; and a shift from permanent to temporary employment contracts, which reduces workers' legal rights. Given that migrant workers (mostly from Nicaragua) now account for approximately one-half of the labor force in Costa Rica's banana sector, the likelihood that workers will mobilize to oppose these conditions is low (ActionAid 2007). Perhaps, however, there is some reason for optimism: In the wake of the debates regarding CAFTA-DR ratification, and in response to corporate social responsibility campaigns, multinational banana companies have begun to acknowledge some of the activists' reports and to – according to their corporate social responsibility reports – upgrade working conditions on plantations.

Again, though, the contrast between the conditions described on plantations and those that prevail in the electronics-sector firms in Costa Rica's free trade zones is a striking one. Intel is often noted as responsible for bringing various best practices to Costa Rica. For instance, following Intel's arrival, Costa Rica's National Insurance Institute (INS) created the country's first job safety and health standard, patterned after Intel's practices in its facilities. Intel's standards in this area are applied to its own facilities as well as to its suppliers and subcontractors (World Bank 2006); at least in the area of individual labor rights, this appears an instance of MNCs transferring best practices to their affiliates overseas.

IV. LESSONS FROM COSTA RICA

The mixed picture for collective labor rights in Costa Rica illustrates the tensions between cost-based competitive pressures related to trade openness and subcontracting and the climb to the top processes linked with directly owned production. The expansion of Costa Rica's EPZs has contributed to export diversification, but MNCs may be drawn to Costa Rica because of its hostility toward – or at least lack of embrace for – organized labor. As the discussion in Chapter 3 anticipates, domestic factors – a history of labor repression and a lack of strong ties between unions and ruling political parties, combined with a sizeable proportion of service-related employment, in which union organization is difficult – can conspire to mute the potential positive effects of FDI, and to reinforce the potential negative effects of trade competition, on collective labor rights.

At the same time, though, if we draw a distinction between collective and individual labor rights, a more optimistic account may emerge. Limited collective labor rights may not detract from protections of individual rights and working conditions, particularly if industrial upgrading occurs and skilled labor becomes better able to bargain with employers (e.g., Moran 2002). Put differently, solidarity associations may interfere with the ability of workers to bargain collectively in the traditional sense; but the absence of this right may be offset by the benefits that come in the form of better jobs and higher wages. Costa Rica's checkered record with regard to process-based rights does not necessarily inhibit the achievement of outcomes-based standards (Barrientos and Smith 2007).

Along these lines, some observers distinguish between Costa Rica's labor laws vis-à-vis unions and its (more favorable) laws vis-à-vis individual workers (Frundt 1998; Schrank and Piore 2007). On the side of individual working conditions, Costa Rica's real wages increased during much of the 1970s, 1980s, and 1990s, in contrast with much of Latin America (Weeks 1999). If we consider non-wage labor costs as indicative of workers' individual conditions (as these cover sick pay, health care, and pensions), Costa Rica has high non-wage labor costs relative to its peers. Non-wage labor costs averaged 26 percent of salary in 2005. These costs rank 33rd of 156 countries surveyed; Costa Rica has lower costs than Sweden (33 percent) but higher costs than Germany (20 percent).[23] Additionally, if we look at the EPZ level, we see marked wage growth between 1997 and 2005. The ratio of minimum salaries of all EPZ workers relative to that of semi-skilled workers elsewhere in the economy was 1.33 in 1997. By 2005, EPZ minimum salaries were more than 1.7 times those of semi-skilled, non-EPZ workers (PROCOMER 2006, 47; also see Madami 1999).

By the same token, these positive effects at the individual level may be felt only in a small set of firms. Rising wages in EPZs benefit the approximately 40,000 individuals currently employed there, but they may offer little to the remainder of Costa Rica's workforce, particular in low-technology, labor-intensive activities. Given, for instance, that much of semiconductor fabrication is automated, the direct employment consequences for Costa Rican workers of Intel's facilities in Costa Rica are quite limited (also see Silver 2003). At the same time, other workers in Costa Rica may experience the negative effects of economic openness, as competitive pressures (via trade and tourism) lead to greater downward pressure on wages, working conditions, and collective rights in the agricultural and service sectors. Whereas much of the value added to Costa Rica's economy is now in the high-technology sectors, the bulk of its employment remains in other sectors. In this way, it is perhaps not entirely different from other low- and middle-income economies, where agriculture remains a significant source of employment.[24] In demonstrating the plausibility of a series of domestic-level variables as important intervening factors, the Costa Rican case lends support to the proposition that national responses to multinational production are contingent on domestic institutions. This assertion is consistent with recent scholarship on industrial upgrading, which identifies it as a necessary – but

---

[23] Data are from the 2005 version of the World Bank's *Doing Business* survey. http://www. doingbusiness.org/ExploreTopics/EmployingWorkers/

[24] Flanagan (2006) notes that agriculture still provides most of the jobs in low-income developing nations and 40 percent of the work in middle-income countries.

not sufficient – condition for positive changes (see Breznitz 1999; 2007; Gereffi 1999).

Given that the case of Costa Rica reveals the value in tracing countries' experience with collective labor rights over time, and in treating domestic factors as important mediating variables, how might it inform future research on multinational production and labor rights? First, analyzing a wider set of cases qualitatively would allow researchers to move beyond probing the plausibility of domestically oriented hypotheses. Ideally, such cases would display different combinations of "multinational production" variables, such as high levels of both directly owned and subcontracted production; low levels of both FDI and subcontracting; high levels of directly owned production but low levels of arm's-length activities; and low levels of direct investment but high levels of subcontracting. Studying this array of cases, with a focus on the mediating effect of domestic factors, would provide a better sense of how different facets of economic globalization interact to affect governments' and firms behavior. Moreover, as I discuss in previous chapters, it may be useful to distinguish between the effects on legal protections for workers' rights and the actual implementation of such rights. Costa Rica's experience suggests that, whereas governments often are slow to enact legal reforms in middle-income nations, the real challenge – and the most noticeable impact of political institutions and ideologies – lies in the fields of implementation, inspection, and enforcement.

Second, and returning to an issue discussed in Chapter 6, such cases could be cast, not only at the national level, but also at the sectoral level. Different types of multinational production may have different consequences for labor rights. Violations of labor rights also may be focused in particular industries. Third and finally, Costa Rica's recent experiences, especially in light of debates regarding ratification of CAFTA-DR there and in the United States, highlight the potential impact of other international forces on labor rights outcomes. Murillo and Schrank's (2005) broader study of Latin America finds that, in traditionally labor-repressive polities (including Costa Rica), unions formed transnational coalitions with U.S. labor unions, bringing U.S. government pressure to bear on their home governments. In Costa Rica, local labor federations worked with the AFL-CIO to petition the U.S. Trade Representative for removal of the country's Generalized System of Preferences (GSP) privileges, alleging violations of internationally recognized core labor standards (Frundt 2002); such pressure may have contributed to the 1993 Labor Code reforms.

Moreover, intergovernmental organizations (e.g., the ILO) and national government agencies (such as USAID and ILAB) may provide direct resources for the improvement of labor rights. As in other policy areas (Brooks 2005; Simmons et al. 2008), the particular orientation and funding strategies of these entities may affect outcomes. Frundt (2002) notes, for instance, that several international funding sources (official and private) recently have directed resources away from labor unions and toward NGO-based support for workers' rights and health, as well as child labor (Vice Ministers 2005, Annex E). By 2001, Central America hosted twenty internationally funded projects on *maquila* issues, but only one that directly supported union organizing. This relates as well to a larger issue raised by Costa Rica: Whereas we tend to assume a connection between collective and individual labor rights, in that the former facilitates the achievement of the latter, this may not always be true in practice. Particularly in technology and capital-intensive sectors, Costa Rica's workers have fared well relative to their counterparts elsewhere in the region. Yet their on-the-ground capacity to organize and act collectively still falls short of international standards, suggesting that such standards may not always be necessary for the achievement of a certain level of individual labor rights outcomes.

8

Conclusions and Issues for the Future

Multinational corporations often are the targets of human and labor rights activists. Whereas some activists view MNCs as partners in corporate social responsibility efforts, the relationship more often is an adversarial one. Labor rights activists are suspicious of MNCs' commitments to improving workers' rights, and they often treat MNCs as agents of repression in developing nations.

The activists, in fact, may have a point. Indeed, some types of global production in which MNCs are involved have negative consequences for workers' rights. We observe these most easily where subcontracting and arm's-length relationships with suppliers are the tools of market entry. In these situations, the cost concerns associated with global competition can generate downward pressures on labor standards. The activists' point lacks nuance, however, as this downward pressure is only part of the story. Directly owned production often has positive consequences for labor rights, as MNCs bring their best practices to their subsidiaries, and as MNCs strive to hire and retain the most productive workers in host economies.

What, then, ought activists and policymakers do? This book suggests two general lessons. First, they should acknowledge the heterogeneity of multinational production. Some modes of firm entry and organization will have positive effects for labor rights, even if MNCs are purely profit-oriented. Other modes, however, can damage labor rights. Second, no matter the pressures emanating from the global economy, many determinants of labor rights outcomes remain internal to states. Democratization, economic growth, and the expansion of the formal economic sector are direct and important pathways to improved labor rights. They deserve at least as much of activists' attention as MNCs receive.

This concluding chapter summarizes the book's main findings, which support these two lessons. Moreover, it offers directions for future research, which take into account, not only unanswered research questions regarding past and current collective labor rights, but also change in the nature of global production, which likely will matter to future labor rights outcomes.

I. ARGUMENTS, FINDINGS, AND EXTENSIONS

One of the primary arguments that I develop and test is that these differences in how low- and middle-income nations participate in global production networks have important implications for the rights of workers to organize, bargain collectively, and strike. In particular, the presence of directly owned multinational operations is likely to be associated with improvements in collective labor rights, as MNCs have incentives to bring best practices (or, more generally, a standardized set of corporate practices) to host countries. These MNCs also tend to hire from the top of local labor markets, generating material incentives for them to attract and retain (via the provision of collective labor rights as well as the maintenance of good working conditions) employees. Moreover, when these MNCs find themselves under scrutiny from transnational and local activists, shareholders, and consumers, such pressures can contribute to their incentives to treat workers well. As a result, the longer-run global trend toward greater foreign direct investment activity, reviewed in Chapter 2, should augur positively for labor rights.

At the same time, however, the global economy certainly generates some pressures for cross-national competition. Some of these forces can lead to a competitive lowering – or, at the very least, a static pattern – of labor rights practices. This is particularly true for multinational production that relies on arm's-length (subcontracted) rather than directly owned production. In arm's-length relationships, the capacity of subcontracting firms to supply a given product at the lowest possible price is key to winning contracts from lead firms in the supply chain. The focus on prices generates concerns with wage rates and non-wage labor costs, as these tend to be viewed as the most variable of firms' production expenses. At the same time, because subcontracting activities tend to involve hundreds or even thousands of suppliers, often in geographically diverse locations, the capacity of lead firms to monitor labor rights practices of their suppliers is quite limited. The prevalence of subcontracting in labor-intensive industries – where the organizational incentives to keep production in-house are few – generates additional downward pressures on the provision and protection of workers' collective rights. Hence, using trade openness as a reasonable proxy for subcontracting activity, increases in trade openness are predicted to negatively affect labor rights.

Whereas the focus of this book is on causal processes related to the global economy, many of the main determinants of labor rights outcomes are domestic. Domestic variables remain important determinants of labor rights outcomes, either acting independently (for instance, more democratic regimes tend to have stronger protections for labor rights), or mediating the influence of global economic factors (so that left-leaning governments may mute the negative pressures generated by trade-based competition).

Another objective of *Labor Rights and Multinational Production* is to facilitate the cross-country, cross-regional and over-time assessment of collective labor rights outcomes. Whereas policymakers, labor rights activists, and political scientists have long been interested in the causal connections between workers' rights and the global economy, their capacity to assess these relationships in a large-N context has been limited by a lack of comparable data. We generate an annual measure of collective labor rights violations, covering every sovereign state in the international system, and spanning the years between 1985 and 2002. This measure serves as the main dependent variable in the various statistical analyses reported in Chapters 5 and 6. Whereas the labor rights measure has its limitations, as I discuss in Chapter 4, it also offers advances over existing cross-national measures. In particular, it focuses specifically on labor – rather than more broadly on human – rights; it considers government and private sector behavior, rather than simply the ratification of international conventions; and it is based on multiple sources of information. The components of the labor rights measure also allow us to differentiate between collective labor rights in law and those in practice, where we may well observe significant differences in outcomes even within the same country and year.

The main findings from the statistical analyses offer support to our key expectations: Country-years characterized by greater foreign direct investment flows do, in fact, have significantly better collective labor rights outcomes. But higher levels of openness to international trade are negatively linked with these same outcomes. At the same time, our empirical analyses highlight the importance of various domestically oriented variables, such as the type of political regime, the ideology of the governing party or executive, and the level of economic development. Additional analyses point to the utility of differentiating between the legal protection of labor rights and the practical implementation of such rights, as the significant correlates of law and practice tend to differ. From a policy point of view, this suggests that we ought to ask not how open an economy is in general, but specifically to what sorts of activities it is open. Although convincing governments to enact legal reforms that follow internationally recognized core labor standards is a good first step, it is not sufficient to guarantee the protection of such rights in practice. For reasons both technical and political, there remains a significant gap between labor rights in law and labor rights in practice.

In Chapter 6, I consider further types of heterogeneity in global production and the implications of these differences for labor rights outcomes. I explore differences in production profiles, export orientations, and foreign direct investment flows, as well as differences in the nationality of foreign direct investors. I consider the impact – via statistical analyses – of production and export profiles on labor rights outcomes. I also assess whether FDI in certain sectors (i.e., automobiles and extractive industries) is significantly linked with labor rights outcomes. Moreover, I analyze firms' views on labor-related issues, finding that developing-country firms in labor-intensive sectors do tend to express a greater concern with labor-related costs and policies. Whereas these empirical tests leave much for future research – both quantitative and qualitative – they also confirm the plausibility of within-country differences in the impact of multinational production on labor rights.

I also posit that there exist differences among multinational corporations on the basis of source country effects. Whereas some of these differences among MNCs regarding labor rights practice occur along sectoral lines (for instance, pharmaceutical versus textile firms), others are likely related to nationality. "Varieties of capitalism" (Hall and Soskice 2001) are associated with differences in corporate cultures, such as that between Anglo-American firms, on the one hand, and Continental European firms, on the other. These differences will persist when firms take their home country "best practices" abroad to their foreign affiliates. I also expect broader differences between firms based in developed countries and those headquartered in developing nations. Whereas the former were the primary sources of direct investment during the post-World War II period, the latter's role as outward investors is growing. If this trend persists, we may observe new – and perhaps worse – sorts of labor rights practices being transferred from home to host countries. From the point of view of public policy, this trend implies that encouraging investment flows between high-standards and low-standards destinations – rather than sanctioning countries with low labor standards – may be the more effective means of improving workers' rights in low- and middle-income countries (also see Flanagan 2006). Such logic also may apply to trade relationships, given recent evidence regarding the bilateral trade-based diffusion of labor rights practices (Greenhill et al. 2009).

Chapter 7 extends the analysis in a different way, by considering longer-run, domestic determinants of labor rights outcomes. I analyze the experiences of Costa Rica in order to illustrate the interaction between domestic political institutions and histories, on the one hand, and global economic forces, on the other. Costa Rica faces contending international pressures, given its relatively high degree of openness to international trade *and* its large amounts of FDI. Costa Rica also has undergone an upgrading in its industrial profile. In particular, the 1990s were characterized by the arrival of foreign direct investment in the electronics and medical devices sectors and by an accompanying decline in the overall economic importance of the agricultural sector.

Yet, at the same time, Costa Rica is characterized by a long history of repression of organized labor groups, which has – despite the structure of the country's labor market – limited efforts at achieving collective labor rights. Whereas the 1990s and early 2000s witnessed some changes in the country's labor laws, bringing them more into conformity with international labor standards, the period also was characterized by difficulties in implementing collective labor laws. Furthermore, the conditions faced by Costa Rica's workforce differ markedly across sectors: although there are few complaints about the labor practices of firms in the high-technology sectors, many allegations of both collective and individual labor rights violations in agriculture remain. Whereas those in skill-intensive industries have experienced many of the benefits of multinational production, these benefits have not necessarily extended to workers elsewhere in the economy. We ought to explore, therefore, the conditions under which firm- and sector-level benefits of multinational production diffuse more broadly throughout host economies.

More generally, scholars of international and comparative political economy can continue to improve our analytical grasp of the linkages between the global economy and labor rights. First, we can refine further our cross-national measures of labor rights outcomes. In addition to expanding the time frame of the collective labor rights indicator, we should develop measures cast at the sectoral, rather than national, level. Labor rights violations may cluster in some sectors of the economy – in the private rather than public sector, or in textiles and apparel rather than in pharmaceuticals and electronics. Our current collective labor rights measure focuses on country-level outcomes, so it does not explore such differences. A more refined measure would allow us to assess more directly the determinants and correlates of collective labor rights. We could, for instance, gain a better sense of the extent to which violations tend to cluster in labor-intensive industries.

Second, we should complement our measures of collective labor rights with cross-national indicators of individual working conditions. These include wages, working hours, health and safety conditions, the prevalence of child labor, and gender-related issues (including discrimination and maternity leave, among others). Whereas we would expect a correlation between these conditions and collective labor rights, it is unlikely a perfect one. With cross-national data on individual conditions, we could investigate the sources of divergence between collective and individual rights as well as the determinants of individual labor rights themselves. Some indicators of these individual labor rights exist already; the challenge is to expand their country and year coverage and to find indicators that accurately reflect conditions on the ground (rather than, for instance, child labor rates reported by national governments).

Additionally, the informal economy plays an important role in many low- and middle-income countries. Concomitant with structural adjustment programs, the size of the informal sector workforce grew in many countries during the 1990s (Visser 2003). National laws and international conventions regarding collective labor rights concern the formal sector, and assessments of labor rights practices also tend to focus on formal sector workers. Informal sector workers often work in rural areas, are relatively unskilled, and enjoy few protections from national labor regulations (Flanagan 2006). Whereas it is difficult to conceive of a cross-national measure of labor or human rights that would assess the labor-related outcomes of these workers (Abouharb and Cingranelli 2008), it is nonetheless important to note their exclusion from our analyses.

Third, scholars should consider how best to treat multinational production, both theoretically and empirically. Whereas scholarly attention to FDI and MNCs has increased markedly during this decade, our empirical analyses tend to rely on national-level data, even while many of our theories focus on firm-level incentives and behavior. For instance, scholarship that considers the linkages between political institutions and foreign direct investment (Büthe and Milner 2008; Jensen 2006; Li 2006) advances various propositions about how individual firms assess investment risk and how various political institutions (international as well as domestic) affect these assessments. This book's theoretical claims are largely at the firm level, in terms of the incentives to focus on production costs or firms' tendency to employ a single set of labor-related practices across firms' supply chains. However, the empirical tests of these propositions tend to rely on country-level data; aggregating from the firm and industry to the national level, however, can obscure much of the diversity among MNCs.

In some ways, this is unavoidable given the (un)availability of sectoral-level direct investment data. However, it also reflects a need for empirical work at the firm level: Multinational companies themselves should feature more prominently as political actors. Some earlier work on MNCs took such an approach (i.e., Bauer et al. 1963; also see Bandelj 2008), and evidence from firm-level surveys and interviews is a useful starting point for doing so. Yet firm-level empirical analyses remain somewhat rare in political science scholarship.[1] Carefully designed studies of individual firms (perhaps firms with operations in a variety of countries and even sectors) could shed greater light on various questions related to the politics of foreign direct investment. Such studies would allow us to explore the impact on labor rights of differences in firm sector, ownership, size, and supplier relations. Recent work by Locke et al. (2007), which investigates the correlates of differences in labor code compliance among Nike supplier factories, illustrates the utility of such an empirical strategy.

II. LABOR RIGHTS IN THE 21ST CENTURY

What lessons do the various arguments and analyses presented in this book hold for the future? Recent trends in the global economy highlight the potential for changes in the connections between multinational production and labor rights. It is nearly impossible to read a popular account of contemporary economic globalization that does not discuss the role of China. Such discussions (i.e., Meredith 2007) often are cast in terms of race to the bottom concerns, in which China's large reserves of unskilled labor, combined with its government's willingness to repress workers' rights and its continued capacity to attract large flows of direct

---

[1] Examples include Mares 2003, Martin and Swank 2001, Milner 1988, and Murphy 2004.

investment from North America, Europe, and elsewhere in Asia, render it a behemoth of global production. Other low- and middle-income countries, the argument goes, have little choice but to compete with China by reducing regulations and lowering wages. Otherwise, foreign-owned firms will move their affiliates and their subcontracting orders to China, leaving a vacuum in much of the rest of the developing world. Moreover, many argue, foreign firms are unable to resist the temptation of China as an export platform: Whereas multinational firms may be willing to withdraw from smaller-scale production locations (such as Burma or Zimbabwe) in response to activists' complaints about human and labor rights violations, very few firms are willing to exclude China from their global production strategies (Elliott and Freeman 2003). As a result, China is perhaps more able than most host country governments to do as it likes vis-à-vis workers, yet still enjoy the benefits of vast direct investment inflows.

These concerns were expressed strongly in the wake of the phaseout of the Multifibre Arrangement (MFA). The MFA, also referred to as the Agreement on Textiles and Clothing, was in force from 1974 to 2004. It provided quotas, by narrowly defined product categories, on the amount of garments and textiles that each developing nation could export to individual developed countries. The agreement allowed many developing nations without clear comparative advantages in the apparel sector to develop textile and clothing industries. Bangladesh, for instance, was provided with unlimited access (no quotas) to the European Union's consumer markets. Cambodia, Lesotho, Indonesia, Mauritius, the Philippines, and Sri Lanka, among many others, also developed significant textile and apparel production. Multinational corporations often manipulated the quota system, deciding where to locate subsidiaries and from where to hire subcontractors on the basis of quota permits.

In the context of the negotiations to create the World Trade Organization, member governments set January 2005 as the end date for the MFA. As this date approached, observers worried that clothing and textile production would quickly concentrate in China, leading to large investment and employment losses in many other developing nations. Indeed, as early as March 2006, observers noted that many of Mauritius' Hong Kong-based foreign investors – accounting for a quarter of the nation's textile employment – had closed their operations, generating a 30 percent contraction in garment manufacturing. In explaining the shift, some in the business community noted that Mauritius had relatively high wage costs and a rigid labor code. Similarly, Laos experienced dramatic initial declines in its textile industry. These were not surprising, given that labor productivity there was one-third lower than in China (or Vietnam); that shipping costs were significantly higher (given the need to ship finished products through Thailand); and that education levels were low, even by the standards of work involving basic tasks. On the other side of the equation, China's textile and apparel exports surged in early 2005, doubling in many product categories. Both the United States and the European Union imposed temporary restrictions on the growth of apparel imports from China, but the longer-term trend indicated that worries about an "all to China" effect were not entirely misplaced.

In terms of the implications for workers' rights, the picture appears a mixed one: The phaseout *did* allow foreign and domestic firms to source and produce textiles without regard to quota allocations. Rather, they could focus on cost and product quality. Some governments responded with attempts to upgrade: Cambodia (see Chapter 3) continued its efforts to position itself as a high labor standards production location, whereas Mauritius' government discussed a combination of upgrading strategies, including positioning itself as a "high quality, fast delivery" textile producer (perhaps akin to Italy and Turkey; see Berger 2005) and shifting toward higher-technology services (the "cybercenter" strategy).

Upgrading and product differentiation are but two possible responses to the competitive pressures generated by the end of the MFA. Another response is the one that concerns globalization's critics – that, in their efforts to win back business from China, other low- and middle-income nations will compete on the basis of costs, generating downward pressure on labor rights. The latter remains a very real possibility, particularly as the more recent global economic downturn reduces consumer demand in high-income economies and as globally oriented firms engage in some retrenchment. The extent to which repression in the apparel sector will increase appears dependent on the interplay between activist and firm-level efforts at socially responsible production, on the one hand, and lead and supplier firms' concerns with cost (as opposed to other considerations), on the other.

With respect to China specifically, we would do well to treat the country as something more than – and not entirely characterized by – a low-cost, labor-intensive production location. During the last decade, several empirical studies have noted the diversity of production within China (Berger 2005; Gallagher 2005; Guthrie 1999; Santoro 2000). Whereas some production in China *does* depend on unskilled or low-skilled workers, many of whom are female migrants from rural areas with limited awareness of or interest in agitating for their collective labor rights, this is not the entire picture. An additional element of China's recent development is a government-backed, private-sector effort to move toward design as well as production and to increase the skill of the labor force. Rather than being content to serve as the assembly line for foreign firms, China has witnessed the construction of large-scale factories that aim to integrate design and production (Sabel 2007). This is one element of the country's broader aim of climbing the development ladder, and it involves reintegrating previously fragmented supply chains. For workers, such a strategy implies efforts to train, recruit, and retain higher-skilled employees. Such attempts – coupled with the Chinese government's efforts to encourage research and development at a variety of universities and think tanks – may expand the segment of China's labor force that is more willing to press for improvements in collective rights and working conditions.

A second important development in China concerns labor market conditions. Despite the popular perception that China benefits from an endless supply of low-cost labor, reports in the mid-2000s suggested a tightening of the labor market, even in labor-intensive production. In the early part of the 2000s, there were – as with the apparel sector – concerns that electronics production would shift from various locations in Southeast Asia to China. Indeed, China's electronics exports increased in the first half of the 2000s. However, by 2006, media reports began to note that several multinational firms were reversing course, building facilities instead in Malaysia, Singapore, and Vietnam. These firms cited rising wage costs generated by a shortage of skilled workers in China's Guangdong Province, the locus of the country's electronics production. In 2006, for instance, wages for electronics sector workers in Guangdong were described as higher than those in Malaysia.

In response to these trends, some U.S.-based multinationals have shifted from an "all China" to a "China plus others" strategy. This diversification away from China is driven by a variety of concerns, including political uncertainty; infrastructure problems (usually, electricity shortages); and, most markedly for MNCs, wage increases. In skilled industries, the annual increase is estimated at 25 percent. Even in textiles and clothing, reports note a rise in wages of 12 percent in 2007 and a further 16 percent in 2008. Perhaps related to these labor market shifts are recent reforms to China's labor laws. Given China's political structure, it remains unclear how these legal reforms will be implemented. The reforms, passed in June 2007, allow collective bargaining (albeit within China's single union structure); require employers to provide written contracts to workers; and restrict firms' use of temporary workers. Most accounts agree that these reforms were largely a response to growing worker unrest in China. Perhaps, then, China is not that different from other low- and middle-income nations: As labor markets tighten and the demands for skilled workers increase, both firms and the government face growing pressures to improve labor rights. Whereas competitive, "race to the bottom" pressures may persist, these are offset by pressures for improvements. The question, of course, is what the balance between these sets of pressures will be in the future.

Turning to global investment generally, current FDI is characterized by a shift toward the services sector. Whereas the extent to which this shift is occurring varies across countries, the share of global direct investment in the services sector has grown in recent years. At the same time, of course, the share of direct investment in extractive and manufacturing industries has declined. This shift has been facilitated by technological change, which allows for the outsourcing and offshoring of firms' previously in-house activities, as well as by privatizations in developing nations (i.e., in telecommunications) and by efforts of global and regional trade bodies to liberalize trade in sectors such as banking and insurance. Indeed, many of the popular claims about the "flattening" of the world economy are based on anecdotal evidence drawn from the services sector – software development and call centers in India, for instance (Friedman 2005).

The shift toward services FDI may have implications for labor rights, just as do shifts from labor-intensive to capital-intensive manufacturing. Service industries tend to be characterized by lower levels of unionization, implying fewer demands for collective labor rights as well as a possible decline in organized labor's domestic political voice (i.e., Iversen and Wren 1998). At the same time, though, service industries vary in their labor intensity and skill intensity. Tourism often tends toward labor-intensive, lower-skilled activities, suggesting that labor costs may be central to firms. However, tourism also is more prone to receive attention from transnational activists and consumers. Banking and finance, on the other hand, are largely skill-intensive activities, which may not employ large numbers of workers but which are likely to offer better working conditions and collective labor rights to employees.

Another trend in global FDI, noted previously, is the gradual rise of developing nations as sources of direct investment outflows. Outward direct investment from Brazil, China, and India, in particular, has increased markedly during the second half of the 2000s. In 2006, for example, Brazil's direct investment outflows exceeded its inflows for the first time in the country's history; this was driven largely by CVRD's (a Brazilian mining company) purchase of Inco, a Canadian nickel producer. During the 2008–2009 downturn, these larger developing nations were – at least initially – a more stable source of outward direct investment than were their developed-country counterparts. Much of the outward investment from the South focuses on the extractive sector, as both public and private entities in developing nations aim to locate new sources of natural resources (UNCTAD 2007). In the extractive sector, it is not yet clear how the shift from high- to middle-income countries as owners of direct investment will affect labor rights outcomes. However, in labor-intensive sectors, where South-South direct investment flows also have grown, we might worry about whether a "China effect" will cancel out the "California effect." That is, if multinational firms bring corporate practices to their subsidiaries and affiliates and if corporate labor practices in developing nations tend to include less respect for collective labor rights, then the shift in the sources of direct investment may have negative implications for workers' rights.

Finally, the overall state of the global economy certainly plays a role in determining the relationships between multinational production and workers' rights. Global downturns tend to be associated with reductions in foreign direct investment activity. These include a decline in the creation or purchase of new foreign affiliates as well as the divestment of existing foreign operations (UNCTAD 2009). As developing countries compete to attract a shrinking pool of FDI and to retain current FDI, they may be tempted to do so on the basis of laxer regulatory environments. Additionally, if global energy prices experience surges similar to those that occurred in 2007 and early 2008, firms may have another incentive to contract their supply chains, at least in terms of the chains' geographic scope (Levinson 2008). Relatively low shipping costs enable the current pattern of often geographically disparate supply chains; should these costs increase in a sustained fashion, firms may find themselves relocating production closer to consumer markets. In this case, factors other than labor costs (or labor productivity) may play a larger role in firm location and subcontracting decisions.[2]

---

[2] The importance of long-distance transportation to the structure of global production chains also can serve to advantage workers in this sector. See Silver 2003.

In terms of consumers and shareholders in developed nations, economic conditions can affect their responsiveness to and demand for corporate social responsibility campaigns. If consumers treat labor standards as luxury items – something they are willing to pay extra for when times are good or when purchasing branded products – then an economic downturn will reduce market-based pressures on firms to address labor rights issues. If, on the other hand, activists are successful in keeping labor rights on the consumer's agenda, firms may face sustained market-based incentives to attend to core labor standards. Along these lines, in October 2008, Wal-Mart announced that it would require manufacturers supplying its stores to adhere to stricter environmental and ethical standards. The company described new requirements for suppliers, which included building longer-term relationships with a smaller set of suppliers, thereby increasing its capacity to conduct monitoring within its supply chain. At the same time, though, Wal-Mart noted that this would not compromise its ability to provide low-cost goods, given its market share and its resulting ability to make demands on suppliers. The broader question for the future is whether, when faced with tradeoffs between labor rights and product costs, firms and consumers will prioritize workers' rights. This, too, remains an open question, both theoretically and empirically.

Appendix

Data and Coding

VARIABLE NAMES AND DESCRIPTIONS

Unless otherwise indicated, data are from the World Bank, *World Development Indicators*.

Asia and Pacific: Dichotomous variable, coded one for Asian and Pacific region nations, zero otherwise.

Caribbean: Dichotomous variable, coded one for Caribbean nations, zero otherwise.

Chemical Products Exports: Chemical products as a percentage of total exports. From UNCTAD. UNCTAD provides information on a country's trade (import and export) profile, using broad categories of products, and based on SITC revision 2: all food items SITC 0 + 1 + 22 + 4); agricultural raw materials (SITC 2 − 22 − 27 − 28); Fuels (SITC 3); Ores and metals (SITC 27 + 28 + 68); Manufactured goods (SITC 5 to 8 less 68); Chemical products (SITC 5); Other manufactured goods (SITC 6 + 8 − 68); Machinery and transport equipment (SITC 7); and Unallocated. Data from UNCTAD's *Handbook of Statistics Online*, Section 4.1 (Trade Structure by Commodity Group); see http://www.unctad.org/Templates/Page.asp?intItemID=1890&lang=1

Civil War: Dummy variable, with one indicating participation in war within states, taken from the Armed Conflict Dataset (Version 1.1). The original data has three categories for the intensity of conflict (1 = minor, 2 = intermediate, and 3 = war). Recoded so that the variable has a value of one if an observation has a score of either two or three on either type of conflict, i.e., internal or internationalized internal conflict. See http://www.prio.no/cwp/ArmedConflict/.

Country Number: Country number; used in Stata to *tsset* data.

Democracy: Combined Polity scale, with a range of −10 (autocracy) to 10 (democracy), taken from the Polity IV database. See www.bsos.umd.edu/cidcm/inscr/polity.

Economic Peers' Practices: The mean score of every other country in the same income per capita decile, calculated annually. Given the theoretical reasoning behind this variable (countries compete with other countries in the same income category, regardless of their geographic location), we

Income Decile	Countries (bold if in reported model)	Average Income Per Capita
1	**Burundi, Congo (Dem. Rep.), Congo (Rep.),** Ethiopia, Eritrea, **Guinea-Bissau, Madagascar, Mali, Malawi, Niger, Nigeria, Sierra Leone,** Tajikistan, **Tanzania, Yemen, Zambia**	$654
2	**Benin, Burkina Faso, Central African Republic, Chad, Cote d'Ivoire, Gambia,** Haiti, **Kenya,** Kyrgyz Republic, Moldova, **Mozambique, Nepal, Rwanda, Senegal, Togo, Uganda**	$1059
3	**Angola, Bangladesh, Cambodia, Cameroon,** Comoros, Djibouti, **Ghana, Guinea,** Laos, **Mauritania, Mongolia, Pakistan,** Solomon Islands, **Sudan,** Uzbekistan, **Vietnam**	$1563
4	Armenia, Azerbaijan, Bolivia, **Ecuador, Egypt,** Georgia, Honduras, **India, Indonesia, Jamaica, Lesotho, Nicaragua,** Papua New Guinea, Sri Lanka, **Syria,** Vanuatu	$2377
5	Albania, Cape Verde, **China,** El Salvador, Fiji, **Guatemala,** Guyana, **Jordan,** Lebanon, Paraguay, **Peru,** Philippines, **Swaziland,** Turkmenistan, Ukraine, Venezuela	$3487
6	**Algeria,** Belarus, Belize, Bosnia and Herzegovina, **Colombia,** Dominica, Gabon, Kazakhstan, Macedonia, Namibia, Panama, Romania, St. Lucia, St. Vincent, **Turkey,** Western Samoa	$4656
7	**Botswana,** Brazil, Bulgaria, Chile, **Costa Rica,** Dominican Republic, Grenada, **Iran,** Latvia, Malaysia, **Mexico,** Russia, **Thailand,** Trinidad and Tobago, Tonga, **Tunisia, Uruguay**	$6137
8	Antigua and Barbuda, **Argentina,** Barbados, Croatia, Czech Republic, Estonia, Hungary, Kuwait, Lithuania, **Mauritius,** Oman, Poland, Saudi Arabia, Slovak Republic, **South Africa,** St. Kitts	$9675

Income Decile	Countries (bold if in reported model)	Average Income Per Capita
9	Bahamas, Bahrain, Finland, Greece, Israel, Italy, Malta, New Zealand, Portugal, Seychelles, Singapore, Slovenia, Spain, South Korea, Sweden, United Kingdom	$15667
10	Australia, Austria, Belgium, Canada, Denmark, France, Germany, Hong Kong, Iceland, Ireland, Luxembourg, Japan, Netherlands, Norway, Switzerland, United States	$22790

generated income deciles using all countries of the world for which there are data on per capita income, rather than only developing (non-OECD, non-former Soviet Union) nations. The table indicates the countries included in each decile as well as the mean income for that decile. Countries listed in bold are those included in the reported statistical analyses.

Employment in Industry: Employment (proportion of total employees) in the industrial sector as a percent of total employment. Industry includes mining and quarrying (including oil production), manufacturing, electricity, gas and water, and construction, corresponding to major ISIC divisions 2–5 (ISIC revision 2).

Exports of Ores and Metals: Ores and metals exports as a percentage of total exports.

External Debt: Total debt owed to nonresidents that is repayable in foreign currency, goods, or services, as a percentage of GDP. Total external debt is the sum of public, publicly guaranteed, and private non-guaranteed long-term debt, use of IMF credit, and short-term debt.

Extractive Sector: Extractive industries as a percentage of gross domestic product. Calculated by subtracting value-added manufacturing from value-added industry as a percentage of GDP. Industry corresponds to ISIC divisions 10–45, including manufacturing, and comprises value added in mining, manufacturing, construction, electricity, water, and gas.

Extractive Sector Exports: Extractive sector exports (fuels, ores, and metals) as a percentage of total exports, taken from *World Trade Analyzer* database.

FDI Flows: Foreign direct investment, defined as net inflows of investment to acquire a lasting management interest (10 percent or more of voting stock) in an enterprise operating in an economy other than that of the investor, as a percentage of GDP.

FDI Stock: Existing stock of foreign direct investment, as a percentage of GDP, taken from UNCTAD's FDI Statistics database, available from http://www.unctad.org/en/subsites/dite/FDIstats_files/FDIstats.htm.

Government Ideology: Dichotomous variable indicating whether the largest governing party in the legislature is left (coded as one), centrist or right (both coded as zero). Based on the Database of Political Institutions (Beck et al. 2001) GOV1RLC variable, indicating the ideology of the largest government party in the legislature. An alternative measure is executive partisanship, coded similarly (using the EXECRLC variable in Beck et al. 2001), but indicating a left (versus center or right) executive. All ideology measures use the 2006 update of the Database, available at http://siteresources.worldbank.org/INTRES/Resources/469232–1107449512766/DPI2006_rev42008.dta

Growth Rate: Annual change in GDP per capita.

Income: Gross domestic product per capita based on purchasing power parity, transformed as a natural logarithm.

Labor Rights: Mosley-Uno measure of collective labor rights, coded as described in text and in Labor Standards Coding Template below. Higher scores indicate better labor rights outcomes.

Latin America: Dummy variable, coded one for Latin American countries (Central and South America), zero otherwise.

Manufacturing: Net output of the manufacturing sector, after adding up all outputs subtracting intermediate inputs, as a percentage of GDP. Manufacturing refers to industries belonging to ISIC divisions 15–37.

NGOs: The total number of human rights NGOs involved in a country (internally) in a given year, from Human Rights Internet's *Master List* of organizations. Data are collected for 1986, 1991, 1994, and 2000 (years in the sample for which the *Master List* is available); intervening years are interpolated; data for 2001 and 2002 are extrapolated. Variable is transformed as a natural logarithm.

North Africa/Middle East: Dummy variable, coded one for North Africa/Middle East countries, zero otherwise.

Population: Calculated based on the de facto definition of population, which counts all residents regardless of legal status or citizenship, except for refugees; natural logarithm.

PLP (Potential Labor Power): The ratio of skilled to unskilled workers in an economy, multiplied by the inverse of a measure of surplus labor. Higher values indicate tight labor markets and a greater proportion of skilled workers. From Rudra (2002).

Regime Type: Dichotomous measure of political regime type (REG, regime classification), from Przeworski et al. (2000); one connotes dictatorship, while zero connotes democracy. Transition years are coded as the regime that emerges that year. Updated data (through 2002) from Adam Przeworski's Web site: http://politics.as.nyu.edu/object/AdamPrzeworski.html, downloaded 11/17/08.

Regional Practices: The mean score of every other country in the same geographic region, calculated annually. Regions are defined as in Figure 4.1 of the text.

Services: Net output of the service sector, after adding up all outputs and subtracting intermediate inputs, as a percentage of GDP. Services correspond to ISIC divisions 50–99 and include value added in wholesale and retail trade (including hotels and restaurants), transport, and government, financial, professional, and personal services (such as education, health care, and real estate services).

Sub-Saharan Africa: Dummy variable, coded one for Sub-Saharan African nations, zero otherwise.

Textiles: Textiles and clothing, percent of value added in manufacturing. The sum of gross output less the value of intermediate inputs used in production for industries classified in ISIC major division 3. Textiles and clothing comprise ISIC division 32.

Trade: Trade in goods (the sum of merchandise exports and imports), as a percentage of GDP.

Veto Players (Political Constraints): Assesses the extent of constraints on national government policy change by estimating the number of independent veto players as well as the spatial differences in their preferences. Henisz generates two main measures of veto players, POLCONIII and POLCONV. Described in Henisz 2002, and available for download from The Political Constraint Index Database, http://www-management.wharton.upenn.edu/henisz/POLCON/ContactInfo.html

OECD, FDI Inward Flows by Geographic Origin: Flows of foreign direct investment in the host economy, by geographical origin, as a percentage share in total foreign direct investment flows from OECD countries, taken from *International Direct Investment Statistics Yearbook 2001*.

OECD, FDI Stock by Geographic Origin: Positions of foreign direct investment in the host economy, by geographical origin, as a percentage share in total foreign direct investment positions from OECD countries, taken from *International Direct Investment Statistics Yearbook 2001*.

United States/United Kingdom/Japan, FDI flows by Industry: Flows of foreign direct investment in the host economy, by industry, as a percentage share in total foreign direct investment flows from the United States, Japan, and the United Kingdom. Data are taken from *U.S. Direct Investment Abroad* (United States), *Foreign Direct Investment Reference Data* (Japan), and *Foreign Direct Investment – Business Monitor M4* (United Kingdom). Data are available from http://www.bea.gov/bea/ai/iidguide.htm#page8 (United States), http://www.mof.go.jp/english/e1c008.htm (Japan), and http://www.statistics.gov.uk/statbase/ssdataset.asp?vlnk=3804&More=Y

(United Kingdom). Where data are missing for one of the three source countries, we calculate using data from two source countries.

United States/United Kingdom/Japan, FDI flows by Geographic Origin: Flows of foreign direct investment in the host economy, by geographical origin, as a percentage share in total foreign direct investment flows from the United States, Japan, and the United Kingdom. Data are taken from *U.S. Direct Investment Abroad* (United States), *Foreign Direct Investment Reference Data* (Japan), and *Foreign Direct Investment – Business Monitor M4* (United Kingdom). Data are available from http://www.bea.gov/bea/ai/iidguide.htm#page8 (United States), http://www.mof.go.jp/english/e1c008.htm (Japan), and http://www.statistics.gov.uk/statbase/ssdataset.asp?vlnk=3804&More=Y (United Kingdom).

United States/United Kingdom/Japan, FDI Stock by Geographic Origin: Positions of foreign direct investment in the host economy, by geographical origin, as a percentage share in total foreign direct investment positions from the United States, Japan, and the United Kingdom. Data are taken from *U.S. Direct Investment Abroad* (United States), *Zaisei Kinyu Tokei Geppo* (Monthly Finance Review) (Japan), and *Foreign Direct Investment – Business Monitor M4* (United Kingdom). Data are available from http://www.bea.gov/bea/di/di1usdbal.htm (United States), http://www.mof.go.jp/kankou/hyou10.htm (Japan), and http://www.statistics.gov.uk/statbase/ssdataset.asp?vlnk=3804&More=Y (United Kingdom).

United States/United Kingdom/Japan, FDI Stock by Industry: Positions of foreign direct investment in the host economy, by industry, as a percentage share in total foreign direct investment positions from the United States, Japan, and the United Kingdom. Data are taken from *U.S. Direct Investment Abroad* (United States), *Zaisei Kinyu Tokei Geppo* (Monthly Finance Review) (Japan), and *Foreign Direct Investment – Business Monitor M4* (United Kingdom). Data are available from http://www.bea.gov/bea/di/di1usdbal.htm (United States), http://www.mof.go.jp/kankou/hyou10.htm (Japan), and http://www.statistics.gov.uk/statbase/ssdataset.asp?vlnk=3804&More=Y (United Kingdom). Where data are missing for one of the three source countries, we calculate using data from two source countries.

NATIONS INCLUDED IN SAMPLE, MAIN MODEL

Algeria	Gabon	Niger
Angola	The Gambia	Nigeria
Argentina	Ghana	Oman
Bangladesh	Guatemala	Pakistan
Benin	Guinea	Panama
Bolivia	Guinea-Bissau	Papua New Guinea
Botswana	Guyana	Paraguay
Brazil	Haiti	Peru
Burkina Faso	Honduras	Philippines
Burundi	India	Rwanda
Cambodia	Indonesia	Senegal
Cameroon	Iran	Sierra Leone
C. African Rep.	Jamaica	South Africa
Chad	Jordan	Sri Lanka
Chile	Kenya	Sudan
China	Laos	Swaziland
Colombia	Lebanon	Syria
Comoros	Lesotho	Tanzania
Congo (Brazzaville)	Madagascar	Thailand
Congo (Dem. Rep.)	Malawi	Togo
Costa Rica	Malaysia	Trinidad & Tobago
Cote d'Ivoire	Mali	Tunisia
Djibouti	Mauritania	Turkey
Dominican Rep.	Mauritius	Uganda
Ecuador	Mexico	Uruguay
Egypt	Mongolia	Venezuela
El Salvador	Morocco	Vietnam
Eritrea	Mozambique	Yemen
Ethiopia	Nepal	Zambia
Fiji	Nicaragua	Zimbabwe

LABOR STANDARDS CODING TEMPLATE

Category	Description	Weight, If Observed
	Freedom of Association/Collective Bargaining Related Liberties	
1	Murder or disappearance of union members or organizers.	2
2	Other violence against union members or organizers.	2
3	Arrest, detention, imprisonment, or forced exile for union membership or activities.	2
4	Interference with union rights of assembly, demonstration, free opinion, or free expression.	2
5	Seizure or destruction of union premises or property.	2
	Right to Establish and Join Union and Worker Organizations	
6	General prohibitions.	10
7	General absence resulting from socio-economic breakdown.	10
8	Previous authorization requirements. *Does not include requirements that unions register with governments, unless these requirements are deemed onerous by the ILO.*	1.5
9	Employment conditional on non-membership in union.	1.5
10	Dismissal or suspension for union membership or activities. *Includes dismissal for strike activities.*	1.5
11	Interference of employers (attempts to dominate unions).	1.5
12	Dissolution or suspension of union by administrative authority.	2
13	Only workers' committees and labor councils permitted.	2
14	Only state-sponsored or other single unions permitted. *Includes allowing only one union per industry or sector.*	1.5
15	Exclusion of tradable/industrial sectors from union membership.	2

Category	Description	Weight, If Observed
16	Exclusion of other sectors or workers from union membership. *Includes exclusion of public-sector workers from union membership. Excluding "essential services" is acceptable, provided the definition of "essential services" is not excessively broad (i.e., following ILO guidelines, limitations on armed forces' union membership are acceptable).*	2
17	Other specific de facto problems or acts of prohibition.	1.5
18	(No) Right to establish and join federations or confederations of unions.	1.5
19	Previous authorization requirements regarding Category 18	1
	Other Union Activities	
20	(No) Right to elect representatives in full freedom. *Includes requirement that union leaders must work full time in a given industry.*	1.5
21	(No) Right to establish constitutions and rules.	1.5
22	General prohibition of union/federation participation in political activities. *Includes limits on union contributions to political parties.*	1.5
23	(No) Union control of finances. *Includes situations in which unions receive a substantial portion of financing from government sources, or rules that unions may not receive financial contributions from abroad or from certain groups.*	1.5
	Right to Collectively Bargain	
24	General prohibitions.	10
25	Prior approval by authorities of collective agreements.	1.5
26	Compulsory binding arbitration. *Includes systems in which compulsory binding arbitration is necessary before a (legal) strike may be called.*	1.5
27	Intervention of authorities. *Includes unilateral setting of wages by authorities.*	1.5

(continued)

(*continued*)

Category	Description	Weight, If Observed
28	Scope of collective bargaining restricted by non-state employers.	1.5
29	Exclusion of tradable/industrial sectors from right to collectively bargain.	1.75
30	Exclusion of other sectors or workers from right to collectively bargain. *Includes the exclusion of civil servants or all public-sector workers. Excluding "essential services" is acceptable, provided the definition of "essential services" is not excessively broad.*	1.75
31	Other specific de facto problems or acts of prohibition. *Includes "no legal right" to bargain collectively (but no legal prohibition on doing so).*	1.5
	Right to Strike	
32	General prohibitions.	2
33	Previous authorization required by authorities. *Includes requirement for official approval prior to strike. A requirement to notify officials prior to a strike is not coded as a violation.*	1.5
34	Exclusion of tradable/industrial sectors from right to strike	1.5
35	Exclusion of other sectors or workers from right to strike. *Includes the exclusion of civil servants or all public-sector workers. Excluding "essential services" is acceptable, provided the definition of "essential services" is not excessively broad.*	1.5
36	Other specific de facto problems or acts of prohibition.	1.5
	Export Processing Zones	
37	Restricted rights in EPZs. *Includes export processing zones, free trade zones, and/or special economic zones.*	2
	Total Score	

Note: *Labor Rights and Multinational Production* coding notes are in italics.

Sources: ICFTU, U.S. State Dept, ILO. Template and methodology are adapted from Kucera (2002).

References

Abouharb, M. Rodwan and David L. Cingranelli. 2006. "The Human Rights Effects of World Bank Structural Adjustment, 1981–2000." International Studies Quarterly (50): 233–262.

Abouharb, Rodwan M. and David Cingranelli. 2008. *Human Rights and Structural Adjustment.* Cambridge: Cambridge University Press.

Abrami, Regina M. 2003. "Worker Rights and Global Trade: The U.S.-Cambodia Bilateral Textile Trade Agreement." Harvard Business School Case 703–034.

Achen, Christopher H. 2000. "Why Lagged Dependent Variables can Suppress the Explanatory Power of Other Independent Variables." *Political Methodology Working Paper* University of Michigan.

ActionAid UK. 2007. "Who Pays? How British Supermarkets are Keeping Women Workers in Poverty." ActionAid Report (April). At http://www.actionaid.org. uk/doc_lib/actionaid_who_pays_report.pdf

Adserá, Aliciá and Carles Boix. 2002. "Trade, Democracy, and the Size of the Public Sector: The Political Underpinnings of Openness." International Organization 56: 229–262.

AFL-CIO. 2001. "Petition to Remove Costa Rica from the List of Beneficiary Developing Countries under the General System of Preferences and from the List of Beneficiary Countries under the Caribbean Basin Economic Recovery Act." Submitted to the United States Trade Representative, June.

Agarwal, Sanjeev and Sridhar N. Ramaswami. 1992. "Choice of Foreign Market Entry Mode: Impact of Ownership, Location and Internalization Factors." Journal of International Business Studies 23: 1–27.

Aggarwal, Mita. 1995. "International Trade, Labor Standards, and Labor Market Conditions: An Evaluation of the Linkages." *Working Paper* 95–06-C. Washington: U.S. International Trade Commission.

Ahlquist, John S. 2006. "Economic Policy, Institutions, and Capital Flows: Portfolio and Direct Investment Flows in Developing Countries." International Studies Quarterly 50: 681–704.

Ahlquist, John S. and Aseem Prakash. 2008. "The Influence of Foreign Direct Investment on Contracting Confidence in Developing Countries." Regulation and Governance 2: 316–339.

Aidt, Toke and Zafiris Tzannaos. 2002. *Unions and Collective Bargaining: Economic Effects in a Global Environment*. Washington: World Bank.

Aizenman, Joshua and Ilan Noy. 2005. "FDI and Trade? Two-Way Linkages?" *NBER Working Paper* No.11403 (June). Cambridge: National Bureau of Economic Research.

American Center for American Labor Solidarity. 2003. *Justice for All: A Guide to Worker Rights in the Global Economy*. Washington: ACILS.

Anner, Mark, Teri Caraway and Stephanie Rickard. 2010. "International Negotiations and Domestic Politics: The Case of IMF Labor Market Conditionality." Paper presented at the Third Annual Conference on the Political Economy of International Organizations, Georgetown University, January 28–30.

Anner, Mark. 2001. "Labor and Economic Globalization in Eastern Europe and Latin America." Labor Studies Journal 26(1): 22–41.

Antràs, Pol. 2005. "Property Rights and the International Organization of Production." American Economic Review 95(2): 25–32.

Apodaca, Clair. 2001. "Global Economic Patterns and Personal Integrity Rights After the Cold War." International Studies Quarterly 45: 587–602.

Arnold, Wayne. 2006. "Not All Roads Lead to China," *New York Times*, February 28, 2006, p. C1.

ASEPROLA. 2005. "Labor Conditions in the Costa Rican Sugar Industry." (in association with International Labor Rights Fund).

Asian Development Bank. 2006. *The Mekong Region: Foreign Direct Investment*. Manila, Philippines: Asian Development Bank.

Avelino, George, David S. Brown and Wendy Hunter. 2005. "The Effects of Capital Mobility, Trade Openness, and Democracy on Social Spending in Latin America, 1980–1999." American Journal of Political Science 49: 625–641.

Bandelj, Nina. 2008. *From Communists to Foreign Capitalists: The Social Foundations of Foreign Direct Investment in Postsocialist Europe*. Princeton: Princeton University Press.

Barboza, 2006. "Labor Shortage in China May Lead to Trade Shift." New York Times, April 3, 2006, p. A1.

Baron, David. 2003. "Private Politics." Journal of Economics and Management Strategy 12: 31–66.

Barrientos, Stephanie and Sally Smith. 2007. "Do Workers Benefit from Ethical Trade? Assessing Codes of Labour Practice in Global Production Systems." Third World Quarterly 28(4): 713–429.

Bartley, Tim. 2003. "Certifying Forests and Factories: States, Social Movements and the Rise of Private Regulation in the Apparel and Forest Products Fields." Politics and Society 31(3): 433–464.

Bartley, Tim. 2005. "Corporate Accountability and the Privatization of Labor Standards: Struggles over Codes of Conduct in the Apparel Industry." Research in Political Sociology 12: 211–244.

Bartley, Tim. 2007. "Institutional Emergence in an Era of Globalization: The Rise of Transnational Private Regulation of Labor and Environmental Conditions." American Journal of Sociology 113(2): 297–351.

Basinger, Scott J. and Mark Hallerberg. 2004. "Remodeling the Competition for Capital: How Domestic Politics Erases the Race to the Bottom." American Political Science Review 98 (2): 261–276.

Bauer, Raymond A., Ithiel de Sola Pool and Lewis Anthony Dexter. 1963. *American Business and Public Policy: The Politics of Foreign Trade*. Cambridge: The MIT Press.

Beck, Nathaniel. 2001. "Time-Series-Cross-Section Data: What Have We Learned in the Past Few Years?" Annual Review of Political Science 4: 271–293.

Beck, Nathaniel and Jonathan N. Katz. 1995. "What to Do (and Not to Do) with Time-Series Cross-Section Data." American Political Science Review 89: 634–647.

Beck, Nathaniel and Jonathan N. Katz. 2004. "Time Series Cross Section Issues: Dynamics, 2004." *Working Paper*. New York University and California Institute of Technology.

Beck, Thorsten, George Clarke, Alberto Groff, Philip Keefer and Patrick Walsh. 2001. "New Tools in Comparative Political Economy: The Database of Political Institutions." World Bank Economic Review 15(1): 165–176.

Becker, David G. and Richard L. Sklar, eds. 1999. *Postimperialism and World Politics*. Westport, CT: Praeger Publishers.

Berger, Suzanne. 2005. *How We Compete: What Companies around the World are Doing to Make it in Today's Global Economy*. New York: Doubleday.

Berger, Suzanne and Ronald Dore, eds. 1996. *National Diversity and Global Capitalism*. Ithaca: Cornell University Press.

Bhagwati, Jagdish. 2004. *In Defense of Globalization*. New York: Oxford University Press.

Biersteker, Thomas J. 1978. *Distortion or Development? Contending Perspectives on the Multinational Corporation*. Cambridge: The MIT Press.

Biglaiser, Glen and Karl DeRouen. 2006. "Economic Reforms and Inflows of Foreign Direct Investment in Latin America." Latin American Research Review 41: 51–75.

Blanchflower, David G. and Alex Bryson. 2003. "Changes over Time in Union Relative Wage Effects in the UK and the US Revisited." In *International Handbook of Trade Unions*, eds. John T. Addison and Claus Schnabel, 197–245. Chelthenham, England and Northhampton, Massachusetts: Edward Elgar.

Blanton, Shannon Lindsey and Robert G. Blanton. 2007. "What Attracts Foreign Investors? An Examination of Human Rights and Foreign Direct Investment." Journal of Politics 69 (1): 143–155.

Blanton, Shannon Lindsey and Robert G. Blanton. 2009. "A Sectoral Analysis of Human Rights and FDI: Does Industry Type Matter?" International Studies Quarterly 53(2): 469–493.

Blonigen, Bruce A. and Miao Wang. 2005. "Inappropriate Pooling of Wealthy and Poor Countries in Empirical FDI Studies." In *Does Foreign Direct Investment*

Promote Development? Theodore H. Moran, Edward M. Graham and Magnus Bloemstrom, eds., 221–244.Washington: Institute for International Economics.

Bognanno, Mario F., Michael P. Keane and Donghoon Yang. 2005. "The Influence of Wages and Industrial Relations Environments on the Production Location Decisions of U.S. Multinational Corporations." Industrial and Labor Relations Review 58 (2): 171–200.

Böhning, W. R. 2005. *Labour Rights in Crisis: Measuring the Achievement of Human Rights in the World of Work*. London: Palgrave.

Boyenge, Jean-Pierre Singa. 2007. "ILO Database on Export Processing Zones (Revised)." *Sectoral Activities Programme Working Paper*. Geneva: ILO.

Bradsher, Keith, 2006. "In Poorest Lands Like Laos, Limited Markets, Skilled Labor and Banks." New York Times, February 28: C1.

Bradsher, Keith. 2008. "Investors Seek Asian Options to Costly China." *New York Times*, June 18, 2008, p. C1.

Brady, David and Michael Wallace. 2000. "Spatialization, Foreign Direct Investment and Labor Outcomes in the American States, 1978–1996." Social Forces 79(1): 67–105.

Braumoeller, Bear. 2004. "Hypothesis Testing and Multiplicative Interaction Terms." International Organization 58: 807–820.

Braun, Sebastian. 2006. "Core Labour Standards and FDI: Friends or Foes? The Case of Child Labour." Discussion Paper 2006–0614. Institute for Economic Theory, Humboldt-Universität zu Berlin, SFB 649.

Breznitz, Daniel. 2007. *Innovation and the State: Political Choice and Strategies for Growth in Israel, Taiwan and Ireland*. New Haven: Yale University Press.

Bronfenbrenner, Kate. 2000. "Uneasy Terrain: The Impact of Capital Mobility on Workers, Wages, and Union Organizing." Submitted to the U.S. Trade Deficit Review Commission, September 6, 2000.

Brooks, Sarah M. 2002. "Social Protection and Economic Integration: The Politics of Pension Reform in an Era of Capital Mobility." Comparative Political Studies 35(5): 491–525.

Brooks, Sarah M. 2005. "Interdependent and Domestic Foundations of Policy Change: The Diffusion of Pension Privatization around the World." International Studies Quarterly 49(2): 273–294.

Brooks, Sarah M. 2009. *Social Protection and the Market in Latin America*. Cambridge: Cambridge University Press.

Brooks, Sarah M. and Marcus J. Kurtz. 2007. "Capital, Trade and the Political Economies of Reform." American Journal of Political Science 51(4).

Brown, Drusilla K., Alan V. Deardorff and Robert M. Stern. 2004. "The Effects of Multinational Production on Wages and Working Conditions in Developing Countries." In *Challenges to Globalization: Analyzing the Economics*, eds. Robert E. Baldwin and L. Alan Winters, 279–330. Chicago: University of Chicago Press.

Brune, Nancy, Geoffrey Garrett and Bruce Kogut. 2004. "The International Monetary Fund and the Global Spread of Privatization." IMF Staff Papers 51(3): 195–219.

Buckley, Peter J. and Pervez N. Ghauri. 2004. "Globalisation, Economic Geography and the Strategy of Multinational Enterprises." Journal of International Business Studies 35: 81–98.

Bueno de Mesquita, Bruce, Alastair Smith, Randolph M. Siverson and James D. Morrow. 2003. *The Logic of Political Survival*. Cambridge: The MIT Press.

Buitelaar, Rudolf and Ramon Padilla Perez. 2000. "Maquila Economic Reform and Corporate Strategies." World Development 28(9): 1627–1642.

Bunce, Valerie. 1995. "Should Transitologists Be Grounded?" Slavic Review (Spring): 111–122.

Busse, Matthias. 2003. "Do Transnational Corporations Care about Labor Standards?" The Journal of Developing Areas 36: 39–57.

Busse, Matthias and Sebastian Braun. 2003. "Trade and Investment Effects of Forced Labour: An Empirical Assessment." International Labour Review 142(1): 49–71.

Busse, Matthias and Sebastian Braun. 2004. "Export Structure, FDI and Child Labour." Journal of Economic Integration 19(4): 804–829.

Büthe, Tim and Helen V. Milner. 2008. "The Politics of Foreign Direct Investment into Developing Countries: Increasing FDI through International Trade Agreements?" American Journal of Political Science 52(4): 741–762.

Büthe, Tim and Helen V. Milner. 2009. "Bilateral Investment Treaties and Foreign Direct Investment: A Political Analysis." In *The Effect of Treaties on Foreign Direct Investment*, eds. Karl P. Sauvant and Lisa E. Sachs, 171–224. Oxford: Oxford University Press.

Cao, Xun and Aseem Prakash. 2010. "Trade Competition and Domestic Pollution: A Panel Study, 1980–2003." International Organization (forthcoming).

Caraway, Teri L. 2006a. "Freedom of Association: Battering Ram or Trojan Horse?" Review of International Political Economy 13(2): 210–232.

Caraway, Teri L. 2006b. "Political Openness and Transnational Activism: Comparative Insights from Labor Activism." Politics and Society 34(2): 277–304.

Caraway, Teri L. 2008. "Explaining the Dominance of Legacy Unions in New Democracies: Insights from Indonesia." Comparative Political Studies 41(10): 1371–1397.

Cardoso, Fernando Henrique and Enzo Faletto. 1971. *Dependency and Development in Latin America*. Berkeley: University of California Press.

Castro, Ruben Chacon. 2003. "Legal, Political and Practical Obstacles to Compliance with the Costa Rican Labor Code." Manuscript, Consulting Group for ASEPROLA. At http://www.laborrights.org/publications/costarica_labor-laws.pdf#search=%22g.%09Legal%2C%20Political%2C%20and%20Practical%20Obstacles%20to%20Compliance%20with%20Costa%20Rican%20Labor%20Code%22

Chan, Anita and Robert Senser. 1997. "China's Troubled Workers." Foreign Affairs 76(2): 104–117.

Chan, Anita and Hong-zen Wang. 2004. "The Impact of the State on Workers' Conditions: Comparing Taiwanese Factories in China and Vietnam." Pacific Affairs 77(4): 629–646.

Chiu, Catherine C. H. 2007. "Workplace Practices in Hong Kong-Invested Garment Factories in Cambodia." Journal of Contemporary Asia 37(4): 431–448.

Chweiroth, Jeffrey. 2007. "Neoliberal Economists and Capital Account Liberalization in Emerging Markets." International Organization 61(2): 443–463.

Cingranelli, David L. 2002. "Democratization, Economic Globalization, and Workers' Rights," In *Democratic Institutional Performance: Research and Policy Perspectives*, eds. Edward McMahon and Thomas Sinclair. New York: Praeger Press.

Cingranelli, David L. and David L. Richards. 1999. "Measuring the Level, Pattern and Sequence of Government Respect for Physical Integrity Rights." International Studies Quarterly 43: 407–417.

Cingranelli, David L and Chang-yen Tsai. 2003. "Democracy, Workers' Rights, and Income Inequality: A Comparative Cross-National Analysis." Paper presented at the 2003 Annual Meeting of the American Political Science Association, Philadelphia, August 28-September 1.

Clark, Mary A. 1997. "Transnational Alliances and Development Policy in Latin America: Nontraditional Export Promotion." Latin American Research Review 32(2): 71–98.

Collier, Ruth Berins and David Collier. 1991. *Shaping the Political Arena: Critical Junctures, the Labor Movement and Regime Dynamics in Latin America*. Princeton: Princeton University Press.

Collinsworth, Terry, J., William Goold and Pharis J. Harvey. 1994. "Labor and Free Trade." Foreign Affairs 77(1): 8–13.

Colonomos, Ariel and Javier Santiso. 2005. "Viva la France! French Multinationals and Human Rights." Human Rights Quarterly 27: 1307–1345.

Compa, Lance and Stephen F. Diamond. 1996. *Human Rights, Labor Rights and International Trade*. Philadelphia: University of Pennsylvania Press.

Compa, Lance and Jeffrey S. Vogt. 2001. The Generalized System of Preferences: A 20-Year Review. Comparative Law and Policy Journal 22(2/3): 199–238.

Cooke, William N. and Deborah S. Noble. 1998. "Industrial Relations Systems and US Foreign Direct Investment Abroad." British Journal of Industrial Relations 36(4): 581–609.

Coppedge, Michael. 1998. "The Dynamic Diversity of Latin American Party Systems." Party Politics 4(4): 547–568.

Cortázar, René, Nora Lustig and Richard Sabot. 1998. "Economic Policy and Labor Market Dynamics" In *Beyond Trade Offs: Market Reform and Equitable Growth in Latin America*, eds. Nancy Birdsall, Carol Graham and Richard Sabot. Washington, DC: Brookings Institution Press.

Croucher, Richard and Elizabeth Cotton. 2009. *Global Unions, Global Business: Global Union Federations and International Business*. London: Middlesex University Press.

Daubler, Wolfgang and Qian Wang. 2009. "Labor Law Developments in China: the New Chinese Employment Law." Comparative Labor Law and Policy Journal 30: 395–408.

de Soysa, Indra and John R. Oneal. 1999. "Boon or Bane? Reassessing the Productivity of Foreign Direct Investment." American Sociological Review 64(October): 766–782.

Doremus, Paul N., William W. Keller, Louis W. Pauly and Simon Reich. 1999. *The Myth of the Global Corporation.* Princeton: Princeton University Press.

Downs, George W., David M. Rocke and Peter N. Barsoom. 1996. "Is the Good News about Compliance Good News about Cooperation?" International Organization 50(3): 379–406.

Drezner, Daniel W. 2001. "Globalization and Policy Convergence." International Studies Review 3(1): 53–78.

Drezner, Daniel W. 2007. *All Politics is Global: Explaining International Regulatory Regimes.* Princeton: Princeton University Press.

Dunning, John H. 1992. *Multinational Enterprises and the Global Economy.* Wokingham, England: Addison-Wesley.

Dunning, John H. 1995. "Reappraising the Eclectic Paradigm in an Age of Alliance Capitalism." Journal of International Business Studies 26(3): 461–491.

Elkins, Zachary, Andrew T. Guzman and Beth A. Simmons. 2006. "Competing for Capital: The Diffusion of Bilateral Investment Treaties, 1960–2000." International Organization 60(4): 811–846.

Elliott, Kimberly Ann and Richard B. Freeman. 2001. "White Hats or Don Quixotes? Human Rights Vigilantes in the Global Economy." *NBER Working Paper* No.8102. Cambridge: National Bureau of Economic Research.

Elliott, Kimberly Ann and Richard B. Freeman. 2003. *Can Labor Standards Improve Under Globalization?* Washington: Institute for International Economics.

Ethical Trading Initiative. 2005. "Moving Production: Stalling the Race to the Bottom." Briefing Paper No. 4. London: Ethical Trading Initiative.

Evans, Peter B. 1971. "National Autonomy and Economic Development: Critical Perspectives on Multinational Corporations in Poor Countries." International Organization 25(3): 675–692.

Evans, Peter B. 1979. *Dependent Development: The Alliance of Multinational, State and Local Capital in Brazil.* Princeton: Princeton University Press.

Falzoni, Anna M. 2000. "Statistics on Foreign Direct Investment and Multinational Corporations: A Survey." Manuscript, University of Bergamo.

Feenstra, Robert C. and Gordon H. Hanson. 1997. "Foreign Direct Investment and Relative Wages: Evidence from Mexico's Maquiladoras." *Journal of International Economics* 42(3–4): 371–393.

Feng, Yi. 2001. "Political Freedom, Political Instability, and Policy Uncertainty: A Study of Political Institutions and Private Investment in Developing Countries." International Studies Quarterly 45: 271–294.

Findlay, Ronald and Kevin H. O'Rourke. 2003. "Commodity Market Integration, 1500–2000." In *Globalization in Historical Perspective,* eds. Michael D. Bordo, Alan M. Taylor, and Jeffrey G. Williamsom, 13–63. Chicago: University of Chicago Press /NBER.

Finnemore, Martha. 1996. *National Interests in International Society.* Ithaca: Cornell University Press.

FLA (Fair Labor Association). 2005. *2005 Annual Public Report.* Washington: Fair Labor Association.

FLA (Fair Labor Association). 2007. *2007 Annual Public Report.* Washington: Fair Labor Association.

Flanagan, Robert J. 2006. *Globalization and Labor Conditions: Working Conditions and Worker Rights in a Global Economy.* Oxford: Oxford University Press.

Frankel, Jeffrey A. 2003. "The Environment and Globalization." *NBER Working Paper* No.10090 (November). Cambridge: National Bureau of Economic Research.

Freeman, Richard B. 2007. "Labor Market Institutions around the World." *NBER Working Paper* No.13242 (July). Cambridge: National Bureau of Economic Research.

Frenkel, Stephen J. 2001. "Globalization, Athletic Footwear Commodity Chains and Employment Relations in China." *Organization Studies* 22(4): 531–562.

Friedman, Thomas. 2005. *The World Is Flat: A Brief History of the Twenty-First Century.* New York: Farrar, Strauss and Giroux.

Frundt, Henry J. 1998. *Trade Conditions and Labor Rights: U.S. Initiatives, Dominican and Central America Responses.* Gainesville, FL: University Press of Florida.

Frundt, Henry J. 2002. "Central American Unions in the Era of Globalization." *Latin American Research Review* 37(3): 7–53.

Gallagher, Mary. 2005. *Contagious Capitalism: Globalization and the Politics of Labor in China.* Princeton: Princeton University Press.

Garcia-Johnson, Ronie. 2000. *Exporting Environmentalism: U.S. Multinational Chemical Corporations in Brazil and Mexico.* Cambridge: The MIT Press.

Garland, Marshall W. and Glen Biglaiser. 2009. "Do Electoral Rules Matter? Political Institutions and Foreign Direct Investment in Latin America." *Comparative Political Studies* 42(2): 224–251.

Garrett, Geoffrey. 1998. "Global Markets and National Politics: Collision Course or Virtuous Circle?" *International Organization* 52(4): 787–824.

Garrett, Geoffrey. 2000. "The Causes of Globalization." *Comparative Political Studies* 33: 941–991.

Gereffi, Gary. 1999. "International Trade and Industrial Upgrading in the Apparel Commodity Chain." *Journal of International Economics* 48: 37–70.

Gereffi, Gary, John Humphrey and Timothy Sturgeon. 2005. "The Governance of Global Value Chains." *Review of International Political Economy* 12(1): 78–104.

Gereffi, Gary and Miguel Korzeniewicz. eds. 1994. *Commodity Chains and Global Capitalism.* New York: Praeger.

Gibbon, Peter, Jennifer Bair and Stefano Ponte. 2008. "Governing Global Value Chains: An Introduction." *Economy and Society* 37(3): 315–338.

Goldstein, Judith and Lisa L. Martin. 2000. "Legalization, Trade Liberalization, and Domestic Politics: A Cautionary Note," *International Organization* 54(3): 603–632.

Gourevitch, Peter and James A. Shinn. 2005. *Political Power and Corporate Control: The New Global Politics of Corporate Governance.* Princeton: Princeton University Press.

Gowa, Joanne. 1994. *Allies, Adversaries and International Trade*. Princeton: Princeton University Press.

Graham, Edward M. 1995. "Foreign Direct Investment in the World Economy." *Working Paper* No. 95/59. Washington, DC: International Monetary Fund.

Graham, Edward M. 1996. *Global Corporations and National Governments*. Washington, DC: Institute for International Economics.

Graham, Edward M. 2000. *Fighting the Wrong Enemy: Antiglobal Activists and Multinational Enterprises*. Washington, DC: Institute for International Economics.

Greenhill, Brian, Layna Mosley and Aseem Prakash. 2009. "Trade-Based Diffusion of Labor Rights: A Panel Study, 1986–2002." *American Political Science Review* 103(4): 169–190.

Guthrie, Douglas. 1999. *Dragon in a Three Piece Suit: The Emergence of Capitalism in China*. Princeton: Princeton University Press.

Hafner-Burton, Emilie. 2005a. "Right or Robust? The Sensitive Nature of Repression to Globalization." Journal of Peace Research 42(6): 679–698.

Hafner-Burton, Emilie. 2005b. "Trading Human Rights: How Preferential Trade Agreements Influence Government Repression." International Organization 59(2): 593–629.

Hafner-Burton, Emilie. 2008. "Sticks and Stones: Naming and Shaming and the Human Rights Enforcement Problem." International Organization 62(4): 689–716.

Hafner-Burton, Emilie. 2009. *Forced to Be Good: Why Trade Agreements Boost Human Rights*. Ithaca: Cornell University Press.

Hafner-Burton, Emilie M. and Kiyoteru Tsutsui. 2005. "Human Rights in a Globalizing World: The Paradox of Empty Promises." American Journal of Sociology 110(5): 1373–1411.

Hafner-Burton, Emilie M. and Kiyoteru Tsutsui. 2007. "Justice Lost! The Failure of Human Rights Law to Matter Where Needed Most." Journal of Peace Research 44(4): 407–425.

Haggard, Stephan and Robert R. Kaufman. 1995. *The Political Economy of Democratic Transitions*. Princeton: Princeton University Press.

Hall, Peter A. and David Soskice. eds. 2001. *Varieties of Capitalism: The Institutional Foundations of Comparative Advantage*. Oxford: Oxford University Press.

Hanson, Gordon H., Matthew Slaughter and Raymond Mataloni. 2002. "Expansion Strategies of U.S. Multinational Firms." In *Brookings Trade Forum 2001*, eds. Dani Rodrik and Susan Collins, 245–282. Washington, DC: Brookings Institution Press.

Hatem, Fabrice. 1998. *International Investment: Towards the Year 2002*. Paris: United Nations/Invest in France Bureau.

Hathaway, Oona A. 2002. "Do Human Rights Treaties Make a Difference?" The Yale Law Journal 118(8): 1935–2042.

Haufler, Virginia. 2000. *A Public Role for the Private Sector: Industry Self-Regulation in a Global Economy*. New York: Carnegie Endowment for International Peace.

Hays, Jude. 2003. "Globalization and Capital Taxation in Consensus and Majoritarian Democracies." World Politics 56: 79–113.

Helpman, Elhanan. 2006. "Trade, FDI and the Organization of Firms." Journal of Economic Perspectives 44: 589–630.

Helpman, Elhanan, Marc J. Melitz and Stephen R. Yeaple. 2004. "Export versus FDI with Heterogeneous Firms." American Economic Review 94(1): 300–316.

Henderson, Jeffrey, Peter Dicken, Martin Hess, Neil Coe and Henry Wai-Chung Yeung. 2002. "Global Production Networks and the Analysis of Economic Development." Review of International Political Economy 9(3): 436–464.

Henisz, Witold J. 2000. "The Institutional Environment for Multinational Investment." Journal of Law, Economics and Organization 16(2): 334–364.

Henisz, Witold J. 2002. "The Institutional Environment for Infrastructure Investment." Industrial and Corporate Change 11(2): 355–389.

Henisz, Witold J. and Jeffrey T. Macher. 2004. "Firm- and Country-Level Tradeoffs and Contingencies in the Evaluation of Foreign Investment: The Semiconductor Industry, 1994–2002." Organization Science 15(5): 537–554.

Henisz, Witold J. and Edward Mansfield. 2006. "Votes and Vetoes: The Political Determinants of Commercial Openness." International Studies Quarterly 50(1): 189–211.

Henisz, Witold J. and Oliver E. Williamson. 1999. "Comparative Economic Organization – Within and Between Countries." Business and Politics 1: 261–277.

Herzenberg, Stephen. 1996. "In From the Margins: Morality, Economics and International Labor Rights." In *Human Rights, Labor Rights and International Trade*, eds. Lance A. Compa and Stephen F. Diamond, 99–117. Philadelphia: University of Pennsylvania Press.

Hewison, Kevin and Catherine C. H. Chiu. 2008. "Hong Kong-Invested Factories in Thailand: Labour Relations and Practices." *Working Paper*, University of North Carolina.

Hiscox, Michael J. 2002. *International Trade and Political Conflict: Commerce, Coalitions and Factor Mobility*. Princeton: Princeton University Press.

Hiscox, Michael J. and Nicholas F. B. Smyth. 2005. "Is There Consumer Demand for Improved Labor Standards? Evidence from Field Experiments in Social Product Labeling." Manuscript, Department of Government, Harvard University.

Hsaio, C. 1986. *Analysis of Panel Data*. New York: Cambridge University Press.

Huber, Evelyne and John D. Stephens. 2001. *Development and Crisis of the Welfare State*. Chicago: University of Chicago Press.

Huber, Evelyne, Francois Nielsen, Jenny Pribble and John D. Stephens. 2006. "Politics and Inequality in Latin America and the Caribbean." Paper delivered at the Meetings of the Latin American Studies Association, San Juan, Puerto Rico, March 15–18.

Human Rights Internet. Various Years. *Human Rights Internet Reporter*. Ottawa, Canada: Human Rights Internet.

Human Rights Watch. 2002. "Tainted Harvest: Child Labor and Obstacles to Organizing on Ecuador's Banana Plantations." New York: Human Rights Watch. At http://www.hrw.org/legacy/reports/2002/ecuador/

Hummels, David L., Jun Ishii and Kei-Mu Yi. 2001. "The Nature and Growth of Vertical Specialization in World Trade." Journal of International Economics 54(1): 75–96.

Hymer, Stephen H. 1979. "The Multinational Corporation and the International Division of Labor." In The Multinational Corporations: A Radical Approach, eds. Robert B. Cohen, Nadine Felton, Morley Nkosi and Jaap van Liere, 140–164. Cambridge: Cambridge University Press.

ICFTU (International Confederation of Free Trade Unions). 2003. "Export Processing Zones: Symbols of Exploitation and a Development Dead-End." Brussels, Belgium: ICFTU. At http://www.icftu.org/www/pdf/wtoepzreport2003-en.pdf

ICFTU (International Confederation of Free Trade Unions). Various Years. *Annual Survey of Violations of Trade Union Rights*. Brussels: ICFTU.

Iglesias Prieto, Norma. 1997. *Beautiful Flowers of the Maquiladora*. Austin: University of Texas Press.

ILO (International Labour Organization). 1998. Economic and Social Effects of Multinational Enterprises in Export Processing Zones. Geneva: ILO.

ILO (International Labour Organization). 2002. *Labour Overview: Latin America and the Caribbean*. Geneva: ILO. At http://www.oit.org.pe/english/260ameri/publ/panorama/2002/

ILO (International Labour Organization). 2003. *Fundamental Principles and Rights at Work: A Labor Law Study. Costa Rica, El Salvador, Guatemala, Honduras, Nicaragua*. Geneva: ILO.

ILO (International Labour Organization). 2005. *Rules of the Game: A Brief Introduction to International Labour Standards*. Geneva: ILO.

ILO (International Labour Organization). 2006. *Financial Report and Audited Financial Statement for the Sixty-Ninth Financial Period*. Geneva: International Labour Organization.

ILO (International Labour Organization). 2007. *Labour and Social Trends in ASEAN 2007: Integration, Challenges and Opportunities*. Bangkok: ILO Regional Office for Asia and the Pacific.

ILRF (International Labor Rights Fund). 2005. "Testimony regarding the Central American Free Trade Agreement (CAFTA)." Prepared by Bama Athreya, Deputy Director (April).

Innes, Judith Eleanor. 1992. "Human Rights Reporting as a Policy Tool: An Examination of the State Department *Country Reports*." In *Human Rights and Statistics: Getting the Record Straight*, eds. Thomas B. Jabine and Richard P. Claude, 235–257. Philadelphia: University of Pennsylvania Press.

International Labour Office Governing Body, Committee on Employment and Social Policy. 2003. "Employment and Social Policy in Respect of Export Processing Zones [EPZs]." Geneva: GB.286/ESP/3, 286th session. At http://www.ilo.org/public/english/standards/relm/gb/docs/gb286/pdf/esp-3.pdf

ITUC (International Trade Union Confederation). 2007. "Internationally-Recognised Core Labour Standards in Costa Rica." Report for the WTO General Council Review of the Trade Policies of Costa Rica (April).

Iversen, Torben and Thomas R. Cusack. 2000. "The Causes of Welfare State Expansion: Deindustrialization or Globalization?" World Politics 52: 313–349

Iversen, Torben and Anne Wren. 1998. "Equality, Employment and Budgetary Restraint: The Trilemma of the Service Economy." World Politics 50(4): 507–546.

Javorcik, Beata Smarzynska and Wei, Shang-Jin. 2004. "Pollution Havens and Foreign Direct Investment: Dirty Secret or Popular Myth?," Contributions to Economic Analysis and Policy 3(2), Article 8. At: http://www.bepress.com/bejeap/contributions/vol3/iss2/art8

Javorcik, Beate Smarzynska and Mariana Spatareanu. 2005. "Do Foreign Investors Care about Labor Market Regulations?" *Rutgers University Newark Working Paper* No.2005–005. Newark: Rutgers University.

JBIC (Japan Bank for International Cooperation). 2005. "Survey Report on Overseas Business Operations by Japanese Manufacturing Companies: Results of JBIC FY 2004 Survey: Outlook for Japanese Foreign Direct Investment (16th Annual Survey)." JBICI Review 13: 1–113.

Jensen, Nathan. 2003. "Democratic Governance and Multinational Corporations: Political Regimes and Inflows of Foreign Direct Investment." International Organization 57(3): 587–616.

Jensen, Nathan. 2006. *Nation States and the Multinational Corporation.* Princeton: Princeton University Press.

Jensen, Nathan M. and Fiona McGillivray. 2005. "Federalism and Foreign Direct Investment." International Interactions 31(4): 303–326.

Jensen, Nathan and Guillermo Rosas. 2007. "Foreign Direct Investment and Income Inequality in Mexico, 1990–2000." International Organization 61(3): 467–487.

Josephs, Hilary K. 2009. "Labor Law Developments in China: Measuring Progress under China's Labor Law – Goals, Processes and Outcomes." Comparative Labor Law and Policy Journal 30: 373–408.

Kaufman, Robert and Alex Segura-Ubiergo. 2001. "Globalization, Domestic Politics, and Welfare Spending in Latin America: A Time-Series Cross-Section Analysis, 1973–1997." World Politics 53(4): 551–585.

Keck, Margaret and Kathryn Sikkink. 1998. *Activists Beyond Borders.* Ithaca: Cornell University Press.

Keefer, Philip and Stephen Knack. 1997. "Why Don't Poor Countries Catch Up? A Cross-National Test of Institutional Explanation." Economic Inquiry 35(3): 590–602.

Kelley, Judith. 2004. *Ethnic Politics in Europe: The Power of Norms and Incentives.* Princeton: Princeton University Press.

Kim, So Young. 2007. "Openness, External Risk and Volatility: Implications for the Compensation Hypothesis." International Organization 61(1): 181–216.

Knack, Stephen and Philip Keefer. 1995. "Institutions and Economic Performance: Cross Country Tests using Alternative Institutional Measures." Economics and Politics 7: 207–227.

Kobrin, Stephen J. 1987. "Testing the Bargaining Hypothesis in the Manufacturing Sector in Developing Countries." International Organization 41: 609–638.

KPMG. 2005. *KPMG International Survey of Corporate Responsibility Reporting.* Amsterdam: KPMG.

Kreps, David M. 1990. "Corporate Culture and Economic Theory," In *Perspectives on Positive Political Economy*, eds. James Alt and Kenneth Shepsle, 90–143. New York: Cambridge University Press.

Kucera, David. 2002. "Core Labour Standards and Foreign Direct Investment." International Labour Review 141(1–2): 31–69.

Kucera, David. ed. 2007. *Qualitative Indicators of Labour Standards: Comparative Methods and Applications.* Netherlands: Springer.

Lall, Sanjaya. 2000. The Technological Structure and Performance of Developing Country Manufactured Exports, 1985–98." Oxford Development Studies 28(3): 337–369.

Lawyers' Committee for Human Rights. 2003. Testimony before the U.S. Congress Committee on International Relations, Subcommittee on International Terrorism, Non-Proliferation and Human Rights, at Hearing on "A Review of the State Department Country Reports on Human Rights Practices," April 30.

Leahy, Dermot and Catia Montagna. 2000. "Unionisation and FDI: Challenging Conventional Wisdom." The Economic Journal 110: C80–C92.

Leary, Virginia A. 1996. "The Paradox of Workers' Rights as Human Rights." In *Human Rights, Labor Rights, and International Trade*, eds. Lance A. Compa and Stephen F. Diamond, 23–47. Philadelphia: University of Pennsylvania Press.

Lerner, Daniel. 1958. *The Passing of Traditional Society: Modernizing the Middle East.* New York: Free Press.

Levinson, Marc. 2008. "Freight Pain: The Rise and Fall of Globalization." Foreign Affairs 87(6): 133–140.

Levy, David L. and Aseem Prakash. 2003. "Bargains Old and New: Multinational Corporations in Global Governance." Business and Politics 5(2): 131–150.

Li, Quan. 2006. "Democracy, Autocracy, and Tax Incentives to Foreign Direct Investors: A Cross-National Analysis." The Journal of Politics 68(1): 62–74.

Li, Quan. 2009. "Democracy, Autocracy and Expropriation of Foreign Direct Investment." Comparative Political Studies 42(8): 1098–1127.

Li, Quan and Adam Resnick. 2003. "Reversal of Fortunes: Democratic Institutions and Foreign Direct Investment Inflows to Developing Countries." International Organization 57: 175–211.

Lim, L. C. 2001. *The Globalization Debate.* Geneva: International Labour Organization.

Lipset, Seymour Martin. 1959. "Some Social Requisites of Democracy: Economic Development and Political Legitimacy." American Political Science Review 53 (March): 69–105.

Lipsey, Robert. 2002. "Home and Host Country Effects of FDI." *NBER Working Paper* No.9293 (October). Cambridge: National Bureau of Economic Research.

Lipsey, Robert and Fredrik Sjöholm. 2002. "Foreign Firms and Indonesian Manufacturing Wages: An Analysis with Panel Data." Economic Development and Cultural Change 55: 201–221.

Lipson, Charles. 1985. *Standing Guard: Protecting Foreign Capital in the Nineteenth and Twentieth Centuries*. Berkeley: University of California Press.

Locke, Richard M. 2003. "The Promise and Perils of Globalization: The Case of Nike." In *Management: Inventing and Delivering its Future*, eds. Richard Schmalenese and Thomas A. Kochan. Cambridge: The MIT Press.

Locke, Richard M., Matthew Amengual and Akshay Mangla. 2009. "Virtue Out of Necessity? Compliance, Commitment and the Improvement of Labor Conditions in Global Supply Chains." Politics and Society 37(3): 319–351.

Locke, Richard M., Fei Qin and Alberto Brause. 2007. "Does Monitoring Improve Labor Standards? Lessons from Nike." Industrial and Labor Relations Review 61(1): 3–31.

Locke, Richard M. and Monica Romis. 2010 "The Promise and Perils of Private Voluntary Regulation: Labor Standards and Work Organization in Two Mexican Garment Factories." Review of International Political Economy 17(1): 45–74.

Madami, Dorsati. 1999. "A Review of the Role and Impact of Export Processing Zones." *World Bank Policy Working Paper*, August. Washington, DC: World Bank.

Madrid, Raúl. 2003. "Labouring against Neoliberalism: Unions and Patterns of Reform in Latin America." Journal of Latin American Studies 35(1): 53–88.

Mahoney, James. 2007. "Qualitative Methods and Comparative Politics." Comparative Political Studies 40(2): 122–144.

Malesky, Edmund J. 2008. "Straight Ahead on Red: How Foreign Direct Investment Empowers Subnational Leaders." Journal of Politics 70(1): 97–119.

Mandle, Jay. 2003. *Globalization and the Poor*. Cambridge: Cambridge University Press.

Mares, Isabela. 2003. "The Sources of Business Interest in Social Insurance: Sectoral vs. National Differences." World Politics 55: 229–258.

Margolis, Joshua Daniel and James Patrick Walsh. 2001. *People and Profits: The Search for a Link between a Company's Social and Financial Performance.* Mahwah, N.J.: Lawrence Erlbaum Associates.

Markusen, James R. 1995. "The Boundaries of Multinational Enterprises and the Theory of International Trade." Journal of Economic Perspectives 9(2): 169–189.

Martin, Cathie Jo and Duane Swank. 2001. "Employers and the Welfare State." Comparative Political Studies 34(8): 889–923.

Martin, Nathan D. and David Brady. 2007. "Workers of the Less Developed World Unite? A Multilevel Analysis of Unionization in Less Developed Countries." American Sociological Review 72: 562–584.

Maskus, Keith E. 1997. "Should Core Labor Standards Be Imposed through International Trade Policy?" *Policy Research Working Paper* No.1817. Washington, DC: World Bank.

Mattli, Walter and Ngaire Woods. eds. 2009. *The Politics of Global Regulation.* Princeton: Princeton University Press.

McGuire, James W. 2002. Compiler. 20 Latin American Countries Database. Accessed April 1, 2007, http://condor.wesleyan.edu/jmcguire/Data.html

McGuire, James W. 2005. Compiler. Development Indicators for 1995 Database. Accessed April 1, 2007, http://condor.wesleyan.edu/jmcguire/Data.html

Melitz, Marc J. 2003. "The Impact of Trade on Intra-Industry Reallocations and Aggregate Industry Productivity." Econometrica 71: 1695–1725.

Meredith, Robyn. 2007. *The Elephant and the Dragon: The Rise of India and China and What It Means for All of Us.* New York: W. W. Norton.

Meseguer, Covadonga. 2004. "What Role for Learning? The Diffusion of Privatization in Industrial and Latin American Countries." Journal of Public Policy 24(3): 229–325.

Metcalf, David. 2003. "Unions and Productivity, Financial Performance and Investment: International Experience." In *International Handbook of Trade Unions*, eds. John T. Addison and Claus Schnabel, 118–171. Chelthenham, England and Northhampton, Massachusetts: Edward Elgar.

Meyer, Klaus E. 2001. Institutions, Transaction Costs and Entry Mode Choice in Eastern Europe. Journal of International Business Studies 32: 357–367.

Meyer, William H. 1996. "Human Rights and MNCs: Theory versus Quantitative Analysis." Human Rights Quarterly 18: 368–397.

Meyer, William H. 1998. *Human Rights and International Political Economy in the Third World Nations: Multinational Corporations, Foreign Aid, and Repression.* Westport: Praeger.

MIGA (Multilateral Investment Guarantee Agency). 2002. *Foreign Direct Investment Survey.* Washington: World Bank, January.

Milner, Helen. 1988. *Resisting Protectionism: Industries for Free Trade.* Princeton: Princeton University Press.

Milner, Helen and Keiko Kubota. 2005. "Why the Move to Free Trade? Democracy and Trade Policy in the Developing Countries." International Organization 59(1):157–193.

Milner, Wesley T., Steven C. Poe and David Leblang. 1999. "Security Rights, Subsistence Rights, and Liberties: A Theoretical Survey of the Empirical Landscape." Human Rights Quarterly 21(2): 403–443.

Mitchell, Ronald. 1994. "Regime Design Matters: International Oil Pollution and Treaty Compliance." International Organization 48(3): 425–458.

Mitchell, Neil J. and James M. McCormick. 1988. "Economic and Political Explanations of Human Rights Violations." World Politics 40(4): 476–498.

Moran, Theodore H. 1974. *Multinational Corporations and the Politics of Dependence.* Princeton: Princeton University Press.

Moran, Theodore H. 2002. *Beyond Sweatshops: Foreign Direct Investment and Globalization in Developing Countries.* Washington: Brookings Institution Press.

Moran, Theodore, Edward M. Graham and Magnus Blomstrom. eds. 2005. *Does Foreign Direct Investment Promote Development?* Washington, DC: Institute for International Economics.

Morici, Peter with Evan Schultz. 2001. *Labor Standards in the Global Trading System.* Washington: Economic Strategy Institute.

Mosley, Layna. 2003. *Global Capital and National Governments.* Cambridge: Cambridge University Press.

Mosley, Layna. 2005. "Globalization and the State: Still Room to Move?" New Political Economy 10(3): 355–362.

Mosley, Layna. 2006. "Collective Labor Rights and Foreign Direct Investment." Paper presented at the FDI Workshop, Duke University, April 8–9.

Mosley, Layna. 2008. "Workers' Rights in Open Economies: Global Production and Domestic Institutions in the Developing World." Comparative Political Studies 41: 674–714.

Mosley, Layna. 2009. "Private Governance for the Public Good? Exploring Private Sector Participation in Global Financial Regulation," In *Power, Interdependence and Non-State Actors in World Politics*, eds. Helen V. Milner and Andrew Moravcsik, 126–146. Princeton: Princeton University Press.

Mosley, Layna and Saika Uno. 2007. "Racing to the Bottom or Climbing to the Top? Economic Globalization and Collective Labor Rights." Comparative Political Studies 40(8): 923–948.

Murillo, M. Victoria. 2001. *Labor Unions, Partisan Coalitions and Market Reforms in Latin America.* Cambridge: Cambridge University Press.

Murillo, M. Victoria. 2005. "Partisanship amidst Convergence: The Politics of Labor Reform in Latin America." Comparative Politics 37(4): 441–458.

Murillo, M. Victoria and Andrew Schrank. 2005. "With a Little Help from My Friends? Partisan Politics, Transnational Alliances, and Labor Rights in Latin America." Comparative Political Studies 38: 971–999.

Murphy, Dale D. 2004. *The Structure of Regulatory Competition: Corporations and Public Policies in a Global Economy.* New York: Oxford University Press.

Mutti, John H. 2003. *Foreign Direct Investment and Tax Competition.* Washington: Institute for International Economics.

National Research Council. 2004. *Monitoring International Labor Standards: Techniques and Sources of Information.* Washington, DC: The National Academies Press.

Navaretti, Giorgio Barba and Anthony J. Venables. 2004. *Multinational Firms in the World Economy.* Princeton: Princeton University Press.

Neumayer, Eric and Indra de Soysa. 2005. "Trade Openness, Foreign Direct Investment and Child Labor." World Development 33(1): 43–63.

Neumayer, Eric and Indra de Soysa. 2006. "Globalization and the Right to Free Association and Collective Bargaining: An Empirical Analysis." World Development 34(1): 31–49.

Ngai, Pun. 2005. "Global Production, Company Codes of Conduct and Labor Conditions in China: A Case Study of Two Factories." The China Journal 54: 101–113.

Nocera, Joe. 2008. "Seeing the Sights of Industrial China: Two Factories, Two Futures." New York Times, April 5, p. C1.

Nunnenkamp, Peter and Julius Spatz. 2002. "Determinants of FDI in Developing Countries: Has Globalization Changed the Rules of the Game?" Transnational Corporations 11(2): 1–34.

O'Donnell, Guillermo. 1988. *Bureaucratic Authoritarianism: Argentina, 1966–1973, in Comparative Perspective*. Berkeley: University of California Press.

O'Rourke, Dara. 2003. "Outsourcing Regulation: Analyzing Non-Governmental Systems of Labor Standards and Monitoring." Policy Studies Journal 31:1–29.

O'Rourke, Dara. 2005. "Market Movements: Non-Governmental Organization Strategies to Influence Global Production and Consumption." Journal of Industrial Ecology 9(1–2): 115–128.

OECD (Organization for Economic Cooperation and Development). 1996. *Trade, Employment and Labour Standards*. Paris: OECD.

OECD (Organization for Economic Cooperation and Development). 2000. *International Trade and Core Labour Standards*. Paris: OECD.

OECD (Organisation for Economic Co-operation and Development). 2001. *Corporate Responsibility: Private Initiatives and Public Goals*. Paris: OECD.

OECD (Organization for Economic Cooperation and Development). 2001. *International Direct Investments Statistic Yearbook*. Paris: OECD.

OECD (Organization for Economic Cooperation and Development). 2002. *Foreign Direct Investment for Development: Maximising Benefits, Minimising Costs*. Paris: OECD.

OECD (Organization for Economic Cooperation and Development). 2005. *International Investment Perspectives 2005*. Paris: OECD.

Office of the United States Trade Representative. 2006. "U.S. Generalized System of Preferences: Guidebook." Washington, DC (January). At http://www.ustr. gov/assets/Trade_Development/Preference_Programs/GSP/asset_upload_ file890_8359.pdf

Oman, Charles. 2000. *Policy Competition for Foreign Direct Investment: A Study of Competition among Governments to Attract FDI*. Paris: OECD Development Center.

Pauly, Louis W. and Simon Reich. 1997. "National Structures and Multinational Corporate Behavior: Enduring Differences in the Age of Globalization." International Organization 51(1): 1–30.

Pinto, Pablo M. and Santiago M. Pinto. 2008. "The Politics of Investment Partisanship and the Sectoral Allocation of Foreign Direct Investment." Economics and Politics 20(2): 216–254.

Piore, Michael J. and Charles F. Sable. 1984. *The Second Industrial Divide: Possibilities for Prosperity*. New York: Basic Books.

Plümper, Thomas, Vera E. Troeger and Philip Manow. 2005. "Panel Data Analysis in Comparative Politics: Linking Method to Theory." European Journal of Political Research 44(2): 327–354.

Plümper, Thomas, Vera E. Troeger and Hannes Winner. 2009. "Why is There No Race to the Bottom in Capital Taxation?" International Studies Quarterly 53(3): 761–786.

Poe, Steven C. and Neal Tate. 1994. "Repression of Human Rights to Personal Integrity in the 1980s: A Global Analysis." American Political Science Review 88: 853–872.

Poe, Steven C., Neal Tate and Linda Camp Keith. 1999. "Repression of the Human Right to Personal Integrity Revisited: A Global Gross-National Study Covering the Years 1976–1993." International Studies Quarterly 43: 291–313.

Poe, Steven C., Tanya Vazquez and Sabine Carey. 2001. "How are these Pictures Different: Assessing the Biases in the U.S. State Department's Country Reports on Human Rights Practices." Human Rights Quarterly 23: 650–677.

Porter, M. E. 1990. *The Competitive Advantage of Nations.* Free Press: New York.

Potoski, Matthew and Aseem Prakash. 2005. "Covenants and Weak Swords: ISO 14001 and Facilities Environmental Performance." Journal of Policy Analysis and Management 24(4): 745–769.

Potoski, Matthew and Aseem Prakash. 2009. "Information Asymmetries as Trade Barriers: ISO 9000 Increases International Commerce." Journal of Policy Analysis and Management 28(2): 221–238.

Prakash, Aseem and Matthew Potoski. 2006. "Racing to the Bottom? Trade, Environmental Governance and ISO 14001." American Journal of Political Science 50(2): 350–364.

Prakash, Aseem and Matthew Potoski. 2007. "Investing Up: FDI and the Cross-Country Diffusion of ISO 14001 Management Systems." International Studies Quarterly 51(4): 723–744.

PROCOMER. 2006. "Balance de las Zonas Francas: Beneficio Neto del Régimen para Costa Rica (1997–2005)." PROCEMER/COMEX Estudio EE-IE-02–2006 (November). At http://www.procomer.com/regimen/Docs-07/ZF/PDF/ZF percent20EE-IE-02–06.pdf

Przeworski, Adam, Michael E. Alvarez, José Antonio Cheibub and Fernando Limongi. 2000. *Democracy and Development: Political Institutions and Well-Being in the World, 1950–1990.* Cambridge: Cambridge University Press.

Reed, John. 2006. "Mauritius: The Ill Winds of Trade Start Blowing Again." *Financial Times* March 14.

Reis, Ana Balcão. 2001. "On the Welfare Effects of Foreign Investment." Journal of International Economics 54: 411–427.

Resnick, Adam L. 2001. "Investors, Turbulence and Transition: Democratic Transition and Foreign Direct Investment in Nineteen Developing Countries." International Interactions 27(4): 381–398.

Reuveny, Rafael and Quan Li. 2003. "Economic Openness, Democracy and Income Inequality: An Empirical Analysis." Comparative Political Studies 36(5): 575–601.

Richards, David L., Ronald D. Gelleny and David H. Sacko. 2001. "Money with a Mean Streak? Foreign Economic Penetration and Government Respect for Human Rights in Developing Countries." International Studies Quarterly 45: 219–239.

Roach, Stephen. 2006. "Globalization's New Underclass." *Morgan Stanley Global Economic Forum* (March 3). At http://www.morganstanley.com/views/gef/archive/2006/20060303-Fri.html

Roberts, Kenneth M. 2002. "Social Inequalities without Class Cleavages in Latin America's Neoliberal Era." Studies in Comparative International Development 36: 3–33.

Roberts, Kenneth M. and Erik Wibbels. 1999. "Party Systems and Electoral Volatility in Latin America: A Test of Economic, Institutional and Structural Explanations." American Political Science Review 93(3): 575–590.

Robertson, Graeme B. 2007. "Strikes and Labor Organization in Hybrid Regimes." American Political Science Review 101(4): 781–798.

Rodríguez-Clare, Andrés. 2001. "Costa Rica's Development Strategy based on Human Capital and Technology: How it Got There, the Impact of Intel, and Lessons for other Countries." Written for the UNDP *Human Development Report*Rodríguez-Garavito, César. 2005. "Global Governance and Labor Rights: Codes of Conduct and Anti-Sweatshop Struggles in Global Apparel Factories in Mexico and Guatemala." Politics and Society 33(2): 203–233.

Rodrik, Dani. 1996. "Labor Standards in International Trade: Do They Matter and What do We Do about Them?" In *Emerging Agenda for Global Trade: High Stakes for Developing Countries*, eds. Robert Z. Lawrence, Dani Rodrik, and John Whalley. Washington, DC: Johns Hopkins University Press.

Rodrik, Dani. 1997. *Has Globalization Gone Too Far?* Washington: Institute for International Economics.

Rodrik, Dani. 1998. "Why Do More Open Economies Have Bigger Governments?" Journal of Political Economy 106(5): 997–1032.

Rodrik, Dani. 2007. *One Economics, Many Recipes: Globalization, Institutions and Economic Growth*. Princeton: Princeton University Press.

Rodrik, Dani and Francisco Rodríguez. 2001. "Trade Policy and Economic Growth: A Skeptic's Guide to the Cross-National Evidence." In *Macroeconomics Annual*, eds. Ben Bernanke and Kenneth S. Rogoff, 261–324. Cambridge: The MIT Press for NBER.

Romero, Ana Teresa. 1995. "Labour Standards and Export Processing Zones: Situation and Pressures for Change." Development Policy Review 13: 247–276.

Ron, James, Howard Ramos and Kathleen Rodgers. 2005. "Transnational Information Politics: NGO Human Rights Reporting, 1986–2000." International Studies Quarterly 49: 557–587.

Rondinelli, D.A. and W.J. Burpitt. 2000. "Do Government Incentives Attract and Retain Foreign Investment? A Study of Foreign Owned Firms in North Carolina." Policy Sciences 33: 181–205.

Rose, Andrew. 2004. "Do WTO Members Have More Liberal Trade Policy?" Journal of International Economics 63: 209–235.

Ross, Michael L. 2001. "Does Oil Hinder Democracy?" World Politics 53: 325–361.

Ross, Michael L. 2008. "Oil, Islam and Women." American Political Science Review 102(1): 107–123.

Rudra, Nita. 2002. "Globalization and the Decline of the Welfare State in Less Developed Countries." International Organization 56(2): 411–445.

Rudra, Nita. 2008. *Globalization and the Race to the Bottom in Developing Countries: Who Really Gets Hurt?* Cambridge: Cambridge University Press.

Rudra, Nita and Stephan Haggard. 2005. "Globalization, Democracy and Effective Welfare Spending in the Developing World." Comparative Political Studies 38(9): 1015–1049.

Rueschemeyer, Dietrich, Evelyne Huber Stephens and John D. Stephens. 1992. *Capitalist Development and Democracy.* Chicago: University of Chicago Press.

Sabel, Charles F., 2007. "Rolling Rule Labor Standards: Why Their Time Has Come, and Why We Should Be Glad of It." In International Labour Organization, *Protecting Labour Rights as Human Rights: Present and Future of International Supervision.* 257–277 Geneva: International Labour Organization.

Sachs, Jeffrey and Andrew Warner. 1995. "Economic Reform and the Process of Global Integration." Brookings Papers on Economic Activity 1: 1–95.

Sachs, Jeffrey and Andrew Warner. 2001. "The Curse of Natural Resources." European Economic Review 45: 827–838.

Sambanis, Nicholas. 2004. "Using Case Studies to Expand Economic Models of Civil War." Perspectives on Politics 2(2): 259–279.

Santoro, Michael A. 2000. *Profits and Principles: Global Capitalists and Human Rights in China.* Ithaca: Cornell University Press.

Schneider, Friedrich. 2006. "Shadow Economies and Corruption all over the World: What Do We Really Know?" Institute for the Study of Labor Discussion Paper 2315. (www.iza.org)

Schrank, Andrew and Michael Piore. 2007. "Norms, Regulations and Labor Standards in Central America." *CEPAL Estudios y Perspectivas* No. 77. Mexico City: CEPAL.

Schumacher-Matos, Edward. 2008. "Killing a Trade Pact." *New York Times,* March 29, 2008.

Schwartz, Thomas and Mathew McCubbins. 1984. "Congressional Oversight Overlooked: Police Patrols vs. Fire Alarms." American Journal of Political Science 28.

Scruggs, Lyle and Peter Lange. 2002. "Where Have All the Members Gone? Globalization, Institutions, and Union Density." Journal of Politics 64: 126–153.

Seligson, Mitchell A. 2002. "Trouble in Paradise?" Latin American Research Review 37(1): 160–185.

Silver, Beverly J. 2003. *Forces of Labor: Workers' Movements and Globalization since 1870.* Cambridge: Cambridge University Press.

Simmons, Beth A. 2000. "International Law and State Behavior: Commitment and Compliance in International Monetary Affairs." American Political Science Review 94: 819–835.

Simmons, Beth A. 2009. *Mobilizing for Human Rights: International Law in Domestic Politics.* New York: Cambridge University Press.

Simmons, Beth A. and Zachary Elkins. 2004. "The Globalization of Liberalization: Policy Diffusion in the International Political Economy." *American Political Science Review* 98(1): 171–189.

Simmons, Beth A., Frank Dobbin and Geoffrey Garrett. eds. 2008. *The Global Diffusion of Markets and Democracy.* Cambridge: Cambridge University Press.

Simmons, Beth A. and Daniel Hopkins. 2005. "The Constraining Power of International Treaties: Theories and Methods." *American Political Science Review* 99: 623–631.

Smith, Gare and Dan Feldman. 2003. *Company Codes of Conduct and International Standards: an Analytical Comparison, Part I of II.* Washington: World Bank Group.

Smith, Jackie, Melissa Bolyard and Anna Ippolito. 1999. "Human Rights and the Global Economy: A Response to Meyer." *Human Rights Quarterly* 21: 207–219.

Spar, Debora L. 1998a. "The Spotlight and the Bottom Line." Foreign Affairs 77 (2): 7–12.

Spar, Debora L. 1998b. "Attracting High Technology Investment: Intel's Costa Rican Plant." FIAS *Occasional Paper* 11. Washington: World Bank.

Spar, Debora L. 1999. "Foreign Investment and Human Rights." Challenge 42(January–February): 55–67.

Spar, Debora L. and L. T. LaMure. 2003. "The Power of Activism." California Management Review. 45(3): 78–101.

Spar, Debora L. and David B. Yoffie. 1999. "Multinational Enterprises and the Prospects for Justice." Journal of International Affairs 52(2): 557–581.

Stern, Robert M. and Katherine Terrell. 2003. "Labor Standards and the World Trade Organization: A Position Paper." University of Michigan, August.

Stiglitz, Joseph E. 2007. *Making Globalization Work.* New York: W.W. Norton.

Tsebelis, George. 2002. *Veto Players: How Political Institutions Work.* Princeton: Princeton University Press.

Tsogas, George. 2001. *Labor Regulation in a Global Economy.* Armonk, NY: M.E. Sharpe.

TUAC (Trade Union Advisory Committee to the OECD). 1996. *Labour Standards in the Global Trade and Investment System* (November). Paris: TUAC.

Tybout, James R. 2000. "Manufacturing Firms in Developing Countries: How Well Do They Do, and Why?" Journal of Economic Literature 38: 11–44.

U.S. Department of Labor, Bureau of International Labor Affairs. 2000. "Wages, Benefits, Poverty Line, and Meeting Workers' Needs in the Apparel and Footwear Industries of Selected Countries."

U.S. State Department. Various Years. *Country Reports on Human Rights Practices.*

Un, C. A. and Cuervo-Cazurra, A. 2008. "Do Subsidiaries of Foreign MNEs Invest More in R&D than Domestic Firms?" Research Policy, 37(10): 1812–1828.

UNCTAD (United Nations Conference on Trade and Development). 1999. *World Investment Report: Foreign Direct Investment and the Challenge of Development.* New York: United Nations.

UNCTAD (United Nations Conference on Trade and Development). 2002. *World Investment Report 2002: Promoting Linkages*. New York and Geneva: United Nations.

UNCTAD (United Nations Conference on Trade and Development). 2004a. *World Investment Report 2004*. New York and Geneva: United Nations.

UNCTAD (United Nations Conference on Trade and Development). 2004b. *World Investment Directory: Volume IX, Latin America and the Caribbean 2004, Parts I and II*. New York and Geneva: United Nations.

UNCTAD (United Nations Conference on Trade and Development). 2006. *World Investment Report 2006*. New York and Geneva: United Nations.

UNCTAD (United Nations Conference on Trade and Development). 2007. *World Investment Report 2007*. New York and Geneva: United Nations.

UNCTAD (United Nations Conference on Trade and Development). 2009. *World Investment Report 2009*. New York and Geneva: United Nations.

Vachudova, Milada. 2005. *Europe Undivided: Democracy, Leverage and Integration after Communism*. Oxford: Oxford University Press.

Verité. 2004. "Excessive Overtime in Chinese Supplier Factories: Causes, Impacts and Recommendations." Amherst, MA: Verité. At http://www.verite.org/research/Excessive%20Overtime%20in%20Chinese%20Factories.pdf

Vernon, Raymond. 1971. *Sovereignty at Bay: The Multinational Spread of U.S. Enterprises*. New York: Basic Books.

Vijaya, Ramya M. and Linda Kaltani. 2007. "Foreign Direct Investment and Wages: A Bargaining Approach." Journal of World Systems Research 13(1): 83–95.

Visser, Jelle. 2003. "Unions and Unionism around the World." In *International Handbook of Trade Unions*, eds. John T. Addison and Claus Schnabel, 366–414. Chelthenham, England and Northhampton, Massachusetts: Edward Elgar.

Visser, Jelle. 2003. "Unions and Unionism around the World." In *International Handbook of Trade Unions*, eds. John T. Addison and Claus Schnabel, 366–414. Chelthenham, England and Northhampton, Massachusetts: Edward Elgar.

Vogel, David. 1995. *Trading Up: Consumer and Environmental Regulation in a Global Economy*. Cambridge, MA: Harvard University Press.

Vogel, David. 2005. *The Market for Virtue*. Washington: Brookings Institution Press.

Vogel, David. 2009. "The Private Regulation of Global Corporate Conduct." In *The Politics of Global Regulation*, eds. Walter Mattli and Ngaire Woods, 151–188. Princeton: Princeton University Press.

von Stein, Jana. 2005. "Do Treaties Constrain or Screen? Selection Bias and Treaty Compliance." American Political Science Review 99: 611–622.

Vreeland, James Raymond. 2008. "Political Institutions and Human Rights: Why Dictatorships enter into the United Nations Convention Against Torture." International Organization 62(1): 65–101.

Weeks, John. 1999. "Wages, Employment and Workers' Rights in Latin America, 1970–1998." International Labour Review 138(2): 151–170.

Weingast, Barry R. 1995. "The Economic Role of Political Institutions: Market-Preserving Federalism and Economic Development." Journal of Law, Economics, and Organization 11: 1–31.

Weisband, Edward and Christopher J. Colvin. 2000. "An Empirical Analysis of International Confederation of Free Trade Unions (ICFTU) Annual Surveys." Human Rights Quarterly 22: 167–186.

Weisband, Edward. 2000. "Discursive Multilateralism: Global Benchmarks, Shame, and Learning in the ILO Labor Standards Monitoring Regime." International Studies Quarterly 44: 643–666.

Weyland, Kurt. 2003. "Theories of Policy Diffusion: An Assessment." Presented at the Annual Meetings of the American Political Science Association, Philadelphia, August 28–31.

Weyland, Kurt. 2007. *Bounded Rationality and Policy Diffusion: Social Sector Reform in Latin America*. Princeton: Princeton University Press.

Wibbels, Eric. 2006. "Dependency Revisited: International Markets, Business Cycles, and Social Spending in the Developing World." International Organization 60: 433–468.

Wibbels, Eric and Moises Arce. 2003. "Globalization, Taxation and Burden-Shifting in Latin America." International Organization 57: 111–136.

Williamson, Oliver. 1985. *The Economic Institutions of Capitalism*. New York: Free Press.

Wilson, Bruce. 1994. "When Social Democrats Choose Neoliberal Economic Policies: The Case of Costa Rica." Comparative Politics 26(2): 149–168.

Wilson, Bruce. 1999. "Leftist Parties, Neoliberal Policies, and Reelection Strategies: The Case of the PLN in Costa Rica." Comparative Political Studies 32(9): 752–779.

Wilson, Bruce and Juan Carlos Rodríguez Cordero. 2006. "Legal Opportunity Structures and Social Movements: The Effects of Institutional Change on Costa Rican Politics." Comparative Political Studies 39(4): 325–351.

Won, Jaeyoun. 2007. "Post-Socialist China: Labour Relations in Korean-Managed Factories." Journal of Contemporary Asia 37(3): 309–325.

Woods, Ngaire. 2008. "Whose Aid? Whose Influence? China, Emerging Donors and the Silent Revolution in Development Assistance." International Affairs 84(6): 1205–1221.

Working Group of the Vice Ministers Responsible for Trade and Labor in Countries of Central America and the Dominican Republic (Vice Ministers). 2005. "The Labor Dimension in Central America and the Dominican Republic. Building on Progress: Strengthening Compliance and Enhancing Capacity." April.

World Bank Group/Multilateral Investment Guarantee Agency (MIGA). 2006. *The Impact of Intel in Costa Rica: Nine Years after the Decision to Invest*. Washington: World Bank Group.

World Bank. 1996. "Japanese Multinationals in Asia: Capabilities and Motivations." *World Bank Policy Research Working Paper 1634*. Washington, DC: World Bank.

World Bank. 2002. *Global Development Finance*. Washington, DC: World Bank.

World Bank. 2006. World Development Report. Washington, DC: World Bank.

World Bank. Various Years. World Development Indicators. At: http://data.worldbank.org/data-catalog/world-development-indicators

WTO (World Trade Organization). 2005. World Trade Report. Geneva: World Trade Organization.

WTO (World Trade Organization). 2007. World Trade Report. Geneva: World Trade Organization.

WTO (World Trade Organization). 2009. World Trade Report. Geneva: World Trade Organization.

Zhao, Yun. 2009. "Labor Law Developments in China: China's New Labor Dispute Resolution Law: A Catalyst for the Establishment of Harmonious Labor Relationship." Comparative Labor Law and Policy Journal 30: 409–425.

Index

Other Books in the Series (*continued from page iii*)